21 Sure-Fire Ways to As Much As Double Your Income in One Year

OTHER BOOKS BY THE AUTHORS

How to Get 20 to 90% Off on Everything You Buy!

and

Start with an Empty Nest by Jean Kinney

Jean and Cle Kinney

21 Sure-Fire Ways to As Much As Double Your Income in One Year

Parker Publishing Company, Inc.,
West Nyack, N.Y.

LIBRARY OF CONGRESS
CATALOG CARD NUMBER: 70–104718

PRINTED IN THE UNITED STATES OF AMERICA
13-934984-7 B & P

Money is like a sixth sense without which
you cannot make a complete use of the other five.

William Somerset Maugham

WHAT THIS BOOK WILL DO FOR YOU

You have opened this book for a reason. You want to make more money. Chances are you have had this aim for some time, but you have not known what steps to take. Now your approach will become clear.

In these pages, you will find more than 20 specific suggestions for increasing your income at once—21 ways to make your earnings twice as large whether your pay is large or small.

This promise is not an exaggeration. Far from it. It tends, in fact, to be an understatement. With the help of this book, you will find it easy before one year from the day you say, "Let's go," to *double* your incoming money or even *triple* it.

Do you find this hard to believe? Are you skeptical? Probably!

"How can these unknown authors tell me how to pyramid my earnings when they know nothing about me or my field?" you may be asking yourself. Good question, but surprisingly enough, the answer is a simple one. Your field, no matter how complicated it may be, just has to fit into one of the following classifications.

Read down the list.

1. You work for a large profit-making organization.
2. You work for a non-profit organization like the YMCA or Red Cross.
3. You provide a service. (You may be a doctor or nurse or masseuse or baby-sitter.)
4. You run your own business. (Maybe you own a lumber yard, a filling station or a beauty parlor.)
5. You work for someone who runs his own business.

6. Your creative work brings you money. (You may be a writer, a dressmaker, an artist.)
7. You promote the creative output of another. (You are not the "star" but you help to promote him, i.e., talent agent or a business manager.)
8. Others pay you rent for something you own.
9. You buy things for one price, sell them for a higher price. (*Example:* you wheel and deal in real estate.)
10. You sell something on a commission or cost plus basis. (You may be a salesman who gets a percentage on each sale or a contractor who works on a cost plus basis.)
11. Your money earns more money. (You may be living on an annuity or on dividends from stocks.)
12. Your money is given to you by another.

Does your money come from more than one source?

Chances are that in the list on the preceding page you can find more than one source from which you get your income (*Example:* You may be working for a large company, but you may be earning money, too, from renting half of your duplex, and receiving dividends, too, from a stock you own.) This is all to the good. In fact, your aim as you read this book should be to find *new* sources for earnings as well as to increase your basic income from one particular source. Diversification not only amplifies your income possibilities but also makes good business sense. Spreading out your dollars, after you are on your way, cuts down on risk.

As a preliminary self-appraisal right now, however, put a check mark in front of the money source which *best* describes your major method of livelihood. From which type of work on pages 6 and 7 do you receive at least 60 percent of the dollars that come to you?

Do you own a meat market? Put a check mark before Number 4.

Rent out cottages at your resort by a lake? Put a check mark before Number 8.

Work as a cashier at a local restaurant? Put a check mark before Number 5.

Finding the right niche

Think about the niche where you now find yourself. Do you want to work in this area for life?

If your answer is *Yes,* you are lucky and every page of this book will be of enormous help to you as you plan your strategy for moving ahead in your chosen field. But now let us consider the alternate. What if your answer is *No?*

Strangely enough, this book will be as helpful (and in some cases, more helpful) to men and women who have not quite found themselves as to those who are all set.

If you know that your present job is wrong for the long haul, here are three positive ways this book can help you to switch painlessly to where you belong.

1. By giving you specific instructions for boosting your income in your present work area, it will help you to acquire the capital to invest in a new business opportunity and/or give you the money you may need to tide you and your family over between your old and new pay check. (Also, with twice what you now earn coming in, you may decide you like your present field and do not want to make a switch after all.)
2. By bringing you examples of more than 100 self-made business people who have at some time in their careers doubled their income in their chosen fields, it enables you to compare their personalities to yours and determine whether you have the talent to do what they have done. At the same time, you can analyze dozens of work possibilities in terms of your personal qualifications. (If you find what is right for another is not right for you, *fine.*) Eliminating in advance what you know isn't right for you can save you painful errors in job or investment selection. On the other hand, by helping you to find what *is* right, the book can lead you to the way of life *everyone* wants deep down: *work that insures personality fulfillment as well as increased dollars.*
3. By explaining how countless entrepreneurs with no more formal education than most of the men and women who are plugging along in jobs they hate have become rich by earning money in one area and investing in one, two or three other areas, the book will open your eyes to the "river" theory of money-making. (With this theory, money that comes from one major source is invested in several separate money-making "brooks," which then flow back to the main stream to expand an ever-widening income.) The book points up investment possibilities all around you that can feed to your "river" every minute of the day.

A book to make you think

You are only on page 8, but already this book has made you question whether you really like what you are doing or will eventually want to switch. It has made you see that there may be investment possibilities open to you that you are now missing. It has suggested that there may be a way for you to invest outside hours in profit-making endeavors that you have never considered before.

Every page of this book will continue to prod your mind. This is one of our main purposes in writing it. We want to make you think about your dollars in relationship to your personality; to make you ponder your own worth as you consider which one (or more) of the 21 specific plans for jumping your income you personally want to follow; to make you consider which plan fits best with what you are and what you can become.

Dream goal

Ever notice that when you are doing something you like to do, you do not notice the passage of time, the gnats of frustration, or even an aching back? You are joyful about what you are doing when your work, as William Saroyan put it, is "related to your identity." This is the real goal of this book, to help you "do your thing," as you have always wanted to do it. This "thing" may now be buried deep in your subconscious. The book will help you to bring it to the surface. Then, work will be a joy, and the money will roll in. At long last, you will find the truth in this little couplet by a modern wise man:

> Work for work's sake; then, may it be
> That money and glory will come to thee.

A dream? To do what you want and get paid for it? No, this is a truth. *When you are doing what you want to do and working without fear and frustration, the money rolls in.* The book will tell you how and why!

How to get out of your rut

When you plug along passively, just go to work in the morning and come home again at night, it is obvious that you don't like what you're doing. "But I do," you say, "I'm just used to it by now."

You may not protest so much when you compare your answers to the seven questions below with the answers given by successful men and women who find their work a constant joy and stimulation.

(We asked 21 enthusiastic people whom we interviewed in connection with this book to take this test. Each one had bettered his financial picture and *daily work position* by following a different one of the 21 plans outlined in Part Two. Work they now do ranges from something as safe and simple as "take student polls on where kids would like to live in Europe" to something as risky as "buy old office buildings and make them into condominiums which I sell in small units." Yet they all answered the questions in exactly the same way.)

Compare your answers with the upside down Yeses and Noes given by enthusiastic workers on their way to acquiring more and more money. If you have more than three "off" answers, you are in a rut, which *can become a trench.* You can find a way out as you read this book.

(1) Would you be willing to work alone, after hours, any night next week, in preference to anything else that might come up, if by so doing you could solve a knotty problem connected with your work?
(2) Would you switch to a completely different type of work tomorrow if you could get a 20 percent increase in salary?
(3) Would you like to be interviewed by a newspaper reporter about the work you do?
(4) Do you dream of a life completely unrelated to what you are now doing?
(5) Is the work you do related in any way to the work in which you got your top grades in school?
(6) Would you object if your child or talented young friend wanted to go into your same line of work?
(7) Are you learning every day from the work you do?

1. Yes, 2. No, 3. Yes, 4. No, 5. Yes, 6. No, 7. Yes.

Like your work and still not happy?

Let's say your answers lined up 100 percent with the Yeses and Noes given by the able people we talked to, but you don't know how to get more money. Don't despair, you are half-way home. With talent* and aptitude on your side, all you have to do is learn the money-making game. In this book, you will find three different plans for skipping the rung in your organization that ordinarily would be your next step. You will learn the way to attract an outside offer and trade it in to your present company for more dollars. If you work for yourself, you will find how to parlay your annual profits to make twice as much. Before you finish this book, you will find a sure way to change your life and improve your lot!

---

* Doing easily what others find difficult is what we term talent.

What this book will help you accomplish

You may be tunneling along in a dull job year after year watching those with less ability pass you by. Or you may have a handsome income but know within your heart that you have "sold out" because you are too timid to do what you really want to do. Or you may like what you are doing and have no desire to make a big splash, but wish that you could take in a little more so that life could be more fun for those around you. The book will help you in the first category to get rid of apathy; in the second, to get rid of fear; in the third, to make up for your lack of drive. With your success blocks out of the way, you will get amazing results.

How to make this book pay off as you read

In this book's chapters up to Section 2, which sets forth the 21 methods for doubling your dollars, you will find personality tests, interest diviners and money quizzes. Each test-yourself exercise is designed to give you a better understanding of your true aptitudes and wants.

Even though you may be in a hurry to begin a plan that is bound to make you money, do not skip over the tests. Each will add to your understanding of self. Only by knowing what to expect of yourself can you move into new areas with confidence.

21 sure-fire ways

When you get to the bottom of this page, do not go immediately to the first chapter of the book. Move over to the Table of Contents and read the 21 chapter headings in Part Two. Undoubtedly, one idea will be particularly intriguing to you. Do not read that chapter, no matter how interesting it may sound, but do write down the title. Later when you come to it, after doing your preliminary test-yourself work, you may find that your interest though still keen in one area is even keener in another avenue to success. Nothing will help you to see more clearly why self-understanding is of paramount importance. Think of the time you will save if you shift to a more compatible field in your long-range money plan in no more hours than it takes you to read this book.

Nine immediate results that will come from reading this book

1. You will change your job without trauma if a move is right for you.
2. Your work hours will become 5, 10, 100 times more enjoyable.
3. You will remember your old dreams and make of them a reality.
4. You will discover talents you didn't know were yours.
5. You will receive money from new sources.
6. You will lose fear, even though you have lived with fear for years.
7. You will see income possibilities everywhere you turn.
8. Making money will change from a chore to a game.
9. Your life will take on glamour.

CONTENTS

Part One
WHAT DO YOU HAVE TO WORK WITH?

1. How to Assess Your Native Money-Making Ability: The Easy Money Pipeline 23

    when can you start making big money: take this test and find out! 24
    next step: count up your talents, hidden and otherwise 28
    what do you like to do? 29
    find your personal fortune formula 30
    are you in the right field? 31
    strive to use all five 32
    woman of many facets 33

2. Are Your Dollars Working as Hard as You Work? 35

    do you have a hard time with figures? 37
    more for your money 38

3. Continuing Goal: Twice as Much Money After Taxes . . 39

    expand your gross income by saving four ways 41
    what we learned from an irs audit 44

Part Two
21 WAYS TO A DOUBLED INCOME

1. Attract a Doubled Offer Because You're Absolutely Tops 49

    three case histories 49
    the magic BE principle and how to put it to use 51

1. Attract a Doubled Offer Because You're Absolutely Tops (*Continued*)

THE LIMELIGHT PAYS OFF 52
THE CASE OF THE PRIZE-WINNING STEER 53
WHEN YOU DON'T KNOW THE EXACT JOB YOU WANT 53
SOME BEGIN AS PROTEGEES 54
SOME FIND INSTANT SUCCESS 54
LISTEN FOR YOUR CALL 55
DO WHAT YOU WANT TO DO 56
TIMING COUNTS A LOT 57
THE STORY OF ADELE SIMPSON 57
EASY, ELEGANT AND BEST MADE 58
PUTTING THE BE PRINCIPLE TO WORK FOR YOU 59
WHAT DO YOU WANT TO BE? 60

2. Achieve Your Goal Through a Strategy Used in Advertising 62

ACCEPTED STRATEGY FOR SELLING AN ADVERTISED PRODUCT 62
FIND A "UNIQUE SELLING PROPOSITION" 63
FIND YOUR USP 63
FOOLPROOF SELLING PHILOSOPHY 65
PUBLICITY 65
WORD OF MOUTH 65
RULE TO REMEMBER: STICK TO YOUR IMAGE-BUILDING 66
THE FINAL PUSH 66
SUPPOSE YOU ARE SELLING A PRODUCT 66
7-POINT PLAN FOR PROMOTING YOUR OWN PRODUCT 67
CASE HISTORY OF A MAN WHO CAPITALIZED ON A TREND 67
WATCH THIS TREND 68

3. Expand the Market for Your Services or Product 70

HOW DOES AN ADVERTISING AGENCY MAKE ITS MONEY? 70
FIVE SPECIFIC WAYS TO EXPAND YOUR PRESENT MARKET FOR YOU OR YOUR PRODUCT 71
SUPPOSE YOU'RE SELLING A PRODUCT 72
MAKE YOUR PRODUCT MAKE MORE MONEY 73
SUPPOSE YOUR PRODUCT IS A COLUMN 74
SOME CAN SEE OPPORTUNITY AND SOME CAN'T 75
LEARN MARKETING TACTICS FROM POLITICIANS 75
ONE MAN WHO SAW OPPORTUNITY 76
EXPLODING POPULATION A MARKETING PLUS 76
IS YOUR PERCENTAGE INCREASING? 77
CASE IN POINT 77

3. Expand the Market for Your Services or Product (*Continued*)

even the clergy has a marketing problem 77
the case of a young lawyer 78

4. Double Your Margin of Profits—Whatever You're Selling 79

what if your product is a house? 80
what if you work for another? 81
if you want a paternal relationship, stay home 81
two-part self-examination to take if you work for another 82
second half of your work sheet test 83
cutting expenses, cutting hours 85
so how can cutting back on expenses and hours on the job double your profits? 85
case history of our typist 85
short stop for taking stock 86

5. Put Your Total Personality to Work for What You Want 87

two new challenges 88
do you do what you do "for fun"? 88
hew to strengths rather than to weaknesses 89
a diamond-cutter's theory 89
know your good points 90
forget past mistakes 91
don't try to saw sawdust 91
don't be afraid to quit when you're ahead 92
enthusiasm gets your heart involved 92
the two unbeatable ds 93
be a happy elephant 93
total involvement pays off 93
from roustabout to head of a $400 million business 94
go back to your strength and weakness test 94
don't get mad at your boss 95
aftermath of analysis 95

6. Use Some More of You 97

the story of rickenbacker 98
are you using all of you? 99
just keep moving along 99
the case of fred adams, jr. 100
you just want to get ahead 100

6. Use Some More of You (*Continued*)

the secret of not getting old 101
simple exercise 101

7. Shift to a Higher-Paying Field 102

the case of the young stockbroker 102
the case of piero gilardi 104

8. Make Your Spare Moments Pay Off 106

seventy percent do work they don't like 107
lots and lots of money for stuff 107
vacation exchange club 108
mr. toynbee's time-saving principle 109

9. Go After the Nitty-Gritty 110

best time to make a deal 111
get an option to buy stock at below-market cost 112
don't be afraid to reach for the moon 112
time out for self-appraisal 113
mickey lolich's nitty-gritty 113

10. Thou Must Have Faith 115

learning from nature 118

11. Become a Selling Writer, Inventor, Painter or Composer Along with Your Regular Work 120

the case of shepherd mead 120
how do you know you can write? 121
five steps to take as you begin to write 121
what about that doubled income? 123
skinned knuckles lead dentist to heat-pain theory 123
from parachutes to seat belts and more 124
what about painting? 124
the story of les rondell 125
the case of the busy toy salesman 125
many top photographers started in other fields 126
the story of ace williams 126
switching over from librarian to author 127
so you want to compose a song 127

11. Become a Selling Writer, Inventor, Painter or Composer Along with Your Regular Work (*Continued*)

take a tip from the uninhibited 128
expose your work 128

12. Do for Yourself What You Have Done for Others . . . 130

private enterprise pays off 130
the story of carole stupell 132
he quit to do better 134
he dared to take new steps 134

13. Buy in Quantity, Sell by the Piece 136

strange story of a great south american diamond 137
a 4c. profit is all you have to have 137
pure sex by mail and otherwise 138
simplify, simplify! 138
a cluttered desk makes for a cluttered mind and vice versa 139
dollars are simply multiples of pennies 139
story of an old rundown wharf 140
mike wallace's estate at sneden's landing 140

14. Find a Foolproof Pattern for What You Want to Do . . 142

where to look for your pattern 142
never mind if you don't know the person you go to for help 143
write to a national expert 144
not just for salesmen 144
read inspirational stories by and about men and women who have made it big 145
jeno paulucci's five specific money-making commandments 145
exercise 146
constructive ideas are now taking hold in your brain 148

15. Get Score to Help You Run a Business of Your Own . . . 149

free advice from retired executives 149
to qualify for aid 150
back to the clerk who wants his own business 150
play it straight 151

15. Get Score to Help You Run a Business of Your Own (*Continued*)

what about going from a big business to a small business? 151
how to start in business for yourself 151
two stories about a man who loved his product 153
up again, old heart 154

16. Run a Mail Order Business on the Side 156

fruit-of-the-month club 156
direct mail success formula 157
check list as you consider selling by direct mail 158
why mail order? 159
story of a mail order writer 159
don't worry about all the moves—just make them 159
learn from mail order about what makes people buy 160
mail order success story 160
n. flayderman & co., inc. 161
get your wife in the act 162

17. Stake Out a Claim on a Timely Idea 164

different kinds of franchises 165
much-discussed trend—our exploding population 166
birth control, food, housing 166
something old in a standardized world 167
attention-getting job in a crowded world 168
supply a growing market 169
stake out new claims as your market shifts 169
from flour to cake mixes 170
from real potatoes to instant 171
from toilet paper to disposable diapers 171
personal experience 171
sense a trend—and go! 172
down to his last city 172
bouncing boys 173
billion dollar business 173
don't wait for the giant thought 174

18. Take an Override on the Work of Others 175

success story in the life insurance business 176
where to find workers 177
exceptions 178

18. Take an Override on the Work of Others (*Continued*)

working grandmothers 178
override of 35 percent 179

19. Skip a Grade 180

more money for what (and whom) you know 181
from 100 houses to 2,200 condominiums in the time it takes to dream 183
things to be learned from skippers 186
how to apply the skipping principle if you work in an organization, not for yourself, alone 186
is there such a thing as luck? 187

20. Use the "Double A" Method to Get Anything You Want . 188

never mind who gets the credit 189
what has this man done in his life that you can learn from? 190
apply what you have learned 190
w. k. kellogg's application 190
don't be afraid to learn from your mate 191
women have it lucky! 192

21. Think of Money-Making as a Game 194

translating rules for poker into rules for making money 195
knowledge of people 196
how much capital can you raise? 197
do you have courage? 198
how to assess your money-making ability so far 200
how to strengthen your hand 200
how to play the game 201
12 rules to remember in poker or business 201

Part Three

10 WAYS TO BEAT YOUR "I CAN'T DO IT" HANG-UP

1. Three Giant Obstacles—and How to Get Around Them . . 207

three negatives that make for a hang-up 207
do you dare to experiment? 211

1. Three Giant Obstacles—and How to Get Around Them (*Continued*)

story of the lone inventor who made $50 million 212
the priceless plus 213

2. Seven Sure-Footed Steps to Take You Where You Want to Go 215

two honest fears 215
cases in point 216
what about you? 217
no more hang-up 218

3. Face Up to Your Alibis 219

Part Four

WHY MONEY IS NICE TO HAVE

1. "Money Is the Seed of Money" 225

top tv personality 225
why need gets in the way 226
when opportunity knocks 226
the stuff of legends 226
money allows for diversity 227

2. Blessed Is the Convenience 228

"being rich is better" 228
possibilities unlimited 228

3. In the End You Can Forget It 230

final goal 231

Bibliography 233

Part One

What Do You Have to Work with?

1

HOW TO ASSESS YOUR NATIVE MONEY-MAKING ABILITY: THE EASY MONEY PIPELINE

You cannot make money unless you (1) want to make it; (2) try to make it; (3) find your own special way to make it. Because everyone's money-making ability is conditioned by the relative strength of his drives in these three directions, there are no "born money-makers" as there are "born artists," "born writers," "born musicians." Still, in every generation there are men and women who seem to have tapped "an Easy Money Pipeline"—who make giant fortunes with what seems to be no more effort than others expend to bring home small weekly paychecks. Why, then, can we not assume that money-making is a natural talent in itself?

Consider for a few seconds the three biggest money-makers in your town or circle. Chances are they differ widely in their vocations, personalities and pursuits.

One may be a vigorous painter with a flair for publicity whose money came as his talent became recognized, talked about and sought after.

Another may be a company president whose fortune was built along the way by an accumulation of shrewd deals he made as he moved up the organization ladder.

The third may be a real estate woman whose disarming charm helps her to get listings from superintendents and property owners who are inclined to resist more aggressive males.

Not at all alike, the born artist, the driving executive, the gracious lady; certainly, none can be called a "born money-maker." Yet, these three (and the three you selected from your circle, too) do have something in common. For very different personal reasons, each one (1) wanted to make money; (2) made an effort to make money; (3) found his or her own way to make money. That much is basic.

Make a mental note of this. Only by wanting, trying, and searching for your own personal way to make money can you hope to do more than drift along financially. Once, however, you get these three fortune-making wheels synchronized, you can pedal along on them (far more easily than you are now pushing through life) to just about anywhere you want to go.

Strangely enough, once you get the knack of making money, you will not think about money nearly as much as you think about it now. It will come to you so much more easily than it has ever come before that you will not have to exert one-tenth the effort to get it that you are now putting forth.

Once you know where you are going, your natural aptitudes can come into play. When your course is set, your talent and acquired skills (in mathematics, designing, stenography, or anything else) will be amplified. Functioning at your optimum, you will progress far more rapidly than you ever dreamed possible.

When can you start making big money? Take this test and find out!

With a little twist in your thinking, can you be on the road to a fortune tomorrow? Probably not, because it has taken you many years to acquire your attitudes toward what you want and can hope to have in life. However, there is a possibility that you may be on the brink of self-discovery and can make an immediate move that will set your course straight. Chances are, though, that you will have to do more work to find your way than these fortunate few. Still, you can do nothing but progress as you increase your understanding of the attitudes that are presently exerting an influence on your behavior.

Following is a *three-part* test that will help you to evaluate your ability to make money. Simply answer YES or NO to each question. (Find the analysis that pertains to you at the end of the questionnaire.)

A

1. Do you ever bet on a long shot (in a football game, horse race, political election)?
2. Do you like movies and plays about rich people?
3. Do you feel better in expensive clothes?
4. Do you prefer going first class in a plane even when you can get there just as fast going coach?

5. Do you take in at least $100 in dividends from your stock investments each year?
6. Do you think it's worth a good tip to get good service in a restaurant or a good seat at a night club?
7. Would you resent an expense account that limited you to airport limousines rather than cabs (or interurban busses rather than planes) when such transportation takes time that you prefer to spend another way?

B

1. Would you move to another city tomorrow if it meant doubling your income in a year?
2. Have you ever sold anything outside of a shop for money? Door to door? Or from your home? Or sold something face to face like real estate, insurance or stock?
3. Do you prefer to play bridge, gin rummy or poker for money rather than "just for fun"?
4. Say you own three acres of land in another part of the state. Today, you get two offers: one for the entire parcel for a third more than you paid for it, the other to sell one acre for two-thirds of what you paid for the whole parcel. Would you sell the acre and make an effort to sell the other two the same way even if it meant some extra bother?
5. Suppose you and your wife, husband, or friend, had a sum of money set aside for a glamour vacation. An emergency wipes out your fund two months before you set out to go. Would you moonlight a job or work extra hours to get the money for the trip rather than give it up?
6. Would you jump at the chance to work with and learn from a self-made man or woman even if that person is difficult?
7. Do you believe it is possible, in today's tough competitive scholastic climate, for a boy (or girl) to work his way through school with no help at all from home?

C

1. As a child, did you ever win a ribbon, medal or prize for being good at anything? (In a swimming meet, perhaps, or a dancing contest or a Boy Scout effort? A cooking contest, art effort, or any other competition?)
2. Think of what you would prefer to be if you could be anything you wanted to be. Is there the remotest possibility of your attaining this? (You cannot be a long-distance track star, for instance, if you are 50, paunchy and have flat feet.)

3. Are you already recognized for your natural ability? Are you a writer, artist, musician? A superior mathematician? Established in a field like oceanography, psychology, medicine, that you mean to stay in for the rest of your life?
4. Do you feel that an artist can do good work even if he pursues money as energetically as does any other business man?
5. Would you pay out one week's income for a three-day battery of tough tests to learn from recognized psychologists specific ways to advance in your field?
6. Can you see yourself going into partnership with someone who is better than you at making money? Are you sure, if you do this, that you have something of importance to contribute?
7. You undoubtedly have one bad habit that you have been telling yourself that you will break some day. (Maybe you smoke too much, or drink too much, or need to lose 20 pounds, or are cheating in some area of your life.) You will be asked during this book to break one habit that you have promised yourself to break. Can you accept the fact that *now is the time?*

If you have five or more Yes answers in any section, mark the letter A, B, or C down as all or part of your key. FIND YOUR ANALYSIS BELOW.

A

You want money, more than most people, but for much of your life, you have been content to dream of the house you would buy, the clothes you would wear, the trips you would take—if you just had the money. Unfortunately, wishful thinking has not led to happiness but to discontent, because you have not as yet learned how to make your thoughts about your dreams come true. As you read this book, you will not give up the life you want to lead; far from it. But now you will find ways to make your wishes come true because you will at long last become as practical and hard-headed as you are visionary. And won't your friends and relatives be surprised!

B

You're half way home because you're a hard worker, always have been. Unfortunately, while the nose-to-the-grindstone type is seldom broke, he can sometimes miss the really Big Time because he concentrates so hard on the job at hand that he has his blinkers on to bigger opportunities. Work for work's sake for this type of man (and woman, too) can become an obsession. This book will help you to sit back and take stock. Now that your good work habits are established, you can do most any job with the organized approach you have perfected. Your job now will be to reassess yourself and your work. You will find that both are under-priced.

C

You excel in your field, and that's great. Long ago, you found that you can write better than most, or paint or play a musical instrument. Or that you can build houses, or are an excellent scholar, or can teach rings around your associates. Or maybe you are a fine chef or a great athlete or an excellent lawyer. But you aren't making the money you should make because of the very talent that makes you know where you belong. So far, you haven't had to think of money too much, because you had your work cut out for you. This book can help you make your God-given talent pay off. Your new income need take nothing from the quality of your work. Rather, you will become better than ever at what you do.

AB

You work so hard for the way you want to live that you aren't enjoying the life you are earning as much as you should be. But you are far more than half-way along to the Big Money you know in your heart should be yours. You want what money can buy and you're willing to work for it. But you are not as well acquainted with your native capabilities as you should be. (This may be due to your doing so many things well.) This book will encourage introspection and that will help you find the *specific* work that can lead you to the big success you are ready for.

BC

It is surprising that you picked up this book because you have had no special craving to live like a millionaire. Life with the Beautiful People in yachts and great houses has not been your constant search. It would be our guess that you want money now because you know that persons with less industry than you and with much less ability in your line of work are earning far more than you. Why? This book will help you to find out. (Here's a hint: perhaps you're *too* hard working, not frivolous *enough.*)

AC

Finding a field that you enjoy is not a difficulty for you. Far from it. You know what you want to do—and you know how you want to live, too. The only trouble is that you do not really care a lot about the *mechanics* of making money. To take a piece of cloth and cut it into two pieces of cloth and sell each piece for a little more than the original piece; and then to cut that again, and sell the pieces for a little more is not especially appealing to you. You would rather do what you want to do and live the way you want to live without giving thought to money. Unfortunately, unless your talent is very rare and the demand for what you can do is enormous, money will not come unbidden. You have to learn the art of making it come to you. This book will help.

ABC

You are one of the fortunate few who right this minute have what it takes to make money. You know how you want to spend it, you are willing to work for it, and you pretty much know what you want to do to get it. All you need is a little nudge here, a little jog here, and a little reminder there. In your advanced state, every chapter in this book will be meaningful to you, and doubling your income should be easy. In fact, if you really go about things right, you can be one of the top earners in your field.

NO LETTERS

Did someone give you this book? It is surprising to us that you have picked it up, because until now you haven't thought a great deal about money, either about how to make it or what you want to do with it after you get it. Maybe you have decided to pay attention to the little gnawing within you, the voice that says, "You can do better." The voice is correct; you *can* do more than you are doing now, much more, and this book will lead the way. The main things to remember right now are these: It is no sin to enjoy what money can buy; and it is not hard to come by, either, for you or anyone else.

A simple test. Yet, just by answering these few questions, you are already more aware of your native abilities that can put more cash in your till. This new awareness is the first step to doubling your income in one year!

Next step: count up your talents, hidden and otherwise

You may be squeamish about letting anyone know that you want to make lots of money.[1] You can get over this reticence (and you will have to, if you are in earnest about doubling your income) by thinking of

[1] If you really want to make money, you've got to admit that's what you're after. Take a tip from one of our top golfers who has won more than 100 tournaments and has made more than a million dollars. This popular pro makes no bones about why he plays golf—he plays for money. "I'm here," he said during a tournament one day in Milwaukee, Wisconsin, "because of that $200,000 in prizes."

money as a medium of exchange, nothing more. It is a ticket, that's all, that allows you and the persons you are responsible for to enter an easier, more convenient and more attractive way of life.

"It has been said," wrote Samuel Butler a hundred years ago, "that the love of money is the root of all evil." He then concluded, "The want of money is so, quite as truly." Shakespeare's thinking was in agreement. "He that wants money, means and content is without three good friends."

Accepting the fact that money is a friend, make up your mind now that you (1) want the friendly companionship of money and (2) that you are going to make a real try for it. Then you will be ready for the next step, the most important of all. Figure out now what assets you, personally, can put to use to double your income. What are your personal money-making tools?

What do you like to do?

You may have noticed that the big money-makers in your acquaintance appear to be having a ball. Far from grubbing along through life like a Dickens' miser, they apparently are doing exactly what they like to do. And do you know something? Chances are, they *are!* For they are doing what they do best, and 99 times out of a hundred what you do best is what you *like* to do best.

Italian style-setter Pucci whose shirts and pants and dresses are everywhere (even serving as uniforms on Braniff stewardesses) says this about money, "If you do something good, money rolls into your lap." This is true, if what you do is in demand and if you are doing it better than anyone else. But to be better than anyone else in any competitive field today takes either a blazing talent, which is rare, or a combination of talents for which you must search to find the key.

Author Truman Capote has a rare talent. Long ago he learned that this talent won't let him do anything *but* write. "Writing has always been an obsession with me," he told a reporter from McCall's Magazine, "quite something I had to do, and I don't understand exactly why this should have been true. It was as if I were an oyster and somebody forced a grain of sand into my shell—a grain of sand that I didn't know was there and didn't particularly welcome. Then, a pearl started forming around the grain, and it irritated me, made me angry, tortured me sometimes. But the oyster can't help but producing the pearl."

If you have the kind of talent that is forcing you to produce a pearl, you know this right now, but maybe you are not doing all you can to help the production along. Your job as you read this book will be to accept your talent as your birthright and to give up the obstructions in life that are holding you back. If your native gift is great, you will do something with it; that is a law! Remember how Gauguin at the age of 33 gave up his banking career in Europe, and even his family, to go to Martinique to paint! You may not make so drastic a change, but you will do *something!* The author of "In Cold Blood" is right. "The oyster can't help but producing the pearl."

Great pearl-producing talents are rare. The majority of success-oriented men and women accomplish what they want through a combination of aptitudes and interests. And in doing this, they find their way not only to a higher and higher income but to an easygoing happiness, too, which sometimes is denied the greatly gifted, who are often driven.

Find your personal fortune formula

Following is a list of 30 different categories. Read down the list. You will have a great interest in some categories; in others, none. In the space after the special category in which you have the *most* interest (whether you have ever worked in this field or not), put down the figure 30. Then, look at the remaining 29 categories. Which of the categories left on the list is the most interesting to you? When you decide, put the figure 29 after it. Now, put a 28 after the category that is third most interesting to you, and so on clear down the list. When you have numbered each designation from 30 down to one, you will know more about yourself.

Allow yourself ten minutes, no longer, to get your figures set down. Then turn to the explanation (following the list) for help in unlocking the combination that can lead you to success.

MUSIC AND/OR DANCING _______
STENOGRAPHY _______
MATHEMATICS _______
SELLING _______
FOOD (PREPARATION OR SERVING) _______
WRITING _______
CARPENTRY OR SEWING OR OTHER HANDIWORK _______
HOTEL, RESTAURANT, OR NIGHT CLUB BUSINESS _______
RESEARCH _______
SCIENCE _______
PEOPLE MANAGEMENT OR PUBLIC RELATIONS _______
FASHION, HOME DECORATION, THE BEAUTY BUSINESS _______

ACTING, PUBLIC SPEAKING, MODELING ______
MONEY MANAGEMENT, BANKING OR INVESTMENTS ______
WELFARE, POLICE OR PRISON WORK ______
MECHANICAL OR ELECTRICAL WORK ______
ENGINEERING, CONSTRUCTION OR ARCHITECTURE ______
MILITARY WORK ______
TEACHING OR THE MINISTRY ______
TRAVEL ______
SPORTS ______
CARE AND MAINTENANCE OF HOME OR BUSINESS PLACE ______
PROMOTION, ADVERTISING, MERCHANDISING ______
MEDICINE, NURSING, DENTISTRY ______
POLITICS OR LAW ______
PAINTING, DESIGN, SCULPTURE ______
TV OR STAGE DIRECTING OR PRODUCTION ______
HISTORY, ARCHAEOLOGY, EXPLORING
CARD-PLAYING AND/OR OTHER GAMES ______
FARMING, CONSERVATION, OUTDOOR WORK ______

In the space provided write down the five categories you numbered from 30 to 26, in that order. (If there are two different types of work in one, like sewing and carpentry, put down the one that you enjoy most.)

1. ____________________ 2. ____________________
3. ____________________ 4. ____________________
5. ____________________

In the coming together of these quite unrelated interests of yours lies the particular *Fortune Formula* that can double your income.

Are you in the right field?

Does what you are doing today make major use of the interest, aptitude or talent you have given a score of *30?* Good! You are well on your way! And does it make good use of at least two of the other interests which you listed above? No need to switch what you're doing. All you will have to do to progress is to incorporate your remaining two enthusiasms in your work and use the simple money-making principles explained in the next few chapters. Do this, and almost immediately your income will begin to go up.

Now what about your future if your major talent is going unused and you have only two or one (or even none) of your five major interests working for you in your present job? You can't possibly go to the top (especially if the interest you have marked 30 is not part of your daily work), and you can't be really happy in what you are doing, either. You may as well face the fact now that if you are going to double your income in the near future, you will have to make a change.

Summing up: If your number one interest and two other major aptitudes in your top five list are already being put to work in your career, you can go ahead. Any less than this, and you're in the wrong job.[2]

Strive to use all five

We are often asked if adherence to our *Fortune Formula* does not prove limiting. No. After years of research, we find that the average person is far more handicapped by not accommodating his five foremost aptitudes in his daily routine than he is in limiting himself to their use alone. The man or woman who is stymied in life needs to expand in order to make a breakthrough, not retreat.

Think for a minute of Lawrence Welk. Chosen in a ballot of 500 colleges and universities to be one of the recipients of our country's annual Horatio Alger awards, this master of "champagne music" has put his major talents to work for him about as well as anyone we can think of. The son of immigrant parents who settled in a sod farmhouse near Strasburg, North Dakota, he earned the first money he ever made by playing his father's accordion at country dances. He points out that it was no great problem to double his take from his "allowance" once he started to play, because that allowance was *exactly 10 cents a year!*

For several years after leaving the farm, Lawrence Welk's annual salary under other band leaders (and even after organizing his own orchestra) remained barely at the subsistence level. Just to exist, he was *forced* to double and re-double his annual income, which he managed to do.

Music has always been Lawrence Welk's mainstay, but he might still

[2] This does not apply if you are one of those persons we mentioned before who has one glorious talent. Surprisingly, however, even when working with your one great interest, you will be happier in your career if other interests can be brought into play, too.

be playing for local groups in the Middle West if he had not put to work other talents, which he says were brought about through necessity. Today, right along with his musical ability, in his success combination, is a talent for managing people; for managing money; for platform appearances; for TV production. He hit the really big time when he put all five talents to work.

Consider now a girl starting out to be a barber in a little country town. This would not seem to be a launching pad to glamour, would it? Yet Mary McLaren, not so long out of high school in Newtown, Connecticut, has seen the Pyramids, gone on an African safari, visited nearly every seaport in South America, Scandinavia and the Mediterranean and has been to most of the seaports of Europe. Just because she wrapped up all of her talents of barbering, public relations, care and maintenance of a place of business, personal attractiveness (she was a cheer leader) and sports (she loves to swim), and sold this package to the "Brasil" cruise ship where she has signed on as the ship's barber. Away she goes!

Even in affluent America where high-paying beginning jobs are easy to come by, there is no need to think you can't succeed if you happen to have started way down from the top. Climbing up from one job to another or up through many areas of one business will deepen your understanding of yourself and your work.

Woman of many facets

When a glamorous redhead named Blossom becomes a tough-minded construction boss in a storybook county with the highest per capita income in the United States, she, too, becomes like someone in fiction. That's what's happening to Mrs. Martin Rosenbaum of Wilton, Connecticut, in estate-studded Fairfield County. A few years ago, when she was in the real estate business, Blossom Rosenbaum found she had a flair for working with blueprints, building plans, and house-building specifications. So she put this unusual aptitude to work. By combining this unique talent with her built-in female insight into the needs of women (who are the key in home-buying situations), she became a construction foreman. Today, she still is overseeing construction projects but now she is company president. As such, she is involved in more house and apartment building projects than her women neighbors are in Country Club activities. And she loves every minute of her life. "On the job, I help with every phase of the entire operation," she told us the other day, "from selecting building materials to checking up on the men. I have a lot of traumatic experiences along the way, but this is my world and I love it." Naturally, Blossom attracts attention—naturally, this attracts more business—

naturally, this makes for an additional income and a storybook life. All because this particular heroine puts not one but many talents to work.

Before you read further, go back to the list of categories and copy down on a small piece of paper the five major assets that are yours to work with. Carry your personal *Fortune Formula* with you always. As you go about your work, whenever you feel vaguely dissatisfied, look at your list of five special interests and try to figure out how to incorporate more of them in your present job (or how to switch to a position that requires more of what you have to offer). In that way, you will be getting closer to what your aim must be if you are going to move ahead. Soon, like Blossom Rosenbaum, you will be functioning at your optimum. Then, you will gain financial success.

2

ARE YOUR DOLLARS WORKING AS HARD AS YOU WORK?

The Bureau of Labor Statistics recently reported that a city family of four, consisting of an employed 38-year-old father, an unemployed wife, a 13-year-old boy and an 8-year-old girl needed more than $9,000 a year to achieve a moderate standard of living—and the kitty has to be heftier with the passing of every year. (In Minneapolis, Chicago, Los Angeles and Cedar Rapids, Iowa, where living expenses are high, the same size family's need is for more; in Honolulu, Boston and New York, a whole lot more; in Cincinnati, Ohio, Nashville, Tennessee, and Austin, Texas, less; and on a midwest farm, *quite a bit less.*) But everywhere there has been a whopping 50 percent or more rise in what is needed in just eight years!

"Sure! Because prices keep going up," is your probable reaction, and this is true, but still this accounts for only a part of the rise. Second reason: there is an increase in the average American family's spending as old dad's earnings speed up. Sad result: the average consumer is "squoze" today, with an income far larger than he ever dreamed possible a few years ago.

Wise resolution as you look ahead to a doubled income: *As my income goes up, I will make my dollars work as hard as I work!* Otherwise, the old push is silly.

In our recent book, *How to Get 20 to 90% Off on Everything You Buy!*[1] which recently went to its fifth printing and is now in paperback, we set down hundreds of ways to save money on everyday purchases. We also

[1] Get free information about this book from Parker Publishing Company, Inc., West Nyack, N.Y. 10994. On an ordinary postal card, send your name and request for brochure.

introduced a simple, see-all-at-a-glance bookkeeping system. On a blank sheet of paper, we said, make four vertical lines, sectioning off the paper into three columns. At the top of the first column write GROSS INCOME; top of the second, GROSS EXPENSES; top of the third, NEW PURCHASES.

GROSS INCOME	GROSS EXPENSES	NEW PURCHASES

In our 20 to 90 percent off book we urge the reader to write down his anticipated income for the next 12 months. (If total income tax is withheld, take-home pay is considered total income. If you pay your own income tax, total income is the starting point and your income tax is lumped with rent, food, clothing and other major expenses in column two.)

The reader of the first book has a two-fold aim: to cut his expenses in the middle column so that he will have more to spend for new purchases, and to get more for his dollar when buying these new purchases. We made no effort to help anyone increase his income.

This book has a different purpose, so this time head your columns like this:

GROSS INCOME	INVESTMENTS	TAXES

This second chart makes possible a simple overall accounting system. In your first column, pencil in what income you can now expect from your major source in the coming year; in the second, what you can expect from your present investments (rents from property you own, stock dividends, capital gains from real estate and stock, interest, etc.); in the third, your taxes on both, based on what you paid this year.

Your job as you read this book will be to (1) raise your income from your major source; (2) increase your income from investments; (3) work out legitimate tax deductions so that you will have more left in your bank account for next year's investment spending.

Do you have a hard time with figures?

The simple approach to economics in this book is easy enough for a 12-year-old to understand, but a few men and women have an unhappy time with arithmetic. If you are cut out of such cloth, go to an expert.

Perhaps your husband or wife is wiser about figures than you; if so, turn your check book and accounting over to him or her. And *no togetherness* here, if you don't want a divorce. According to James P. Rorris, former lecturer of Domestic Relations at William Mitchell College of Law and a fellow of the American Academy of Matrimonial Lawyers, *money* is our chief cause of divorce. (Sex problems, he says, cause the least.) Here's the way he puts it. "Money problems cause the resentment that leads to the hitting and the beating and the chasing around."

Don't feel that turning your simple accounting over to another means that you have no money sense. There is nothing that says you have to be an able bookkeeper to double your income.

Ten minutes before Debra Dene Barnes, of Moran, Kansas, became Miss America of 1968 she wouldn't have known how to make out an ordinary business man's income tax return if her college tuition depended on it. Yet her own income from personal appearances in 1968 exceeded $40,000.

Recently, another pretty girl, who happens to be a barmaid, told us that a year ago she was a waitress in a hotel dining room, averaging $17 a day in tips. She switched to the cocktail lounge when a girl there told her that *her* tips were running as high as $50 a night. "I didn't have to be much of a bookkeeper to find a reason to move," she told us.

You don't have to be a bookkeeper to see ways to double your income but you do have to have a good investment program to make money work, once you get it. Don't let pride stand in the way of your getting help from your mate.

An army chief of staff we know whose pay recently went up $123.60 a month called his wife when he got the news. "More work for you, baby," he told her. He may be a big wheel in the Army, but she's the one who's good at figures. He's glad to turn over to her all of his accounting problems.

Maybe neither you nor your wife is good at figures. Then get a good accountant to work with you, not only on your income tax but all the time. He will charge you from $75 to $125 for an average-size tax figuring job, and he will be worth it. Besides, you can deduct his fee from your gross income, so his service costs you little. And year after year, as he makes out your tax report, he can point out ways for you to save on your tax the next year.

We have been talking here of relatively small incomes on the double. If you have a giant income, no one needs to tell you that even with your big yearly take you can't build a fortune unless you possess the financial brilliance of a Howard Ahmanson, California's rich savings and loan man, whose friends call "a genius at tax law." To make a giant fortune, your financial genius must be built in or you must hire a genius for your tax lawyer.

The principle, whether you are your own tax man or depend on another, is simply this: you can't afford to risk your capital in a business venture if you have to absorb all losses and the Government gets to skim off 9 out of 10 of the dollars you make in profit. The only way you can make really big money is to know how to make your money work as hard as you work when it once starts rolling in.

More for your money

As we have stated before, this is not a "How to Buy for Less" book, but still it stresses the principle of getting the most for your money. This principle is as sound for the business man investing capital in new businesses as it is for the housewife who is shopping for food.

Any smart homemaker will tell you that she is going to end up with more money to spend for the new dress she wants if she can cut the cost of her food bill from $18 per family member per week to $14 per family member per week. The same principle applies in business even as your income goes up. You are going to have more money to buy stock or real estate or oil fields or anything else if you (1) find a legitimate way to save on your taxes and (2) get the most for your dollar on investment spending. This book addresses itself to both.

3

CONTINUING GOAL: TWICE AS MUCH MONEY AFTER TAXES

A small town in many ways is less insular than any given business circle in New York City. On a recent Sunday morning, a graduate from Dartmouth with an advanced degree in marketing was having coffee with us in our kitchen when a canny local contractor came in and drew up a chair. The proud young wife of the new graduate was telling us at the table about the big salary her husband had just accepted in New York City. $12,000 per year for his first job out of school! As everybody sat around congratulating our friend, the contractor said, "So what are you going to be putting your money in?"

The boy laughed and began reeling off his expenses. $195 a month for their apartment in Hartsdale, $34 a month for commuting, $100 for food, more than $2,000 federal and state taxes; and, then, there would be the monthly payments for his new car, plus expenses coming up for the new baby and payments on that loan he had contracted for during his last year in school.

"You poor guy," the contractor said, sympathetically. "The first year I made what you're making, I bought three houses."

The fledgling marketing man is no dope. "Which proves again," he said quickly, "that it isn't what you take in that counts, but how you put your money to work." He told us later that that would be the last time he or his wife would brag about his salary, whatever he made. "That's not what counts."

What counts is how you put your money to work, and you can't put money to work if you're paying it out in taxes.

The first bite out of your income is income tax. Every dollar you spend there is one that you can't invest. So, it follows that this bill to the government is the one that you should give most careful attention to. Yet many taxpayers pay as billed without question.

We have seen dozens of men and women who would argue to high heaven about a 3 dollar over-charge on a cleaning bill yet overpay on income tax, even when an allowed deduction is pointed out to them. After a lot of thought we believe there are five reasons for this:

1. The taxpayer may be unsure of his grounds on *old* returns; he overpays now rather than "open up a can of worms."
2. He thinks of IRS as an enemy, and has such an unreasonable fear of being audited that he will not even ask IRS for a ruling.
3. Unsophisticated about tax rulings, he still won't pay a good accountant, even though the accountant's fee is deductible. Priding himself on being a rugged individualist, he has to do everything "all by myself."
4. He keeps slipshod accounts which he turns over to an accountant whom he instructs to "save me money"; tells himself "that's his job." Because he hasn't played fair, he secretly fears neither he nor his accountant will be able to defend all the figures on his return.
5. He can't see the logic in tax laws, which, except in rare instances, is at the base of every ruling.

Coming up here is a short true and false test designed to test your understanding of tax laws. (Even if you are not an expert, you should be able to see the logic at work in government rulings. The test indicates your grasp of current rules.)

ANSWER TRUE OR FALSE

1. If you receive a gift[1] of a piece of property and later sell it, you figure your gain from the basis of what the person paid for the property in the first place rather than an FMV[2] cost of the property when it was given to you.
2. If a debt owed you proves to be worthless in 1970, you can postpone taking a deduction for this until 1971 when it may give you a better tax picture.
3. If someone gives you a sweepstakes ticket and you win, you have to pay taxes on your winnings but not on the cost of the ticket.
4. The reduction of value of property because it is near a disaster area and there is a possibility that the disaster may repeat itself is a casualty loss. This property loss is allowed in addition to the actual physical damage resulting from the casualty.

[1] Ruling applies to gifts made after 1/1/21.
[2] Fair Market Value.

5. Your 8-year-old child who is a full-time student in a professional children's school earns $6,000 a year as a child actor in commercials. If you contribute one-half of his support, you can claim him as a dependent on your return, and can claim him as an exemption for himself, too, on the return you file for him.
6. Even though divorced, you and your former wife can file a joint return for any part of the year you lived together as man and wife.
7. Gain or loss from the sale of a house or stock held for more than six months is never taxed more than 25 percent of its actual gain.[3]
8. In estimating your tax, you can waive the number of exemptions you claim and thereby increase your withholding tax payments, but you cannot then claim the "waived" exemptions on your final tax return.

(*Answers:* 1, 3, 5, 7 are TRUE; 2, 4, 6, 8 are FALSE.)

Even though you have no immediate need for any of the information included in these eight statements, read carefully to see if you can deduce the logic in each ruling. This will help you with your own tax planning later on.

Your new knowledge of tax savings available to you will be the second most valuable asset available to you as a result of reading this book. (First will be your increased earning capacity.) Only by realizing that your tax savings are money in the bank can you plan wisely for the investments you will be making next year to double your income. While the doubled income in this book, when we are figuring for the individual, will refer to your gross income, money saved on taxes will be added to your working capital which you will be using to swell that gross income.

Expand your gross income by saving four ways

One way to get more money to invest is to *save*. Save all you can in four areas: (1) on basic business and living costs; (2) on your own time; (3) on stocks, land and other investments; (4) on taxes.

This is the last chapter in which we will address ourselves to saving money on living costs. But such savings (especially if you work for yourself from home as an artist, writer, insurance man, real estate broker or anything else) are important if they are (1) big and (2) consistent. Suppose, for instance, you have two homes on a piece of property which

[3] Unless you are a real estate broker or a dealer in securities.

is appreciating in value. The rental of one home can help support the operating costs of the second in which you live and work. Along with this, you can figure depreciation on your rental property which will help you save on taxes. Now your lowered living costs, plus your tax savings, will give you money to invest in more property or a new business as your previous property investment is paying off. An invest-as-you-live-plan can lead to a doubled income almost without your thinking about it once you get your basic work-and-live strategy worked out.

Big savings are possible in the way of life we have just described. In this book, we will address ourselves to no other type of saving at home, believing, as we do, that exaggerated attention to little savings eats up *time,* which as George Romney once said, "is the ingredient of life."

Suppose you are trying to make up your mind whether to drive 20 miles to a filling station and back and battle a crowd there for an hour or so to save $12 on four new tires. Here's a convenient way for you to figure whether the trip is worth your time.

First, figure what your time is worth per hour. *Changing Times, The Kiplinger Magazine,* figures that you are paid for working 244 eight-hour working days out of 365 when your salary is figured by the year. Thus, if you are making $8,500 a year, your time is worth $4.35 an hour; at $15,000, your time is worth $7.68 an hour.[4]

Figuring as above if you work for a salary, or for more hours if you work for yourself, what is the hourly rate someone else (or you) pays for your work? Once you have that hourly figure, think again about those tires. Is the bargain really a bargain? Maybe not now, unless (1) you are going to do many errands and make several money-saving buys on this trip, or (2) you decide to pay someone making less than you to do the errand for you.

Treat your time as if someone else were paying for what you are doing, whatever you do, and you will not only become more efficient but you will also automatically throw out of your life the time-filling pushes that aren't worth your while. Let somebody else sit in line for an hour getting extra stamps today for buying a tankful of gas; you spend the hour

---

[4] *Your time is valuable*
(Based on 244 eight-hour working days a year)

If your salary is	*One hour is worth*	*One minute is worth*
$ 5,000	$ 2.56	$ .0426
7,500	3.84	.0640
8,500	4.35	.0726
10,000	5.12	.0852
12,000	6.15	.1025
15,000	7.68	.1278
20,000	10.25	.1708

By *Changing Times, The Kiplinger Magazine,* September, 1967.

shopping for a better deal on your mortgage (1/2 a percent there can save you thousands), or for that car you need (get it in September when your dealer has to get rid of last year's cars before the new ones come in), or find out what real estate is selling for in your county, or study the stock market page.

Three years ago we asked three young account men just starting to work in a New York agency what each one did as he commuted to work from White Plains each morning. The first got his last night's homework ready for the office; the second, a whiz at bridge in college, played in a regular train foursome, often earning enough to pay for his lunch; the third analyzed why stocks in day's *High* column had taken a spurt, why those in the *Low* column had dipped. Today, the first man is making $2,000 more in his same agency. The second has switched both agencies and bridge foursomes, makes $3,000 a year more in his new job which he heard about on the train, sometimes wins now and sometimes loses at bridge (his new game is a tougher one). The third man has switched jobs, also makes $3,000 more a year, and invests some of his increase in the stock market where he picked his best buy out of the *Low* column a few mornings after the English pound was devalued.

Should each man work out a "What I'm Worth" sheet today, the third would be in the best position. Whether this will always be true remains to be seen, but certainly the number three man is beginning to sense what makes for a bargain in the stock market, which is something the other two know nothing about.

Shrewd money-makers look for bargains in stocks, in interest rates, in real estate the way housewives look for bargains in meat and canned goods. And just as the good woman shopper knows that you can't find a bargain unless you know one when you see one, the canny investor realizes the same thing. He keeps up on real estate values wherever he is, knows what the stock market is doing and tries to figure out why, shops for better interest rates on everything he buys. First rule, then, as you look for a better overall income: *Look for bargains in investments just as you look for a good buy in a car.*

As you begin to know a good investment when you see one, you will find a way to take advantage of an opportunity when it comes along. The same insight that makes you spot a bargain in the stock market will open your eyes to the way to make or put aside the money you have to have to take advantage of such bargains. Once again, let us remind you that the best place to look for extra money is in a tax saving.

Money saved after taxes is money already earned by you, not new money you have to pay tax on. Once again: *the more you can keep after taxes, the more you will have to invest.* As our accountant once said, "The dollars you keep after taxes are tax free." *They are dollars to do what you want with.*

What we learned from an IRS audit

Last year we were audited for the first time in either of our experiences in long years of working for others and ourselves. When the call came from Danbury that an agent was coming, we had just read an article in Reader's Digest that recounted stories of bullying and unfairness on the part of IRS. Even though our work has made us knowledgeable about money, we felt anxiety about our first audit by federal agents. We were in for a pleasant surprise.

Jack Perun went over two years of our records with an eagle eye, discussing with our accountant the whys and wherefores of our tax indebtedness which is complicated in that it is figured on income from dividends, interest, rents, royalties, advertising agency fees and real estate commissions. We groaned when one of several adjustments (question of whether the calculation of depreciation on two pieces of rental property should be figured to end at 20 or 33 years) resulted in a ruling against us. Still, looking back at the audit, we figure we came out ahead.

Here are services rendered by the agent, who:

1. Helped us to set up a see-at-a-glance accounting system consisting of cash receipts and a disbursement ledger. Not only will this streamlined two-way record save us time in figuring our income tax for next year, but it will also explain our expenditures in minutes to the IRS should we ever be audited again.
2. Suggested that we include as income our expenses which were reimbursed by advertising clients and publishers. Because our actual expenses exceeded the reimbursements, we were allowed a deduction from the excess.
3. Encouraged us to maintain a daily diary in which we now record all travel and entertainment expenses. (A pamphlet from the IRS office suggests this, too.)
4. Pointed out different IRS methods for calculating depreciation on a business automobile. (In our case, we were allowed expenses and depreciation on a portion of two cars, one used in research and advertising work, the other in real estate.) Told us that expenses can be calculated on a mileage basis, if preferred—10 cents a mile for the first 15,000 miles, 7 cents a mile after that.

In spite of the fact that we paid an additional tax, with interest, as the result of this audit, we figure we are the winners for three reasons: (1) We have lost our fear of an audit. Should we be called again, we will know what to expect and will have everything in readiness for IRS. (2) The time for our tax-figuring will be cut down this year not just in hours but in *days.* (3) We have a telephone number we can call for information that we can use to advantage as we plan our work ahead. When we ask a question, we get a thoughtful answer. (*Example:* Should we figure purchase price and remodeling cost for an old Iowa schoolhouse we intend to remake, photograph and describe in a book as capital for a year's operating cost for a job? Or shall we call the schoolhouse a working studio, figure depreciation as in any work place and declare a profit when the building is sold?) Danbury IRS people suggested we write directly to Washington for a ruling. (When we get our answer, we will proceed according to the most beneficial tax plan.)

Concluding suggestion: Think of the IRS as an adjunct to your business. Call at your nearest office for beneficial tax information as you work out your business plans for next year.

"He bids fair to grow wise
who discovers that he is not so"
. . . Pubillius Syrus, 42 B.C.

7 SUPPLEMENTARY OPPORTUNITIES TO LEARN MORE ABOUT WHAT YOU WANT TO KNOW

Daily Help: *Sylvia Porter,* syndicated financial column, probably in your local paper. (Also read *local* financial writers.)

By Your Side: *Your Income Tax* by J. K. Lasser, $1.95, at bookstores. (Easy reading, sound advice.)

Monthly Magazine: *Changing Times, The Kiplinger Magazine,* 1729 H. Street NW, Washington, D.C. (Publishes tax changes, price changes in various areas, merchandise supply and demand.) $6 per year.

Nearby: *Your own accountant.* (Call him as needed, not just at income tax time. His fee is deductible.)

Always Available: *IRS assistance.* (Remember that S after Internal Revenue stands for Service. Don't be afraid to ask a government auditor for help whenever you need it.)

Money-saving Book: *How to Get 20 to 90% Off on Everything You Buy,* now in paper back at bookstores, $1.95. (Tells how to cut down in all areas without sacrificing quality or good living.)

Daily Exercise: *Stock Market Report.* (Select three area stocks—one listed on the American Stock Exchange, another on New York Stock Exchange, another on National Over-the-Counter. For six months, if you read nothing else in the financial section, read what is happening to these three stocks sold by companies in your local area.)

The more you read and listen to what others know about making, saving and investing money, the more sophisticated you will become about financial matters.

The Next Section of This Book Can Change Your Life

One message (or a combination of messages) in Part II of this book can alter your entire future. To get the most out of this important section, obey these three rules:

1. Do not begin reading Part II when overtired.
2. Pause at the end of each chapter to think about what you have read.
3. Do not try to absorb more than seven chapters at one sitting, no matter how enthusiastic you may be.

You have traveled long with your old methods of doing things. You will need time to shift your thinking to something new.

Part Two

21 Ways to a Doubled Income

1

ATTRACT A DOUBLED OFFER BECAUSE YOU'RE ABSOLUTELY TOPS

There is one beautiful way to double your income. That is to have someone offer you twice what you are now being paid for whatever it is that you do. When this happens, all you have to do is accept with thanks and swing along without missing a beat. The only major change: your next check will be twice as high.

A laughable hypothesis? Not at all. Such offers come every day to men and women (and even children) who are absolutely tops in their field and whose skills are in demand. Whether you can realistically expect to receive an offer out of the blue for double whatever you're making depends on your answering yes to these three questions.

1. Do you get an enormous kick from what you do?
2. Are you working all the time to be 10 times better than anyone else in your field?
3. Is there a limited supply of persons who do what you do? (Or do it as well as you?)

Three case histories

There is a simple "ironing woman" (whom we will call Mrs. J) in our town who thinks of work she does for others as a "profession." And there are many busy housewives in this same community who have washers and dryers to do the washing but no one to do the ironing. So Mrs. J's work is much in demand. For many years, she charged $5 to iron an average-size load of family wash. But this year, when one woman, then two, then three offered double what she was charging if she could work them into her schedule, she began accepting $10 rather than $5 for the same size wash. Today she averages $100 a week rather than the $50 she was making for the same amount of time and work a year ago.

One of the top advertising men in Europe told us not long ago that he does little today that he wasn't doing 25 years ago as a high school kid in upper New York State. The son of a skilled cabinetmaker, he began writing ads for his dad in high school. With his keen analytical mind, he formulated a sure-fire plan early in life to sell what he wanted to sell. He made an effort to "get into the product" and tell prospective buyers what there was about what he was selling that was different from any other. In talking about cabinets in his first classified ads for his father's cabinets, he explained in detail how a drawer in each of his father's cabinets was made. Results impressed the town newspaper, which asked him to help sell products for space buyers other than his father. Now he got paid for what he had been doing for free. The next year, in his college town nearby, a furniture store which had advertised in his local newspaper asked him to do their 1,000-line retail ads in a bigger paper. By the time he had finished school, his skill as an ad man who could "dig into the product and find a good selling idea" was recognized by many and he was offered a job in a small New York agency. From there, he went to a larger one at a doubled income, and then to a larger agency at a higher salary—until finally he got into one of the giant agencies with Procter & Gamble as a client. He moved quickly to the top and last year moved to London as a supervisor on a giant soap account there. "And yet," he told us recently, "I still use the same basic method I used when I was writing ads for my dad back in high school. I simply try to find a plus in the product I'm selling that's bound to make sense to prospective buyers."

A one-time time salesman for a small midwest radio station has had much the same pattern. In his first job with a tiny 500-watt station early in his career, he took a creative approach to selling. "I never went out and talked about what a great station I was selling for," he said. "Instead, I analyzed what market a sports shop or garage or seed manufacturer was trying to sell before I went to talk to the guy and approached him with a plan. In my first call, I told him how many fishermen or car drivers or farmers he could reach by buying the spot I wanted him to buy." The time salesman soon became Commercial Manager and then Manager (at a doubled salary) of the small station, which was affiliated with a network of stations. Eventually, he moved to a larger station in the network as Commercial Manager and eventually became top boss of that. "And I still work exactly as I did as a salesman in my first job," he told us recently. "No, not quite, because as Manager I don't work as hard as I used to. I still do the old mental spade work before we approach a new client, but younger men make the calls."

Superficially, the three persons you have just read about have major differences. One is a grey-haired woman; one man is an easterner now living in London; one was once a farm boy. And there are other differences. The ironing woman has always been on her own. The ad man has worked for a series of bosses. The time salesman has worked for one company all his life. Yet these three people have two characteristics in common. They have long known what they could do well, and they have done it and done it and done it. As a result, in each case an upped income has come. If you have a calling, and you do your work well, your income will go up. This is a law. But there is no law that guarantees that it will double in a year. To accomplish this, (1) you must be noticed by a prospective buyer of wares; and (2) that buyer must believe *on his own* that you are worth twice what you are now charging for whatever it is you are selling. In all three case histories just described, the individuals who doubled their incomes were visible to one or more prospective buyers of their wares and worth to those buyers twice what they were currently charging at a lower level.

Let's say now that you like what you do and that you do it well. But you know you should be making twice as much. The trick for you is to get yourself noticed by a prospective buyer who will offer you twice what you're now taking in. Our suggestion: a psychologically sound approach called the *be* principle.

The magic be principle and how to put it to use

Girls in New York offices who want better jobs (or want to get married) use the *be* principle. From observation and from a consultation with an eminent psychologist, we know their simple approach is as sound, workable and easy to put into practice for a business man as for a girl in her first job.

To understand how the foolproof principle works, let's take a look at the new girl in the typing pool who wants to become a private secretary. What she must do, devotees of the *be* principle explain, is to take a long look at private secretaries who are successful in her organization. Then, she must begin to dress as if she were *already* one of them and conduct herself as she would if she had their job. If she is not as skillful at her work as they are at their work, she must become so. Soon, one of the executives who needs a new secretary will look out in the typing pool and find the ideal secretary right under his nose.

Now suppose there is another girl who wants to get married. She will decide, if she is following *be*, what man (or perhaps, simply what kind of man) she wants to spend her life with. Then she must get ready to be the wife of such a man, in dress, in attitude, in conduct. With this approach, say psychologists, if she keeps circulating, the man is bound to appear. Then she will get what she wants. "All she will really have to do is be there," insisted the psychologist who talked about this to us.

Analyze the *be* principle and you will see that it has two parts. If you want to be asked to accept what you want, (1) *be ready,* and (2) *be there.* Take these two steps, and the next step will take care of itself. Anyone in the performing arts knows this principle instinctively.

A young Broadway actress in a bit part pushes her talent to the limit whenever she goes on stage, knowing that a Hollywood producer may be out front. The folk singer gives his all on amateur night hoping with all his heart that a TV emcee is in the audience. The kid violinist plays his heart out in his year-end recital so that the older violinist who may be there will help him get to the New York teacher who will coach him through the whopper door. Silly kids? Not on your life. That is what breaks are made of, not just in the arts, but in all fields.

Barbara Walters was a behind-the-scenes reporter for NBC's Today show before moving into the chair beside Hugh Downs. As she did her work conscientiously, she listened to men on the show talk about the "ideal woman" they wanted out front. There she was all the time, looking the part, wanting the part, capable of handling the part and thinking to herself all the time, "Hey, fellows, what about me?" Eventually, the "fellows" saw their "ideal woman" right there beside them in the studio. Barbara Walters was invited on stage where she has been ever since.

In principle, this is not an unusual case. Look deep into the turning point of any person's life and you will discover that (1) he or she was ready; (2) he or she was there.

The limelight pays off

Viewers of the annual televised Academy Awards show can begin to see within a week's time how winning an Oscar pays off for actors, actresses, producers, composers, studios, everyone. Once they are winners, performers scarcely known by the public before the Awards show suddenly are all over the place on television and radio; films that drew only moderate crowds the first time around, pack houses when first-place awards are advertised; year-old pictures singled out as great get far greater ballyhoo the second time around than the first.

According to a 1969 *Time* magazine report,[1] "An award for a film can mean more than $1,000,000 in increased grosses. For an actor, the impact is greater: Walter Matthau's salary quintupled after he received his Oscar. George Kennedy's story is twice as good: his fee went from

[1] Reprinted by permission from *Time,* The Weekly Newsmagazine; Copyright Time Inc. 1969.

$20,000 to $200,000 per film. 'Before Cat Ballou,' recalls Lee Marvin, 'I was what they call a good back-up actor. I was getting money in five figures before the Oscar. For the last one, *Paint Your Wagon,* I got a million dollars, plus 10%. From 1965 to 1969, that's a pretty nice climb.'" Climbs in income after an award comes are sufficient reason to make a Hollywood performer (or his agent or backer) want to make headlines with a win. Similar take-offs in income after awards come in other fields are just as spectacular (and welcome), as any person can tell you who is sophisticated about the way money follows a headlined award-winning performer in any field.

The case of the prize-winning steer

At Annabel Irving's 500-acre Iron Mountain Farm in the Berkshire foothills in South Kent, Connecticut, a young Aberdeen Angus steer was purchased in November, 1967, by Litchfield County 4-H club member, Paul Schwanka, of Terryville, Connecticut. Price paid: $100.[2] For one year, according to Mrs. Irving, the steer was loved, fattened, groomed by its 18-year-old owner haltered at rehearsal for show and even sung to. All of this Tender Loving Care paid off. In September, 1968, Paul's steer from Iron Mountain Farm was named Grand Champion Steer at the big Eastern States Exposition at Springfield, Massachusetts. The following day it brought in a bid from Stop & Shop Markets for $3,202.50, total. So, in one year, far from doubling the amount he paid for his steer, Paul got back more than 30 times his original investment. And Annabel Irving received a certificate of an award from the Aberdeen Angus Association from St. Joseph, Missouri, which encourages many 4-H members and others to look to her herds for quality steers for upcoming showings.

Whether it's a steer, dog, cat or anything else in competition, groom your entry to win. It will pay off in increased profits.

When you don't know the exact job you want

There are times when you know exactly what you want (i.e., you are in the typing pool and have your eye on the job of one of the private secretaries who is leaving to be married; you are graduating in engineering and want to go into business with your uncle, a real estate developer). At such times, applying the *be* principle is easy. (1) You get ready

[2] After careful examination, Paul paid the going price for a light-weight steer with good formation that looked to him like a winner.

for the job you want. (2) You see to it that the person who can decide your destiny is aware of your readiness. What you want, if you are right for the job, will come to you.

Now, let's consider how you will prepare for the next step when you're not sure what you want that next step to be. In some ways, this is the toughest assignment you will ever have; in others, the most fun.

Some begin as protegees

As a result of a proxy fight in 1954, lawyer Ben W. Heineman took over control of the small Minneapolis & St. Louis Railway, and requested the help of Arthur Andersen & Co., accounting firm, to help him straighten things out. In came Larry S. Provo, 27, who proved so helpful to Heineman that he hired him away from Andersen and made him a vice president. Two years later, when he took over Chicago and North Western as President, Heineman took Provo along. Today, in his 40s, Provo, still with Heineman, is President and Chief Executive Officer of C & NW. (Heineman is chairman.)

In 1966, American League pitcher Jim McGlothlin, farmed out to Seattle by the California Angels, caught the attention of Bob Lemon, one-time ace pitcher for the Cleveland Indians. Lemon taught Jim one of the most important lessons any man can learn. "The big ones are human, too, like everybody else." No longer in awe of major league hitters, Jim became the pro pitcher he was always meant to be. A year later, he was pitching in the All Star Game.

Some find instant success

Francine LeFrak became an associate in a boutique[3] in one of Manhattan's most successful department stores before she had had any business experience of any kind because her groovy good looks attracted the attention of a young man just going into business. The man was Jonathan Farkas, son of board chairman of Alexander's Department Store, 58th St. and Lexington Ave., New York City. Admiring the clothes and hairdo and just plain *style* of Francine, who pals nightly with seeing-the-action debutantes, young Jonathan invited her to become his colleague in his

[3] Name of the shop: *The 59th Street Bridge Shop for Feeling Groovy,* now called "The Groovy Shop" in Alexander's eight stores where it has become a permanent department.

New York boutique. Overnight, Francine found herself playing a major role in an instant success story. Today, she is having the time of her life, putting to work her good taste and the knowledge she has of the wants of her contemporaries in Alexander's 3rd floor boutique, which is a real hit.

In this case, Francine had not groomed herself for something she wanted; she simply was being herself. Success came because a young man saw that she could be invaluable to him (and to herself!) in business. Without ever having heard of the *be* principle, Francine benefited from the way it works.

Listen for your call

Suppose that everytime you think of this job, that job, the other job, you feel no enthusiasm. You know you could do any of the jobs offered to you, but none gives you a lift. Before committing yourself, go off for a week alone (or for a few hours every day for a week, if going away is impossible) and ask yourself what you really do want to do, no matter how impossible it may seem as you think of it. Want to be a writer? An artist? A musician? A lawyer? A teacher? An architect? Think deeply, clearly, alone, about what would give you the greatest pleasure, and you will feel your call. Then, no matter what job is offered to you that takes you away from the field you want, turn it down.

Once you sense your right direction (whether what you want is to be a manicurist, a mortician, a mining engineer, or anything else), take even the lowliest job that gets you coursing along in the channel you want. "Don't worry about the breaks," say the psychologists. "Just do what you like to do as well as you can possibly do it, and the breaks will come."

"Each man has his own vocation," Emerson wrote.[4] "The talent is the call. There is one direction in which all space is open to him. He has faculties silently inviting him thither to endless exertion. He is like a ship in a river; he runs against obstructions on every side but one, on that side all obstruction is taken away and he sweeps serenely over a deepening channel into an infinite sea. This talent and this call depend on his organization, or the mode in which the general soul incarnates itself in him. He inclines to do something which is easy to him and good when it is done, but which no other man can do. He has no rival. For the more truly he consults his own powers, the more difference will his work exhibit

[4] Ralph Waldo Emerson, "The Spiritual Laws," *The Complete Essays and Other Writings* (New York: Random House, Inc. [Modern Library], n.d.), pp. 195, 196.

from the work of any other. His ambition is exactly proportioned to his powers. The height of the pinnacle is determined by the breadth of the base. Every man has this call of the power to do somewhat unique, and no man has any other call. The pretence that he has another call, a summons by name and personal election and outward 'signs that mark him extraordinary and not in the roll of common men,' is fanaticism, and betrays obtuseness to perceive that there is one mind in all the individuals, and no respect of persons therein."

Do what you want to do

Olivia de Havilland wanted to be a great actress but didn't push for great roles; she simply worked to be ready when her break came. It did, in the part of Melanie, in the movie classic of our time, *Gone With the Wind.* The part was first offered to Joan Fontaine, Olivia's sister, who had been turned down for the Scarlett O'Hara role, which was the one she wanted. According to *Time* magazine, "Get Olivia to read for Melanie," is what Joan said. David Selznick did exactly that, and the rest is history.

Millionaire John Diebold, just over 40, became interested in the use of computers in 1950 at the Harvard Business School, and helped prepare a report on the new science of automating factories. Out of his report grew his book, *Automation,*[5] which drew attention to the word and to Diebold. His first job with Griffenhagen & Associates in Chicago, however, paid him less than that of any man in his Business School class at Harvard. Soon, in order to apply his ideas on the business application of computers, he returned to New York and opened his own small office. Today his companies have offices from San Francisco to Madrid as he helps the largest business concerns in the world blend technology and business techniques. Remember, he started out to know everything that he could know about the subject that interested him most, *advanced business technology.* Success just naturally followed.

Daniel Barry, a vigorous, hard-working painter near us, has a romantic heart and a scientific mind. Most of each week, he paints brilliant florals, serene nudes and seemingly unposed men and children much in demand internationally by leading galleries and museums for their wit, expert draftsmanship and deep perception. Then he switches to conceiving science fiction exploits for Flash Gordon. Author of the strip for 18 years, he was interviewed extensively when Neil Armstrong landed on the moon. For it was Daniel who first put on paper the idea for a separate

[5] Diebold, *Automation: The Advent of the Automatic Factory* (Princeton: D. Van Nostrand Co., 1952).

moon-landing vehicle similar to the Eagle. The Flash Gordon series provides Dan with an outlet for his restless versatility. It also publicizes his name, which helps to sell his paintings, his real love.

Timing counts a lot

Now that America is focusing attention on the malcontent of the Negro, many Negroes who have trained to be good at what they are doing, are getting a break. Not a break that comes through kindness, but through the need of society to know that the Negro knows. Kenneth Mines, 38, son of a chauffeur turned landscaper, is an esteemed Negro lawyer in Detroit's Labor Department; Cereta Perry, the child of a janitor, is a prominent Negro teacher in Washington; William Lucas, highly intelligent Negro in Connecticut, is a much needed urban planner. The prepared Negro who can help America do what has to be done in any field today is getting a break. Again, that word "prepared" is the key.

Once again: Prepare yourself for the career you want. Work to be good at this career. (Be *ready;* be *there!*) *Your break will come.*

The story of Adele Simpson

When we were considering what designer of women's clothes we should write about in this book, we researched women shoppers on floors where better clothes are sold in Dayton's Store in Minneapolis, Higbee's Store in Cleveland, Armstrong's in Cedar Rapids, Bloomingdale's in New York, asking them, "What American designer do you especially admire?" Over and over again we got the answer, "Adele Simpson."

"Let's tell the story of Adele Simpson," we said to each other, "somewhere along the line she must have doubled her income."

That she did! At an age when most girls are still in college she was hard at work on 7th Avenue in New York and earning a reputation for tailoring wonderful-looking but easy-to-move-around-in clothes that women were taking to. (She was first to engineer the set-in sleeve; made dresses that could be stepped into, not pulled over the head; paired easy-walking skirts with matching coats.) "I wasn't out to make money," she told us when we visited her at her 28-acre estate in Greenwich, Connecticut, on a recent Sunday afternoon, "I was just designing dresses." A graduate of a two-year course at Pratt Institute, where she went to study cutting, she was soon making $15,000 a year; and before long, as her reputation grew, she got a call from a rival manufacturer who wanted her to move over there as a designer at double her salary. She did and so found herself making *$30,000 a year before she was 21 years old.*

"As I look back," she says now, "although this was a giant step, it didn't make very much of an impression on me. I just knew that I was very busy and doing what I wanted to do."

Easy, elegant and best made

A small (she's 4′ 9″) quiet-voiced woman who moves through life with rhythm and speed, Adele Simpson has a sure knowledge of the needs of today's woman who is too busy for fussiness but still wants to look elegant wherever she finds herself. So she designs dresses and suits (and often the fabric that goes into them) to fit the life she knows intuitively is led by her customers. Result: clothes considered by the fashion world as best made for their price category ($90 to $350 retail); clothes said by women everywhere to demand less altering than women's clothes designed by any other American designer.

Today Adele Simpson, Inc., with 12 factories busy year-round, is the largest volume house in its category, using over a million yards of fabric a year. And the tiny designer who is president and many times a millionaire will still tell you that she is simply "doing what she likes to do." What she likes to do has brought her into contact with some of the best-known women in the world. (She's a favorite designer of Mrs. Lyndon Johnson, Mrs. Norman Vincent Peale, and many more.) It has also brought her the Cotton Fashion Award, the Neiman-Marcus Award, the International Silk Association Award, the Woolens and Worsteds citation, and NBC's Today Show award, plus dozens more and keys to more cities than she will ever have time to know—although like the women she designs for she is an enthusiastic traveler. Her trips to everywhere in the world feed her need for constant fashion research, produce ideas for styles, designs and fabrics and bring her in contact with people, all kinds of people, whom she finds stimulating. "My own travels have made me more aware than ever that clothes must fit properly, must not be contrived. No woman can be comfortable when traveling, or any other time, if her clothes have to be fussed over."

Mrs. Simpson's life, itself, seems to move along as smoothly as the clothes she designs—yet it is a full life that takes her attention in many different areas. Wife of a successful textile manufacturer for 40 years, mother of two productive children in the dress business, grandmother of three, she sees to the running of her handsome four-floor Manhattan town house, her home in the country and her 47-foot yacht with the same seemingly effortless attention to detail and the comfort of her guests as she has always put into the making of her dresses.

"A remarkable woman," a male competitor said of her, "very shrewd."

"A great talent," said one of the women who have worked with her in New York's famous Fashion Group, "along with a rare sense of today."

"Obviously, a practicer of *be*," said a friend of our daughter's who read our account.

All are correct, even our young friend, and this in spite of the fact that Adele Simpson probably never has heard of the *be* principle. Still, she has been using it effectively most of her life because of the kind of woman she happens to be, because of the talent which has always been hers.

"I didn't set out to make a fortune," is what we remember her saying, "I just did what I knew how to do."

And did it, and did it, and did it, until she got to be better at what she could do than all the rest. Then, the money came.

Putting the be principle to work for you

"That's fine for a natural-born designer," you may be saying to yourself, "but, ho, ho, ho, if *I* tried to do that."

Or as one of our house guests put it last weekend, "As Alice B. Toklas said, 'What is sauce for the goose may be sauce for the gander but it is not necessarily sauce for the chicken, the duck, the turkey or the guinea hen.'"

So you're not a gander! You can still use the principle of doing what you do well naturally, and doing it and doing it, until you get to be so good at what you do that your services will be sought. Don't worry that you won't be sought after when there is a population explosion making for more and more of a demand from more and more people for what you have to give.

The naturally gifted garage mechanic whose sensitive hands understand machines and whose sensitive brain understands the needs and desires of his customers will have no trouble in doubling his salary in a year as his reputation for service and competence keeps getting better and better. The boy who washes windows better than any other boy in the neighborhood and is fast and remembers that his customer likes the bucket and sponge to be put away afterward, where he found them, is going to be so in demand that he will be asked to work for another at twice what he's getting now, whatever that happens to be. The conscientious baby-sitter who thinks of the children and the mother and the house where she finds herself and does her best for all three is going to be twice as busy next month when other mothers hear about how she works. The business will come, and when she gets so busy she can't take on more, a higher hourly offer will come, and then more offers that are even higher. If you are unusually good at what you do, you will get an offer to do what you do for more money. That is a law!

Now, suppose the mechanic wants to be manager of the garage that he is in; the window washer wants a steady Saturday job as yard boy, waiter, chauffeur, family helper in the house where he's working; the girl wants to earn more money as a tutor for older children rather than as a baby sitter for small children.

All can put *be* to use in the way it was designed to be used.

The mechanic, according to the principle, will begin right now to function as a manager, think as a manager, talk to customers as a manager. Automatically, he will take on a management viewpoint; he will get to work earlier, stay later, do what he can to cut expenses, produce more profits; naturally, his work will continue to be just as good under the hood of the car and that will bring in more business. The owner of this business or of a rival business is bound some day to take note. "That fellow would make a great manager," he will say to himself. When the offer comes, the mechanic will not be surprised; in fact, he will hardly notice. He will have been functioning as a manager for a long time.

The window washer at the house that can use a Saturday helper can use *be* the same way. As the family helper, he will do a great job of washing windows, of course, but he will see and do more. As he sees and does what is needed at the house, the owner will see. The job will come.

The girl who wants to be a tutor instead of a baby sitter will function as one. First, she will be good enough in her own right to know inside herself that she is ready to tutor others. Then when she baby-sits she will read to the small children with a more careful understanding of their reactions, and when they are in bed, she will help the older children in the house with their lessons. Their work will soon reflect this extra help at home and at school. The girl who is doing the tutoring will be "discovered."

What do you want to be?

As you have read this chapter, you have mentally discarded the notion of being a mechanic, perhaps, or a baby sitter, or a designer, or a computer programmer or a window washer, because none of these jobs exactly fit you. So what do you want to do? Do you know? If not, don't worry about this. As you read, you will see. And when this happens, you can put the *be* principle to work to get what you know you want.

From This Chapter . . .

First Financial Recipe for Doubling Your Income

1. Get to be 10 times better at what you're doing than anyone else around.
2. Make yourself ready to function in a job paying twice as much. (Dress, talk and *feel* the part now.)
3. Get as close as possible to the person who has a doubled income to offer. Stay in view.

Never fear, the call will come!

2

ACHIEVE YOUR GOAL THROUGH A STRATEGY USED IN ADVERTISING

Adding up the time we have spent individually in the advertising business, we arrive at a figure of 40 years as a total for Authors' Years Spent on Madison Avenue. For this reason, we tend to think in terms of this business more than of others as we talk of ways to get ahead financially. Normally, we would avoid leaning on examples concerned with one profession; in this book, however, we will turn to the business of advertising often for stories that can help you in your pursuit of a higher income, whatever your business may be.

There are two reasons for this.

1. Principles used by shrewd creative men and women to get ahead in the world of advertising are ones that you can adapt easily for your own use.
2. Methods used by men and women to sell package goods in a highly competitive market place are methods you can adapt to sell the most important product you will ever be involved with, *yourself*.

The *number two* factor is the one that we will address ourselves to in this chapter.

Accepted strategy for selling an advertised product

"We have always maintained," Dick Lord, 43-year-old president of the young, hot New York ad agency, Lord, Geller, Federico and Partners, Inc., said recently in explaining his agency's philosophy, "that the only difference between two similar products is *the idea*."

Think of this for a minute.

You are about to buy a shaving cream. You have your choice of a cream that smells like lime or one that makes abundant lather or one that comes out hot or one that contains an astringent to heal nicks as you shave. Four basic ideas built into four different products so that each product can be advertised by different agencies as something new, desirable, right for *you.*

Or you are a woman about to buy a hair spray. One tells you that it contains silicone so it holds better in any weather; another, that it contains lemon so it makes your hair shine as it holds; another, that it contains special conditioners that restore body to hair that's washed often; another, that it contains an atomized cream rinse so it holds but lets hair move. Four different ideas that have been built into four different sprays.

Which shaving cream and which hair spray will get the biggest share of market? The answer is easy. The product with the built-in idea that appeals to the most people. But we are talking about *you!* How can you build an idea into *you* that will make a man or a company in a position to double your income reach out for you? The answer again is a simple one. Use the method employed by advertising people when they are building a selling story for a specific product.

Find a "Unique Selling Proposition"

Rosser Reeves, for many years the board chairman of the giant agency, Ted Bates & Company, made the initials USP as well known in advertising agency circles as the initials JFK were in politics. "Find a Unique Selling Proposition," was his theory, "that is built on a product advantage that is of real interest to the consumer." Typical campaign built on this theory: "Like a doctor's prescription, *Anacin gives fast, fast, fast relief.*" To the man or woman with a headache, an Anacin commercial with its three streams of bubbles flowing up to do away with pain causers in three boxes in the head conveyed that this tablet had *not one but a combination of the pain-relieving ingredients.* The convinced sufferer bought Anacin.

Now let's take the USP theory and apply it to *you!*

Find your USP

You know from the self-analyzing you did in Part I of this book what kind of work you like to do. Now, if you are already in this field, we are going to help you to sell yourself for twice the money you are now making. You will do this by finding your personal USP.

Suppose you are a carpenter working for yourself in a small town.

Maybe you're as busy as you want to be in the summer but not in the winter. Now, there may be a contractor in your town who has a small string of carpenters he guarantees work for during a given number of weeks per year on jobs he contracts for. You know he won't pay you double per hour what you are now getting, but he may be able to get half again as much for your services as you are getting on your own and he can keep you busy in the winter when you are now idle. The combination of more pay and more hours may well double your income. So how do you encourage him, in a town of many carpenters, to select you as one of his string? The contractor obviously wants to make money or he wouldn't be in business. Should he hire you, he will expect to make more money with you than he did without you. Why, then, are *you* his man?

Never had an accident? That's a plus. Accident-prone carpenters cost money.

Not a heavy drinker? Good. Drinkers tend to be slipshod.

Not sickly? Fine. Absenteeism won't be a problem.

But these are simply the absence of negatives. What's the great big positive about you that sets you apart from other carpenters?

Are you dedicated to doing a good job? (Would you work an extra hour even if you didn't get paid for it to make the hardware on a cupboard look the way the lady of the house wants it to look?) This is going to be something a contractor will appreciate.

Are you faster than other men he can hire? Your speed is going to make him money because he can compete with other contractors if he knows he can finish a job faster than they can finish it.

Are you creative? Is it easy for you to see how a spiral stairway will dress up a room, how a skylight will lighten up a reading place, how chestnut beams in a library will add character? The contractor can go after jobs other contractors will never be considered for.

Are you unusually efficient? See ways the whole job can be speeded up, find ways in which work done by every man on the job can be made less complicated? Great. You can free the contractor from routine work so that he can go out and sell more jobs.

Do you have access to supplies not available to him without you? Got a brother in the lumber business, own land with gravel on it, own a pick-up truck or a bulldozer or a big power motor? Your contacts and/or equipment may save on his overhead.

What the carpenter sells in the hypothetical exercise we have so far addressed to *you* depends on what kind of a town you live in. If most of the workmen in the town are lazy, you will sell dedication; if there is a great deal of work to be had if a contractor just had time to go out and get it, you will sell efficiency; if the town is one in which wealthy persons are restoring old homes, you will sell creativeness.

But how? How will you sell your creative ability in case this is the way the contractor wants to go?

Foolproof selling philosophy

When advertising consultant Bill Tyler, well-known columnist for "Advertising Age," was creative director of Benton & Bowles Advertising Agency, he worked out for the agency an advertising philosophy which is foolproof. "A strong simple selling idea, dramatically presented." The philosophy goes a step beyond a unique selling proposition, to the presentation of that idea. According to Bill, that presentation must have drama. "Then, it will be memorable."

So how does the carpenter who knows that he is more creative in his approach than are other carpenters in town go about dramatizing this ability for any contractor to see? Just talking about his creativity isn't enough; it may actually turn people off.

The answer is *publicity.*

Publicity

If a carpenter has a creative mind, somewhere along the line he has put this mind to work in an unusual project. One carpenter we know built a suspension tree house between two trees in his yard which attracted children for blocks around; another built a glassed-in sun porch around a 150-year-old maple tree which provides cooling shade on the hottest summer days; another engineered a horizontal clothes chute from the bathroom to the laundry in his one-floor house which carried soiled clothes on a cable. So far as we know none of these projects ever made the newspapers—yet each was worthy of a story.

In our plan for our carpenter, we urge that he get someone to tell a feature writer on his local paper (they want stories) about one of his projects which couldn't have been done by a carpenter without imagination. A story in the paper will do him a lot of good with his contractor.

Word of mouth

If the carpenter is truly creative, he is going to have ideas about many projects, whether he is working on those projects or not. In the beginning, as he builds his reputation, it will be worthwhile for him to put his ideas in front of the public even when he doesn't get paid.

The town may be building a new bridge and need fill for the project. He may have an idea as to where to get it. Rather than remain silent, he should give this idea to the town, through a letter to the town clerk, the mayor, the newspaper or the engineer on the job. The idea he gives away will enhance his reputation for being a man with ideas.

The man next door may be trying to build a TV set into an antique chest. Our carpenter may see a way to incorporate the chest into a built-in bookcase by taking the legs off the chest and turning it upside down and suspending it from the ceiling. If he has the energy, after his day's work, he might help the man with the job. The resulting word-of-mouth publicity will attract attention.

Anything that he can do now, whether he gets paid as he will eventually get paid or not, is worthwhile in this job-bettering stage *if it underscores the reputation that our carpenter is trying to build.*

Sometimes a man's wife is the best salesman he can have. In the case of the carpenter, anything he does in his own home of an inventive nature will be observed and commented on by friends of his wife. Therefore, his house should be filled with creative touches not usual in homes in his circle. His work will be his best press agent.

Rule to remember: STICK to your image-building

As far as the carpenter is concerned, his aim is to get known as a carpenter who is creative. Any publicity that helps him in this aim is something he will welcome, but just any publicity won't do. (He won't write a letter to the paper on why there should be an earlier curfew during this period; he *will* write a letter about how to restore the steeple on the famous old church in town.)

The final push

Once his reputation for having a creative mind has begun to build, our carpenter can go to the contractor he wants to work for with pictures of his projects, stories of what he has done, a list of unusual things he has built. Probably he won't have to. Undoubtedly, the contractor will have heard of his work and will have called him first.

Suppose you are selling a product

Now, suppose you are not trying to sell yourself to a person or a business who can use your services but that you are in business for yourself and want your own product to be bought by twice as many consumers. What do you do? Again, our answer: Do what the advertising people do.

7-Point plan for promoting your own product

1. Determine what people are in (or can be brought into) the market for your product.
2. Find out what competition you have for this market.
3. Discover what your major competitors are saying about their products.
4. Decide whether or not you can beat your competitors' price and/or quality and still make a good profit. (This means careful figuring of all marketing costs.)
5. Determine what is there about your product that is different (or can be made to seem different) from what your competitors are offering.
6. Publicize your story.
7. Advertise your product.

Case history of a man who capitalized on a trend

In 1964 at a court auction in Connecticut we bought an old rundown 50-acre tobacco farm for the bargain price of $18,000. Bordering the old dirt road which ran through the property were two silvery-grey chestnut barns, one upright, the other, a collapsed jumble of great grey beams and sidewalls. Immediately, we began converting the upright barn to a house, lining it with richly-textured aged wood from its own outside, borrowing beams from the blown-down barn. The barn, after it evolved into a two-living room, two bath, two-bedroom Gold Medallion Electric Home, became a show place. As we entertained friends there, we were congratulated over and over again on our lucky find of weathered chestnut. "If you had enough of this old wood," one of our advertising friends said one night, "you could make a fortune. All some guy would have to do is comb the country for old barns, and sell the siding and beams to builders and decorators." Well, *somebody did.*

For years, County Judge Gerald Jolin, now in his 50s, of Appleton, Wisconsin, hunted old barns for architect friends as a sideline. As America's appetite for hand-hewn beams and wood exteriors increased, so did the demand for Mr. Jolin's siding. In 1965, sensing the vast potential for the product he was interested in, former Judge Jolin went into the barn business full time. Now he keeps a man busy roving back-country roads through his native state, searching for barns built of pine and hemlock which have been sufficiently weathered. And he sells his "authentic antiquity" all over the country.

Recently, *Time* Magazine printed a picture of Jolin in front of an old barn over the caption, *Harvest of Age,* and ran a story about the former judge's Wisconsin operation. Less than a month later, we received in the mail a reprint of the *Time* story from Decor Materials, Route 2, Appleton, Wisconsin, Mr. Jolin's company, with a strong selling story for barn boards (half-century minimum), shingles (half-century minimum) and beams (half-century minimum).

Gerald Jolin is selling "authentic antiquity" to a nostalgic world with modern marketing methods. He knows that his market will be waiting for his product for as long as his supply lasts. Mr. Jolin started out with a winning idea and he knows how to sell it.

Watch this trend

As city problems increase in modern America, a desire for the peace that used-to-be is going to make American antiques of every kind more desirable to buyers. This is true of everything but especially true of handsomely weathered woods (used now for cabinets, picture frames, woodwork, as well as indoor paneling); and the rarer the wood, the higher the price.[1]

At 23, Bill Krawski, from a Connecticut tobacco farming family, decided to harvest barns instead of tobacco. By the time he was 28 he had stripped 120 barns, some of which were used to restore Mystic Village in the old Connecticut seaport. But his supply is running out because tobacco barns are rare; Bill says there may not be 100 left.

As the old barns go, lumber companies are rough-sawing plywood to give it a textured look, and some companies have begun to make synthetic barn boards. The Abitibi Corporation markets a hard-board paneling called "Barnboard," and Armstrong Cork has put "Sturbridge paneling," made of compressed wood fibers, on the market.

If you have access to old American latches, window frames, picture frames, anything of that nature, think of marketing them to builders, contractors, decorators. Sell them with modern marketing methods, as Jolin in Wisconsin knows how to do.

Whatever your product, whether it is an old latch or a new cocktail party appetizer or *you,* take a tip from today's advertising geniuses and

---

[1] The chestnut blight in the early 1900s makes durable weathered chestnut, which is a handsome silvery grey, as valuable today as marble.

follow the seven-point marketing plan you read in this chapter. Your income will not only double; if you plan a wise campaign, it will sky-rocket.

End of Chapter Exercise

Your aim: to be making twice as much per month one year from today as you are making today. *Write down what that figure will be.* Directly under that figure write down what product you will be promoting that will earn you that increased income. With these two entries, you have your goal and your product. (This product may be a product like barn siding or it may be a combination of products such as drug items in your own drug store. Or it may be a service: i.e., your services as a dentist. Or it may be your ability: i.e., your skill as a secretary.)

Once you know what you want to sell, go back and read again the 7 *points for promoting your own product.* Write down the seven steps you personally can take to increase your income from whatever it is you are planning to sell.[2]

Tape your plan with Scotch tape beside the mirror where you put on your make-up or do your shaving. Refer to it daily as you get ready for work. The plan will soon become a part of your daily thinking. You are on your way!

From This Chapter . . .

Second Financial Recipe for Doubling Your Income

1. Develop the right *selling strategy.* (Determine through careful analysis what message will attract the largest number of buyers of what you have to sell.)
2. Tie your effort in with a current trend.
3. Follow the 7-Point Plan for promoting your product or service.

---

[2] If you are a dentist or doctor or anyone else in an ethical business, you may not be able to do actual advertising as you would for a product. But you can still work to build an "image" of yourself. Once this "image" is established, word-of-mouth publicity by your satisfied patients will do the rest.

3

EXPAND THE MARKET FOR YOUR SERVICES OR PRODUCT

To help you get the income you have in mind, we will encourage you again in this chapter to use methods worked out by the world's most sophisticated advertisers. In doing so, we shall study another phase of marketing which gets the attention of America's largest advertising agencies.

How does an advertising agency make its money?

An advertising agency has no product of its own (other than its ability to sell a product). So (1) where does it get its products to sell? And (2) how does it get paid?

The answer to the first question is easy to understand. The agency sells the product or services of a client which may be a manufacturer or food processor or insurance company or railroad or airline or any other concern with something to sell. The advertiser (client) simply appoints the agency of its choice to create and place its advertising.

The answer to the second question is not so easy to understand, because the advertiser does not pay the agency for the work it does; someone else does. Without going into the complicated fee systems worked out by a few advertisers and their agencies, we will simply say that most agencies are paid by the TV or radio network or magazine where the advertising is placed. The system can best be explained as follows:

If you, as an average woman or man, place an ad costing $100 in your newspaper, on your own, it will cost you $100. If you place it through an advertising agency, it will cost you the same, but the agency will get $15 from the paper. Now if you are a giant industry placing $100 million in advertising a year, your agency will get back $15 million from magazines, newspapers, TV networks, radio stations, etc., for the ads and commercials it creates and places. So the agency business is a giant business, too. Therefore, it behooves an agency to make sales grow for any product it helps to sell. (The more sales made for the product of its advertisers, the bigger the advertising budget and the more dollars back for the agency.)

So let's take a long look at two ways used by agencies to double *their* income.

The first is the obvious way. Go after and get a new account, which will place as much advertising as the agency is already placing for its other clients.

The second approach is the one we will discuss in this chapter. *Double the market for the product (or products) you are now selling.* Adapt this principle used by advertising agencies to double their income, and you will double *yours!*

Five specific ways to expand your present market for you or your product

Let's take as basic an example as you can think of.

You are a cleaning woman who is currently being paid $14 a day—and you work three days a week.

To double your income, you can charge twice as much per day as you are now charging, but you may get no takers in your area. Here are five ways to double your income outside of the obvious way.

1. Work six days a week instead of three. This means you must expand your market by going out and getting one, two or three more women who need your services.
2. If you are working your three days a week for a career woman with a family, think of ways to save her money so that she can afford to pay you double for the days you now work. (Launder her husband's shirts, thus saving a professional laundry bill; offer to do the shopping twice a week on *your* time, saving a third on what she now pays for ordering; say you will get dinner three nights a week, thus saving what she and her husband spend to take the children out when she is "too tired to cook.")
3. Look for a new employer. (If you are good with children, look for a career woman who needs someone to baby sit as well as to clean the house. This way you will qualify as a nurse as well as a cleaning lady.

Or maybe you are an exceptionally *fast* cleaning woman. If so, go to the owner of an office building and tell him you will clean twice as fast as the cleaning people he now employs and do a better job for half again more. You can come close to doubling your income in the same hours a week if you can convince the building owner you will save him some headaches and you're willing to work nights.)

4. Start a small house-cleaning agency. On your three days when you are not working, line up three women who are willing to do house cleaning under confidential and excellent home conditions. By finding each of these women three days of work apiece for $20 a day (you take the $6 commission, give each woman $14) you will take in $54 a week in addition to the $42 that you now make. The price you pay: responsibility. It will be up to you to see that each woman is happy and her employers are happy, too—but it can be worth it.
5. Work for more persons for shorter periods, charging more for each period. Instead of charging $14 a day for one day's work for each of three employers in different parts of the city, work a third of a day three days a week for three women in the same apartment house. Charge each woman $9 for doing whatever you have to do to keep her apartment going. Instead of making $42 per week, you will get $81 a week and you save additional dollars on carfare and/or wear and tear connected with long-distance travel to many places. Principle to remember: You make more per hour when you work short periods of time, because such help is needed and hard to find. Also, you get less resistance when you charge by the job than by the hour.

As we said, we have purposely selected as basic a work example as possible to prove there are many ways to expand a market for your services, whatever your services may be. Now let's look at what to do for a product you are thinking about selling. Again, we will take an example that anyone can understand.

Suppose you're selling a product

Let's say you have earned a reputation in your little town for making great ginger marmalade. During the last year, you have been persuaded to let your marmalade be sold at your church fair, by a local gourmet shop and by one farmer who comes into town with a wagon of farm produce and home baked goods. There has been a big story in the paper about your marmalade, and wherever it is sold, you find the seller is quickly sold out. Now you are saying to yourself, "If I am going to do this at all, I should be making money from it." How should you proceed?

The answer again is simple. *You should proceed exactly as the woman who does housecleaning should proceed.*

Make your product make more money

The woman with the ginger marmalade can do far more than double her income; she can build a fortune.

Here are simple ways she can begin:

1. Get more outlets for her product. (If her present outlets average a total of 12 jars a week, getting five gourmet shops with bigger volume businesses in neighboring towns may boost that total to 100 jars a week. If she continues to make the marmalade as she has been doing, she should more than double her income with this additional volume.)
2. Give more, get more. (The woman can look for a small unique "marmalade jar" which can be used on the table when empty of marmalade for other jellies. With her combined profit on the "gift jar" and the marmalade, she can double her profit from the 12 sales a week.)
3. Increase demand through publicity. (Perhaps the story which has already been in the paper is one that simply told that the woman's ginger marmalade was the big hit at the church fair. Fine, but not enough. Each time that she gets her product in a store in a neighboring town she should talk to a reporter about how she happened to go to that town. Perhaps the church suppers there have the largest attendance of any in the county; or there are more people there of Dutch descent, who have a special liking for ginger; or maybe the town is English in character and ginger marmalade has long been a treat at tea on scones; or maybe this town has the highest income of any for miles around and the inhabitants appreciate good living and this calls for a gourmet product such as ginger marmalade. A local angle appeals to a local newspaper and makes for a good radio news item, too.) Our woman should work out five different "slants" for stories that she can "plant" in papers and on radio shows, too, from time to time. (*Examples:* (1) Does her ginger come from Jamaica? Why? Through what outlet? Any trouble getting it, in any kind of weather? How does she store it? (2) When did she first start making this marmalade? As a child in Europe? In the deep South? With her grandmother in Victoria? This is a story *we* would like to read. (3) How did she happen to sell her first jar of marmalade? Did someone call her after tasting it in her home or at a church supper?

(4) There may be a story in pectin. Ever wonder where it comes from? Or maybe our woman adds another fruit to her ginger marmalade (cranberries? currants?) that has lots of pectin in it. A food editor will like this story. (5) There's a marketing story in the woman's business. How does she plan to continue? As a small business or as a big business like Arnold's Bread, which had a small beginning, too. The financial editor will listen to this story. The main thing is to get the marmalade talked about.

4. Offer to sell marmalades, jams or jellies made by other women. With this approach, the maker of the marmalade actually becomes a salesman for three of her friends who may make great mint jelly, currant jam, orange preserves. By taking a commission on the sales of the jellies and jams not hers and selling and packaging and selling *with hers* she can make twice as much for the same number of unit retail sales.
5. Sell marmalade with home-baked English scones to local colleges and schools and women's clubs for special teas and other parties. Now the woman can charge more for she is providing more than a product; she is filling a need with a special service.

Even a casual reader with no interest in selling marmalade can see where promotion can take our lady with the ginger. And what she can do to expand her market, you can do, too. This is true, wherever you happen to be reading this book and whatever you're doing for a living.

Suppose your product is a column

When Arkady Leokum, author of the popular column, "Tell Me Why," was creative director of the Grey Agency in New York City, he got into the habit of digging deep into any product he was working on to find a selling story that would be sure to appeal to a large segment of the market. Later, when he retired to do full-time editorial writing, the old habit stuck. So it follows that should he decide to write a column he would search for an appealing idea that would just naturally get the attention of a large group of readers. "I will answer questions that children (and their parents) want the answers to," he said to himself. The result was "Tell Me Why," which answers questions like "Why does a bull charge at a red cloth?", "What are freckles?" and "How can you tell poisonous mushrooms?" put to the local newspaper by young readers.

Almost from its conception, Arkady's column has had an inspired merchandising tie-in with Encyclopaedia Britannica which is also a result of the author's past advertising experience. Each day a full set of Encyclopaedias is given to the boy or girl writing in the question of the day selected for print. From the first his question column and unusual gift offer has attracted readers. And his income has gone up and up as more and more large city papers have carried his work.[1]

Once his column became a hit, Arkady's next step was a collection of columns which he put into a book for Grosset & Dunlap under the title, *Tell Me Why*. The book became a best seller for children and led to a second book. All of the time Arkady's income was growing as he went on to do plays and other books along with his column. Today, he earns the money he needs to support the life he wants. He is a happy man.

Some can see opportunity and some can't

"There is plenty of opportunity," Leonard J. Matchan, British board chairman of Cope Allman International, Ltd., a huge holding company that operates in 74 countries, said recently as he relaxed in a New York hotel suite, "but some have the guts to follow up on things, others don't."

The son of a sewing machine repairman whose salary grew from $2.00 a week to over $600,000 a year, Matchan, close to 60, has retired twice, doesn't like doing nothing, says he works for the interests it gives him. "It's the thrill of the chase," he insists.

The thrill of the chase is always there when you can see opportunity and go after it. To help you see opportunity is the first purpose of this book. Once you see, you will begin to take simple steps, such as the ones set forth in this chapter, which will expand your income and start you on your way.

Learn marketing tactics from politicians

In our town where Republican voters outnumber registered Democrats three to two, we elect three town selectmen every two years, naming two from one party, one from the other. In a recent town election, the Democrats had a good two-way strategy: (1) Run one of the town's most popular business men, Paul Richmond, as second selectman, as a strong back up for a less known top man on the ticket; (2) push to switch Republicans to the Democratic ticket and run ads naming prominent members of the opposing party who were pledged to do just that. Good

[1] Papers pay for a column according to circulation. A paper with a small circulation pays little; a large city paper pays proportionately more. The author, who gets a percentage, profits accordingly.

strategy, but the incumbent first selectman (a Republican running for his 5th term) countered with a shrewd move. Counting on many committed Republicans to hew to the line, no matter what man was running for the Democrats, he urged voters four days before the election to vote for the *Democratic* second selectman. This way he kept Republicans, tempted to bolt the party to vote for the opposing team, by telling them to split their vote so as to vote for him and the opposition's second spot candidate. This way he was bound to get in and he took only one gamble: *his own second man might lose out!* Enough Republicans came through, as he anticipated, so this did not happen, and the popular second selectman on the opposing ticket became third selectman, as he also anticipated.

Most good politicians are shrewd marketing men *instinctively*. Watch the moves they use to garner votes. As you become aware of why they're doing what they're doing, you will become a better marketing man in all your business transactions.

One man who saw opportunity

The discoverer-manager of the Beatles, Brian Epstein, made $14 million in five years, and lived opulently with a valet in a London town house. Unhappily, he died at 32, but in his short life he brought fame to four young novelty singers and fortune to himself by following up on a hunch that a young quartette he knew about would appeal to others—a hunch that paid off. Should you trace his method, you will find that it incorporated the simple marketing principles recommended here for a cleaning woman and the maker of marmalade. He simply set out to expand the market for his product, and he did it.

Something to remember: The steps to success are not complicated. The main thing is to know where you want to go and to start walking.

Exploding population a marketing plus

We live in Litchfield County, only 79 miles from New York, in one of the fastest-growing population centers in this part of the country. In just five years, we have seen our town change from a sleepy village to a busy town with new roads, new businesses and new people coming in every day, a fact that is decried by conservation experts but welcomed by business men. A doubled population can mean a doubled business for contractors, real estate men, grocers, discount stores, doctors, lawyers, almost everyone.

If you live where a fast-growing population is making you rich without half trying, don't pat yourself on the back for being a great business man unless you are getting an increased percentage of the business available to you. That *percentage* yardstick is the one used by professional marketing men to keep their accomplishments in perspective.

Is your percentage increasing?

Let's say you are the owner of a small gourmet grocery store in a high rent apartment district. Suddenly, with the coming of a great new high-rise apartment, your business doubles in a year. You may be able to convince your wife that you are a genius but you know you aren't doing as well as you could be doing if another gourmet grocer down at the end of your block quadruples his business as population increases.

Case in point

If you have 10 percent of the available real estate, law, optometry, grocery or any other business in a town where the population has sky-rocketed, and you have doubled your income, don't pat yourself on your back until you check your percentage of available business. If you have only 7 percent of the available business now, your marketing picture is less favorable than it was last year, according to sophisticated marketing men, even if your income has gone up.

Even the clergy has a marketing problem

The expert in every field, even your clergyman, has to take into account the "numbers" in his market and what they mean. On a sunny June Sunday, when many members of our town's local high school graduating class attended his church, the Rev. E. B. Hamlin, rector of St. John's Episcopal Church, gave them this marketing problem from the pulpit.

"How would you make your church inviting to young people (and their mothers and fathers, too) should you be faced with these figures, recently released by Dr. George Gallup of Princeton? *Ninety-eight percent of all Americans believe in God; only 43 percent of all Americans attend church; and 67 percent of all Americans believe that there is a diminishing interest in religion in the United States.* Add to this the fact that *more college students are signing up for courses in religion and religious history than ever before in history*, and you have a puzzler. *How do you reconcile these figures?* What do you think the church can do today to be more helpful than ever before to this country filled with men, women and children who believe in God?"

Obviously, this is a marketing puzzler if there ever was one, as well as a religious challenge.

The case of a young lawyer

Legal ethics keep me from using the name of the young lawyer who came fresh out of a Boston law school five years ago to hang up his shingle in our town. When we first met him, he did not have one client. Soon, however, his intelligence, honesty, and involvement in any problem put to him became apparent to all who came in contact with him, and clients came. At the end of his first year, his income, of course, was more than double that from his first month in his office. And then, in his second year, he was invited to become a partner in a recognized firm in a neighboring town, and his income doubled again. As population in our area jumped so did the business of his firm, and, as his reputation as a good lawyer grew, so did a special demand for his services. Far from just being doubled in his fourth year, his income sailed. Today, he owns his own home and tracts of land on the side.

Two things to remember: (1) If your business depends on people, go where the population is going up; (2) once there, remember it's your share of market, not just more income, that spells success.

From This Chapter . . .

Third Financial Recipe for Doubling Your Income

1. Use the methods of sophisticated marketing men to up your income whether you're selling a product or yourself.
2. Get you and/or your product known so that word-of-mouth advertising helps to build your business.
3. Does your present business have a good growth potential in your particular community? If not, *move!*
4. Keep your eye on your share of market, not just on your income alone.

4

DOUBLE YOUR MARGIN OF PROFITS—WHATEVER YOU'RE SELLING

You can give less attention to your daily work than you are now giving, sell no more of your product or your services than you are now selling, and still come out far better than you are coming out now, if you can stretch the margin between what you pay out and what you take in to get your job done. In this chapter we will tell you how to do this whether you are selling a product or your services and whether you work for yourself or for another.

Two primary ways to increase your profits

There are two primary ways to boost the amount of money you have left after selling a product or services. You can (1) charge a higher price for what you are selling; (2) cut down on what it costs you to sell it.

To make our point, let's go back again to the cleaning woman who makes $14 a day. Say she's a widow and works for five different women five days a week, making a total of $70 per week. In our town, which is without buses or taxis, she has to arrange her own transportation by getting a ride or paying to be part of a car pool.

Now in this same town, the going price for a live-in maid is $55 a week. By living in, our cleaning lady could save on food, room rent, transportation, utilities—in fact, on everything but clothing (and even on that if she wore a uniform). With one switch—from cleaning lady to live-in maid—she can more than double what she has left each week after expenses are paid.

Next, let's look at the lady with the marmalade. Suppose she gets 89 cents a jar for her marmalade and can put it up for 39 cents a jar. In selling her 12 jars a week, she makes $6.00. Now she finds a chain that can sell 100 jars a week. Should she jump at this? Of course, if she can still put up the marmalade herself. Then she will make $50 profit for working each week, rather than $6.00. But what if she has to pay a woman $42 for three days' work a week to help keep the whole thing going? There go the profits; *no good!*

Simple rule to remember: *It isn't just what you get that counts; it's what it costs to get it. Keep your overhead down!*

What if your product is a house?

In the real estate business, in our part of Connecticut, we occasionally come upon an old harness shop, schoolhouse or chestnut barn that we know, if we put some money and effort into restoring it, can become a show place. Because both of us are interested in old places and enthusiastic about what we can do with them, we have to hold ourselves back from buying every relic we see.

Here are questions we ask ourselves before buying, say, an old railroad station which we think we can make into a house.

1. Are we sure that we really want to put the effort into this to turn it into a home? If yes, fine. But if we are going to be tempted to sell (let's say, at a $5,000 profit, tomorrow) we should forget this. Sell tomorrow, and we pay a short-term gains tax on our $5,000. Take longer than six months to turn it into a home, and we are allowed a long-term gain which means a maximum tax of only 25 percent.
2. Can we sell this property in January as well as in October? Good! Then we can take a profit and not pay taxes on our gain for a year. Sell in October and we have to pay taxes the following April. Sell in January and we can have the use of the money we make for almost a year longer.[1]
3. Will our station make a desirable home where it is or will we have to move it? Move it, and *kerplunk* go the profits. To move a building today can cost as much as the building itself.

---

[1] Larry Greenhaus, our accountant, points out another real estate tax break if you are over 65. *Should you sell your principal residence, the capital gain attributable to the first $20,000 of the selling price may be excluded when your income tax is prepared.*

4. Are there bathrooms in this station or did passengers and the station master use an outhouse? If there were bathrooms, there was water; if there were none, probably not. And digging a well can dig away at profits.
5. Will this home be easy to rent if we decide not to use it ourselves? If the answer is yes, we're in clover, because if we rent the property we can take depreciation.[2]

We will not go down the entire list now of all the considerations that you have to think about when buying a building you want to spiff up. We simply make the point here that just saying to yourself, "What great possibilities!" isn't enough. "Will our expenses be so great we can never sell at a profit" is a much sounder approach.

What if you work for another?

Is this chapter one that you should skip if you work for someone else?

Not on your life, because even if you are employed by another, you are working all of the time, if you are smart, *for yourself!*

If you want a paternal relationship, stay home

Once you go to work for another, keep this in mind. Your employer isn't keeping you around because he likes you; he pays you a salary because he believes that by paying you he can make more than he could without you. Accept this, and you will do better for your employer and yourself.

For the next week, take part in this easy test. Each night ask yourself if your employer made more on this day because you were working for him than he would have had you not been working for him. If your answer is yes, you're worth every cent you're making and probably a whole lot more; if no, you are not worth what you are getting and your job is precarious. This is a business reality.

---

[2] Depreciation is an expense reduction on your income tax. If you rent a house to another, you can charge off what you paid for the house and for improvements, taking as an expense each year an installment on what you paid spread over the estimated years of the building's useful life. Furniture in a rented house is figured separately, and because its life will obviously be shorter than the life of the house, your charge-off will be speedier. Thus, it pays to rent a house furnished (to the right tenants, of course).

The above test is not a method for determining your job security. We simply want you to get a proper perspective on yourself in whatever business situation you find yourself in.

Don't look to your employer for parental care. Look to him for money. With this attitude, you will give more for what you get, and your employer will therefore make more money from everything you do. When this happens, and as you can see this happen, your pay will go up. This is a law.

Two-part self-examination to take if you work for another

This is a self-examination test that you will not actually take until a week from today. Read the questions through once now; then put a dollar bill for a book mark here and come back to it in another week after you have rated yourself when your work is done each day, as suggested on the following page. Next week, then, fill in the answers below.

1. How many days in the week that you tested yourself did you earn your company or employer 20 percent over and beyond what you cost the company per day? (If you are a secretary, your immediate boss should be free to accomplish at least 40 percent more work per day than he or she can accomplish without you.)
2. How much money did you spend out of pocket each day from the time you left home to go to work until you got home again at night?
3. How much of this, if any, can you charge to your expense account?
4. How much of this, if any, can you deduct from your income tax?
5. How much are you paid per hour for the time you actually work on the job? (Figure what you make per day and divide that by the hours you have committed yourself to work.) Looks pretty good per hour, doesn't it? Now figure the time it takes you to get to work, to get home from work, your lunch time, that drink you usually have with a client or co-worker, everything you do that you wouldn't be doing if you weren't working for this particular place. Add up the total number of hours you spend away from home in pursuit of your job from the time you leave in the morning until you get home at night. From now on, we will refer to this time as *door-to-door time.* Add to this your unreimbursed out-of-pocket expenses. So, *now* how much do you earn per hour per day when you figure *door-to-door?*

Here is a simple method for figuring what your employer is making from your day and what you are making. Enter the figure in each column as instructed at the base of the columns.

My Employer Pays per Hour for My Work	My Employer Gets Back per Hour for My Work	I Get Back per Hour for the Time I Spend

In column number one write down what your employer pays you per hour, when you add your reimbursed expenses to your hourly pay. In column number two, put down what you honestly believe your employer realizes from your work. What he pays you and 10 percent more? 20 percent more? 50 percent more? Put that *total* hourly return to him in column number two. (If you feel he makes nothing on your work, nor does he improve his own efficiency so that he can make more, write down Loss in column number two.) Now, in column number three, let's figure what you are worth to yourself. Right now add your average reimbursed expenses per day to what you make *per day* (not per hour). Now subtract from this figure what you spend away from home each day which cannot be deducted from your income tax. The result is your present per diem earning. Now count the hours you spend *door-to-door* to do your job. Divide this into your per diem pay and you will know what you are paid per hour for leaving home to go to work each day. Not much? You have some thinking to do.

Let's take an example. For the sake of simplicity, let's say your employer is paying out $10 an hour for your combined expenses and salary. But because of you, he is taking in *at least* $25 an hour that he wouldn't take in without you. That means $15 an hour profit to him—for what you do. But what about you? Let's say you eat a good lunch with the office people, have a couple of drinks with them at night, pick up your own tab and commute from hell and gone (it takes you 12 hours from door-to-door). For your work day, figuring door-to-door, you are probably making about $5.38 an hour. So who's a better business man, you or your boss—and what are you going to do about it?

Second half of your work sheet test

If there is a big difference in the figure the boss pays out for you in column one and what he takes in from your work in column two, fine. The more he receives from his investment in you, the more valuable you are to him and the sooner you're due for a raise. (If it doesn't come from what you will learn in this book, you should leave anyway.) But that is not your big concern right now. Your concern is to narrow the gap between what your boss pays for your work in column one and what you actually take home for doing the job in column three. The closer these two figures are to each other, the better your personal profit picture. If there is a big gap, ask yourself these questions.

1. Can I move closer to my work if the extra hours I spend are due to a long train commute? (If not, can I put the commuting hours to work for me on some job other than this one? This time saving alone will raise my hourly rate for my main job, and may bring in money from a second source.)
2. Am I frittering away money as well as time with people I would never seek out—if it weren't for this job? (Beginning now, I will spend my lunch hour at a museum or gallery or exhibit or spend it checking merchandising trends in a store or at a men's or women's fashion show or in going to the stock exchange or even to the library or the zoo. This I will treat as work apart from my job because I know that every step like this that I take will lead me to something that will eventually help me to earn money from a new source.)
3. Am I spending more on liquor and cigarettes than I would if I were not bored with my job or nervous about it? (If the answer is yes, give up one or the other for a month and at the same time do one thing to improve your physical well-being—diet, maybe, or take a long walk every day or do gym work. This you will not count as work on your present job.)
4. Am I spending more than I should on cabs or on any other method of transportation for which I am not reimbursed? Is there a way next week I can cut back on this spending? (Find the way.)
5. Am I spending more time on unpaid-for office home work than is needed? (To check this, compare your total time spent on your job with what your company realizes for that total time. If your company is getting less than 20 percent above what it pays you, the extra work you are doing is getting you nowhere. Face it, you're in the wrong job. If it is getting more than 60 percent, you are underpaid and probably should be in business for yourself.) Now is the time to take a long look.

Time and ability in exchange for money, that's all you have to trade at the market place when you are working for another who is also in business to make money. Surely, you should be as wise about selling yourself as the marmalade lady is about selling her product. Are you? This chapter should begin to help you know.

Cutting expenses, cutting hours

You surely see how cutting expenses as you go to and from your job brightens your profit picture, but can you see how cutting time spent on the job does the same? Think about it. If you are worth $10 an hour to an employer, you are worth that to yourself, surely, *whatever you do*. Every hour, then, that you are not being paid by another is an hour in your bank to do something for yourself. Make that time count. Use it for *you*, to prepare for the next step in your climb to success.

So how can cutting back on expenses and hours on the job double your profits?

Say you are now averaging $5.38 per hour for that seven-hour-a-day job that pays you $10 per hour. If you cut time spent in connection with this job to the minimum, you will come close to making $10 per hour; say, for the sake of clarity, you can bring it up to $9 per hour. By using the time wisely that you used to spend unconsciously on the job, you can think of a way, surely, to make $2 an hour for the five hours you no longer waste. (Maybe you will become a shark at bridge in these hours and pick up extra money from this pursuit, or study the market, or study art and do sketches on your own time, or take a photography course and sell news pictures to papers from the town where you live at the end of that long commute.) Get to think of your time as money, and the money will come.

Case history of our typist

Our supplementary typist, Linda Smart, of Brookfield, Connecticut, typed the first draft of this book and began to think about how to put what she had learned in this chapter to use. The plan she came up with doubled her income the first month.

Before reading this chapter, she drove from her home to ours to do typing, averaging three hours a day. Her driving time was 45 minutes each way; thus, her time away from home averaged almost five hours, for which she often had to pay a baby sitter.

After reading, she suggested that on straight manuscript typing she have her son pick up typing at our house on his way from work near us the night before work was to be done. Then he could return it the day after she had finished typing and pick up a fresh assignment. She thus saves one and a half hours a day driving time which, as a result of an ad she ran in the paper, she devotes along with another one and a half hours to typing for others. Result: six hours paid for instead of three; no car expenses; no babysitting fee. "And I don't have the wear and tear on *me*," she told us.

Short stop for taking stock

Is there a simple way for you to cut down on the expenditure of time and money to make your profit picture better? *Take stock.*

From This Chapter . . .

Fourth Financial Recipe for Doubling Your Income

1. Charge more per item whatever you're selling.
2. Spend less on the production of everything you sell.
3. Figure time as well as money as a production expense, and work to double your *hourly* take.

5

PUT YOUR TOTAL PERSONALITY TO WORK FOR WHAT YOU WANT

More than once, in his long-time study of history, Arnold J. Toynbee made this observation: *Each society progresses only to the point that it meets its challenges.* Something similar happens, we believe, in the life of an individual. Man is challenged and reacts with a forward action. If he fails to meet the challenge he has accepted, he falls back. If he succeeds, he moves ahead. In his push, he is inner directed, and his success or failure depends on the force or lack of force of his personal dynamos.

In his 80th year, when his book *Experiences* was published by Oxford University Press, Mr. Toynbee's analysis in the book of what has made him work was published in *Saturday Review*. Here he admitted to having been driven to hard work by anxiety and conscience, two motivating forces which in extreme can be negative. Fortunately, Mr. Toynbee's personality included also a third major motivation: *the desire to see and understand.* Here in his words is his personal analysis of the forces that propelled him: "Anxiety and conscience are a powerful pair of dynamos. Between them, they have ensured that I shall work hard, but they cannot ensure that one shall work at anything worthwhile. They are blind forces, which drive but do not direct. Fortunately, I have also been moved by a third motive: the wish to see and understand. . . . Curiosity is a positive motive for action . . . one of the points in which human beings differ from each other markedly. The charge of curiosity with which I have been endowed happens to be high. This is a gift of the gods, and I am heartily grateful for it."[1]

Mr. Toynbee's clear understanding of his inner motivations is as rare as

[1] Permission from Oxford University Press given to reprint material from *Saturday Review* story "Why and How I Work," by Arnold J. Toynbee.

his attitude toward the work of his lifetime (the study of history) which he told more than one reporter he did "for fun." These two unusual attitudes of self-acceptance and joy in work added up to a constant appreciation of life which he revealed in this way when he was 80. "If I could have my life over again, I would spend it in the same way again."[2]

Two new challenges

You have accepted a major challenge in opening this book. You want to be paid more for the work you put out and you are willing to practice new methods to accomplish this. You are even prepared to give up old negative attitudes *if a change in you can help you reach your goal.* But now we ask you to face up to two *new* challenges.

Challenge number one: Are you willing to face up to your *total* personality, looking at weaknesses as well as strengths, and accept yourself as you are with no apology? This you must do if you are going to work without distraction.

Challenge number two: Can you accept your work as "fun" not only in your own mind but as you refer to it to others? Can you give up martyrdom? Without apology for yourself or a martyred attitude toward the work you can do, you can begin to move as if jet propelled. This is providing, of course, that you are doing work that is right for you.

Do you do what you do "for fun"?

You have taken many self-analysis tests in this book to find out whether your major talents are being utilized in your daily work. If not, you are going to move to another field, but, if so, you should be getting pleasure all day long from work that gives you pleasure. But ask yourself: "*Does* it?" Or is there a streak of puritanism in your make-up that tells you that life is a struggle and work is work and no job is to be enjoyed? This is puritanism that is bound to hold you back. Your problem will be to get rid of this attitude if it is making you feel heavy-laden.

We have seen in the Toynbee story that conscience can be a prod, so accept this force that drives you to your work. At the same time, once you start to work brush away thoughts of how hard you are working or that this is something you must do in order to merit an occasional vacation in life. Do you really have more fun on a vacation than you do when you're functioning at your best in work you like to do? If it is your nature to talk about what you do, begin conveying little pleasures connected with your

[2] Ibid.

work when you talk to family and friends. If you are not a talker, begin questioning any down-trodden feelings within yourself. This heavy-laden approach is a bad habit like smoking that you can give up. Challenge yourself to do this. Think of work as fun, and you not only can have more enjoyment on the job but you can also move ahead twice as fast as the world of complainers around you.

Hew to strengths rather than to weaknesses

You may not have the rare ability to put all inner drives to work for you positively instead of negatively. Don't worry about this. Simply set your direction, and then forget about negative pulls. Soon, inner motivations like conscience and anxiety which may be making you uncomfortable will exert a push that will propel you toward your goal. For your weaknesses which may actually be detrimental, you may need to get help from an expert. (If you are an alcoholic, call on Alcoholics Anonymous; if you have some neurotic fears, talk to a psychiatrist or a psychologist; if you lack the education you need for what you want to do, go back to school.)

When weaknesses can be bolstered as a lame leg can be helped by a cane, be grateful for any help you can get. When they cannot, forget about your drawbacks and lean on your strengths.

A diamond-cutter's theory

Morris B. Zale, founder and chairman of Zale jewelry chain with 750 stores[3] and annual sales of $230 million, has a simple formula for keeping people happy in his vast merchandising network. "Our policy toward our people is not much different from the way we cut diamonds—we hew to their strengths, rather than to their weaknesses." A sound principle to follow as you evaluate others, and vital for you to remember as you assay your own worth.

Fashion leaders Diana Vreeland, editor of *Vogue* magazine, and Nancy White, editor of *Harper's Bazaar,* adhere to this "diamond-cutting principle" as they advise women of all ages on how to dress, how to apply make-up, how to be attractive. And notice next time you look at either magazine, how the photographers highlight a model's beautiful eyes, play down her so-so nose—play up good points, play down bad. If a woman has bad legs, fashion editors advise her to forget bizarre stockings, and

[3] More than three times as many stores as next biggest jewelry chain.

suggest that she call the eye of the beholder to a tiny waist. All the way along, fashion experts urge hewing to good points. For beautiful hands, an attention-attracting ring; for elegant feet, eye-catching shoes; for a slim waist, an unusual belt. No bikini for an unshapely body—instead, a sensational hairdo for glorious hair.

"Simply good sense," you say, and you agree to bolster weaknesses where you can and hew to strengths in your basic personality. But now let's look at less basic strengths and weaknesses that come into play in your daily work. The excellence of your work is going to depend on your playing down weak points and playing up the good.

Know your good points

Here is a list of 15 personal attributes. Read down the list with a pencil in hand, and without stopping to ponder too long, write an S for Strength or a W for Weakness after each item.

1. Good personal appearance
2. Good clothes and color sense
3. Good at entertaining others, at home and out
4. Work well in any job without supervision
5. Responsible in handling personal finances
6. Do my best when no one else is around
7. Need no assignment to keep busy alone or with others
8. Can follow instructions to the letter
9. Can help others to produce more
10. Not a worrier
11. Enjoy seeing a job completed to the last detail
12. Am a good salesman
13. Will work with my hands as well as my head to get job on the road
14. Like to travel in my work
15. Always see the big financial picture

You may be in an organization where you want to end up, eventually, as president. In checking your strengths and weaknesses, you can know in a minute's introspection whether the work you are doing every day is presenting your strong points to today's management as you want those strengths presented. If not, *shift* within the organization so that you are using your strong points, because in so doing, you will automatically succeed and your strengths will be seen and depended on. You will be propelled to the top.

If you are dissatisfied in your job and are not using your strong points, you can evaluate now whether you should make the break to go into business for yourself.

Suppose you are a great salesman in a company where the boss does all the selling and you are simply assigned follow-up work. Your dream is to be your own boss, but in checking your strengths you have to put a W after Items 5 and 15 that have to do with finances. Obviously, you can't start a one-man business and make a sure go of it. Your choice: switch to another organization where you can do selling or manage a group of salesmen and let the organization handle the finances—or go into business with a partner who is a financial man. Don't waste time bemoaning the fact that you are weak in the figures department. Do get to work at what you do best: *selling.* Your strength in this department will take you where you want to go.

Forget past mistakes

A simple evaluation such as you have just made with the Weakness and Strength test will make such good sense to you that you may find yourself kicking yourself for having made a wrong turn along the way. "I used to do great as a salesman," you may say to yourself as you look at the big S after Item 12, "so how come I let this guy I work for talk me into a crazy deal like the one I'm in now?" Forget it. You are where you are but you don't have to stay there. If you don't like where you find yourself, move, *but don't blame yourself for wrong moves in the past.*

Don't try to saw sawdust

Gerry Naves, area manager near us for the Dale Carnegie Courses, has a gift for making old truths meaningful with a colorful quote. One night in his Danbury class a woman asked to be excused from speaking until better prepared, and admitted to being embarrassed about her showing the previous week. "Remember what the editor of the Philadelphia Bulletin told a college graduating class," Gerry suggested; *"don't try to saw sawdust."* His point: *Don't go back over things that are already sawed; tackle the next log.*

Think about this when you find yourself saying, "It's too late now, I should have done that when . . ." With our longer life spans and increased vitality, it isn't too late to do anything you want to do 90 percent of the time, especially something to increase your ability.

Dale Carnegie Courses (and Dorothy Carnegie Courses for women) aid in self-discovery. And while not designed to increase your income, the courses help to uncover what is blocking your ability to communicate and sell what you know, so they are bound to lead you to a more productive business life. In off hours, take a course that increases self-confidence. And never say, "Not now, I should have done that years ago." That's *sawing sawdust.* Tackle the log.

Don't be afraid to quit when you're ahead

Dr. H. Bentley Glass, internationally known geneticist and national president of Phi Beta Kappa, tells a revealing story about his first teaching experience 40 years ago at an East Texas high school.

Interested in science, the young teacher was surprised to be asked to coach football. As part of his job, he accepted his assignment and enrolled in a coaching class at Southern Methodist University where he learned the principles of the game from football genius Knute Rockne and Ray Morrison, a pioneer of the forward pass. The next fall his high school team lost only one game and tied its great rival. It was the best record in the history of the school.

"With that kind of success I did the only thing a sensible man could do," Dr. Glass says now. "I resigned."

Science, not sports, was to be the lifework of Bentley Glass, and he knew this from the beginning. In the wrong slot, he edged out, even though winning at the time. No need to tell you that success of the kind he wanted came in the field he knew was for him.

Sum up: *Don't be afraid to move out of a job where you seem to be successful if you know in your heart the work you are doing isn't for you.*

Enthusiasm gets your heart involved

When you're using your strengths, you become enthusiastic about what you are doing because you're doing it well. Enthusiasm gets your heart involved, and that is the key to success.

Charles M. Schwab, who started in the steel industry with a surveying crew at a dollar a day and ended up as chairman of the board of Bethlehem Steel, said more than once, "A man can succeed at anything when he is enthusiastic." We agree, and take the observation one step further. "Indeed, he can," we say, "because any man who is enthusiastic about his work is one who is doing that work well. That follows as the night the day. And such a man is leaning on his strengths, not fumbling along with his weaknesses."

The two unbeatable Ds

"The secret of business success is simple," the founder of the Zale Corporation, whom we referred to earlier in this chapter, has said many times. "It's drive and desire." Recently, this soft-spoken Texan who started his first store in Wichita Falls, Texas, in 1924, and whose jewelry chain now does five times the volume of its nearest competitor, told a New York Times reporter, "It's downright amazing how few people really have drive and desire. Enthusiasm is contagious. When you are enthusiastic, others are *with* you, want you to succeed, will help you on your way."

Be a happy elephant

The late Henry Kaiser, steel tycoon, aluminum king, dam-builder, ship-builder, road-builder, you name it, believed there was no such thing as work. "It's all occupation." A tough, hard-driving man, he was respected by road crews and executives alike. "Henry's a happy elephant," one associate said. "He smiles and leans against you—and after awhile you move along in that same direction because there's really nothing else you can do."

Go where you go *with enthusiasm,* and others will go along!

Total involvement pays off

C. Jay Parkinson, the Utah lawyer who climbed from company counsel of Anaconda in 1940 to chairman and chief executive in 1968, gets deeply involved in everything he does, in and out of business. As a young college graduate, he spent time in England as a missionary for his Church of the Latter Day Saints (Mormons). Back in Utah, he became involved next in politics, was a chairman of the Republican party when he was 21. Today, heading the world's largest copper producing company which has sales of more than a billion dollars a year, he still gets totally involved in away-from-the-office projects as well as business. He's director of the Downtown Lower Manhattan Association, vice president of New York Chamber of Commerce and of the National Advisory Council of Muscular Dystrophy Associations. We could go on and on. The point is that C. Jay Parkinson has a fantastic ability to become totally involved in whatever he becomes interested in—and that even includes cabinet making.

(He shares this hobby with a friend who is a partner in a downtown brokerage house. The two make between 15 to 20 pieces of furniture a year at a workshop they maintain at 57th Street and Second Avenue.)

"Just for therapy," Mr. Parkinson explained recently to a New York Times reporter. Other hobbies of Anaconda's chief include golf and reading (five books a week!).

No man or woman can accomplish so much so successfully without having mastered the ability to concentrate. Mr. Parkinson's fantastic ability in this direction comes from his lifetime habit of becoming totally (not partially) involved in everything that he finds interesting.

From roustabout to head of a $400 million business

The president of one of the largest oil and gas companies in the world and the only Canadian oil and gas company on the New York Stock Exchange is a man who knows the oil business from rig to board room. Starting as a roustabout on an oil rig in the 30s, this rugged worker kept learning the oil business year after year from under the ground up. Eventually, he was asked to be a production manager of an American company's Canadian operations. Along he went, working and learning in the business he enjoyed, and in a few years more he was sought out by another company (his present one) to come in as a vice president. And then in a few more years, he was named president. Since then, until this writing, company profits have increased 20% a year.[4] There are dozens of dramatic stories like this about men to whom success has come as the result of their getting more and more experience in the business they knew best.

Go back to your strength and weakness test

Suppose when you took the Strength and Weakness test you had to put a W after "Do my best when no one else is around," another one after "Am a good salesman," and another after "Always see the big financial

[4] Among his company's assets: 14 million acres of land in Canada thought to contain over 100 billion barrels of oil. More than 100,000 acres owned by the company is on the Canadian side of the North Slope only a few hundred miles from the site of Atlantic Richfield's great oil discovery on the Alaskan side. This land which was bought for approximately $500,000 (5 to 10 cents an acre) is now worth about $16 million.

picture." Let's say your S's were after "Can follow instructions to the letter" and "Enjoy seeing a job completed to the last detail." You may not have the disposition to be the number one executive in a company, but the man or woman who gets you as "a second man" or a secretary is going to do ten times as much work as he could do without you! All you have to be sure of is that you get a boss who knows this!

Don't get mad at your boss

When Mary Ann Seibert of St. Cloud, Minnesota, was named International Secretary of the Year by the National Secretaries Association, she was asked by a reporter, "What things about your boss make you mad?" She said the thought had never crossed her mind.

"If things about your boss irritate you, you can't be loyal and you ought to quit."

Miss Seibert also said, "You shouldn't run to your boss with every petty gripe, either; you should know what's important to him and his firm and what you shouldn't bother him with." Here is the perfect back-up person for a high-powered *doer*, and such a person always does as well in his or her way as the more aggressive front runner does in his.

Aftermath of analysis

When a man or woman undergoes a successful analysis under the care of a psychologist, he ends up with an awareness of self that he has never had before. "We help the patient to bolster his weaknesses, lean on his strengths," an outstanding doctor told us. "And when this is accomplished, it is like taking the muffler off a Cadillac."

"That's right," another psychologist agreed, "I've seen amazing things happen once a man has a flash of insight about his own worth. And it isn't always necessary to go through analysis to have that happen, either; sometimes the simple desire to get ahead can do the unlocking."

You may not have exactly the same qualities as these people, but you have your own strengths. Locate those strengths and depend on them. Pay attention to flashes of insight that tell you what you can do. Once you know, move ahead with all the thrust of your total personality to the life that is right for you.

From This Chapter . . .

Fifth Financial Recipe for Doubling Your Income

1. Give up martyrdom and apology.
2. Meet a challenge with your total personality.
3. Pay attention to flashes of insight.
4. Bolster your weaknesses, when possible; otherwise, forget them and move on.
5. Put your strong points to work every hour.
6. Quit even when you're ahead if your work isn't what you really want to do.

6

USE SOME MORE OF YOU

You may not entirely agree with the political views of California's Governor Reagan, but you cannot make light of the "success talent" which has been obvious in his make-up since way back when he was playing football "for life or death" in Dixon, Illinois. His good high school athletic record led him to a scholarship for half his tuition and a board job at nearby Eureka College. In this small midwestern school, he got caught up in college dramatics, entered a national contest at Northwestern, won an award and knew, then, that some form of show business was to be his career. But this was the depression! How was he to start?

Well, he was good at football and he was good at speech-making. Of course, he could be a football announcer! He got a job at tiny WOC, in Davenport, Iowa, one of the world's first radio stations; soon moved on to 50,000 watt WHO in Des Moines to broadcast track as well as football. Shortly after that, he began broadcasting the Chicago Cubs and White Sox games, via telegraphic report. "Dutch" Reagan, as he was known in those days, was doing what was to be part of his pattern for life. Once he had something mastered, he reached out for something additional to add to what he was doing—something extra that would put to work *some more of him.*

Ronald Reagan first put words to this need of his to go on and on expanding his talent in 1941 when he was playing King's Row for Warner Brothers, his best picture.

In the story, Reagan has both legs amputated by a sadistic doctor whose daughter he has dated; doesn't realize this until he awakens after an operation in a hospital bed near nurse Anne Sheridan. Reaching for where his legs should be, he calls out to her, "Where's the rest of me?"

Reagan says this line comes back to him every time he reaches a point in his life where he knows that it's time to put some more of himself to work.

Ronald Reagan more than doubled his salary in 1937 when he went from $75 a week as a radio announcer to $200 a week as a movie actor as the result of a screen test in California, where he had gone with the Cubs on a training trip. From then on, he moved ahead, using new facets of himself whenever he had mastered the use of a particular facet. Horseback riding for the movies led to horseback riding for the cavalry reserve in World War II; in turn, that led to an assignment with a motion picture unit of the Air Force where he worked with Irving Berlin. Reagan came out of the war a true patriot, and began making speeches to this effect. Back in Hollywood, he got interested in the Screen Actors Guild, became president, made speeches that helped that cause. As TV came alive, he moved into that medium, became emcee for the GE Theatre, began making speeches now on tour for the sponsor. All of his talent was now coming into play, on screen and off. Following his pattern, he was obviously on his way to a new career, politics.

As Ronald Reagan's enriched personality took on stature, so did his bank account. Learning to handle money as he had learned to handle himself, he invested in real estate, got more than double his investment time after time when he sold. As he moved through life, he put more and more of himself to work, a paramount aim for every man who wants to get ahead.

The story of Rickenbacker

Edward V. Rickenbacker's life reads like the adventure of a swashbuckling fictional TV character. First a successful professional racing-car driver; later, owner of the Indianapolis Speedway. One time ace flyer in a World War; winner of the Congressional Medal of Honor. Designer and producer of his own line of automobiles; creator of an airline that became the world's greatest. Along the way, death-nudging accidents which he came through with a ruthless will to survive. Now a tycoon! Next, a best selling book[1] with this italicized quotation which could become his epitaph: *He who does most, lives most. He who lives most, gives most.* Of all men, anywhere, here is a man who used more and more of himself as he moved through life.

---

[1] Edward V. Rickenbacker, *Rickenbacker* (Englewood Cliffs, N.J.: Prentice Hall, Inc., 1967).

Are you using all of you?

Think of your personality as a river that should become wider and wider as you move through life. Are you using all of you? Of course not; there is always more to be used. This does not mean that you will work more hours; it simply means that as you work you will use more and more of your talent.

The amateur golfer who becomes a professional golfer and then becomes a pro at a Country Club and continues to play in tournaments, is putting more and more of himself to work in the sport he loves. The fashion model who becomes a spokeswoman in TV commercials and eventually moves on to acting in motion pictures is progressing the same way. The baby-sitter who gets so interested in children she goes to school to expand her knowledge of pre-school children, and eventually organizes her own day care center is putting more and more of *herself* to work, too. Whatever your field, ask yourself if you are putting more of yourself to work this year than last. This will be much easier for you, of course, if you are in work you really enjoy.

Just keep moving along

Our son Peter and his wife Dale are art historians, who took their undergraduate work at Syracuse and their graduate work at New York University's Institute of Fine Arts. Their classrooms were in the Doris Duke mansion when they were getting their MA degrees; their laboratory, the Metropolitan Museum of Art. By the time they had finished their orals for their doctorates, their obvious dedication to their combined lifetime career attracted job offers to catalogue collections, authenticate paintings and do research material for faculty authors faster than they could say yes. Publicity as a result of Peter's being president of NYU's Graduate Student Club and Dale's being editor of the school newspaper also help to make their names well known in and out of their circle. Grants and awards, as well as job offers, now began to come in, and when it came time for them to take off for Europe to work on their dissertations, money was the least of their problems.

Peter, who had received a fellowship tuition of $1,200 in his last year as a graduate student at NYU, now received one of the 217 Woodrow Wilson Dissertation Fellowships of $3,000 annually to outstanding students for travel. This was enough to finance the digging he wanted to do into the life of the sculptor Bartolommeo Ammanati in Florence and

Venice. His wife received a Fulbright Fellowship ($1,700) plus $2,500 from the Samuel H. Kress Foundation to study a 12th century church in Rome, which was to be the subject of her thesis.

If you should ask Peter and Dale today if the acquisition of money is their number one aim, they would say *no,* yet their income is doubling annually even as they breathe because their concentration on perfecting their abilities in their chosen field is undeviating.

The case of Fred Adams, Jr.

Fred Adams, Jr., of Jackson, Mississippi, started out as a truck driver; now he is a legend in the annals of free enterprise. First, a truck driver; then a salesman; and soon, before he was 35, owner of the largest egg factory in the world! Today, the Adams' industries distribute eggs in 16 states and to many foreign countries.

What's the reason for Fred Adams' success? Is it because he wasn't afraid to start out as a truck driver? Or that he worked hard? Of course not. But he did start out as a truck driver and he did work hard, and today he does understand trucking, and selling, and breeders and layers and packaging and everything else connected with the egg business. Besides that, he has a people sense (he employs 600) and a money sense (his sales were up over $10 million last year). That is quite a package of abilities and he is making good use of them. Fred Adams has a lot to work with, and today he is using everything he's got and functioning at his optimum.

You just want to get ahead

"But I have no great talent," you insist. "I'm just an ordinary person who wants to get ahead!" So was young Barbara Bennett, divorced mother of two, who lives near us in Kent, Connecticut. "I knew nothing much except ordinary homemaking skills," she told us. "But I decided to put what I had to use to give my children the kind of lives I wanted them to have."

Her first job: cook at a private school in her home town. "The hours were good; I could work when the children were in school." As she mastered this job, she decided to work with another homemaking talent: *sewing.* She began making slipcovers, curtains, even dresses for women in her community. Soon the money that came in from sewing was twice what she was making at the school job, so she let the first one drop away. Now she could be home all day and still earn money. The more she sewed, the more obvious became her ability. Soon she began to design clothes for women in her town; then she raised her prices. All of the time, she remembered her major function: to be a good mother to her children. Naturally, being attractive to men, she soon married a man with children. Now she has a good marriage, a big family and a career. She's the busiest "little French seamstress" in Connecticut.

The secret of not getting old

Persons whose lives become wider and wider, not narrower and narrower, never become old. Grandma Moses, Helena Rubenstein and popular Marianne Moore, octogenarian poet, allowed their lives to move *out,* and so became more and more attractive as senior citizens. Students who never knew Miss Moore's poetry came to admire her through her lectures and television appearances.

Simple exercise

Write down the talent you are now making most use of. Maybe it is *typing.* Perhaps you, like our typist, are copying manuscripts for others at home. How can you widen that talent? Perhaps you can make it include *dictaphone transcription.* (This may mean taking a short course.) Once you do that, you may have more business than you can handle and can get other typists to work with you. See—you are on your way.

We cannot see into your mind from where we sit. But we still know that you have *something* you do every day as a matter of course. Write down what you now do. Then beside it put the first thing that comes to your mind that will provide an expansion for that daily occupation. (Probably you have already thought in this direction.) Now go to work to make this expansion a reality. When you master this, do the next thing. You will be on your way to a doubled income and then more and more as you continue to expand what you have to give. *Give more, get more*—that's the way!

From This Chapter . . .

Sixth Financial Recipe for Doubling Your Income

1. Study, read and search for new ways to use your talent. As your talent expands, so will your ability to make money. Put this expanded ability to work to bring in more.
2. The minute you achieve any success, look for a way to use more of you.

7

SHIFT TO A HIGHER-PAYING FIELD

Sometimes, doing just what you are now doing in another field can more than double your income. Examples: A writer of commercial radio spots for a local radio station can up his income by moving to an advertising agency where he writes commercial radio spots for a national advertiser to be distributed to many radio stations. An insurance salesman can sell sickness compensation policy to an individual for a small commission, or he can work out this same kind of policy for many individuals under a group plan and sell it to a company for a giant commission. A real estate broker can spend an afternoon finding a young couple a $150-a-month house to rent and come out with a $15-a-month commission for a 12-month period; or he can help that same couple work out a way to buy the house for $15,000 and end up with a $900 seller's commission.

Are you using your talent and time in a way to make it pay off as it should be paying off?

The case of the young stockbroker

D. Douglas Stevenson, Jr., in Minneapolis, is a registered representative with a local branch of a New York Stock Exchange Minneapolis firm. His story is a case in point.

A graduate of Dartmouth as an Economics major in 1956, Doug went on with his training at the Amos Tuck School of Business Administration for one semester, the University of Minnesota Graduate School of Business for another semester and the American Institute of Banking for a third semester. Then he went to work.

After three months as a commercial loan trainee with the Guaranty Trust Company of New York, he was called to three years of active duty with USAF-SAC. With an honorable discharge in his pocket, he went to work afterward for one of the National Banks in Minnesota, for the first year and a half as a commercial loan trainee and then for two and a half years with the Trust Investment Division.

By this time, he was close to 30 years old, married, a homeowner and the father of two. He was making $6,840 a year as a security analyst and portfolio manager, happy, hard-working and productive, but he wanted a higher income.

"I began to see that the best way for me to make more money was to find a job in which I could make more money for others. I decided to go after a job in a brokerage firm."

He did, and got the job he applied for at a Minneapolis brokerage house. That was early in 1965. He recently made up a chart for us of his earnings from 1965 through 1968.

The chart shows a total income of $7,200 in 1965; $14,436 in 1966; $22,000 in 1967—and in 1968, $42,000! A doubled income, then a tripled one, and then, double the triple income—with no great upheaval in his life. (His office is only a few blocks from where he used to work in the bank but he does have a new house, a real lalapalooza!) Why did he succeed? Because he took what he knew about investing money to a field where this knowledge could pay off for specific clients and thus earn him a larger commission.

Here is the letter we received from Doug when we told him we wanted to tell his story:

> Dear Jean and Cle:
>
> The knowledge gained as a security analyst and investment portfolio manager at a major Trust Department was one of the particular skills which I have been able to apply in my new position.
>
> The essential ingredients for success in this business, however, are product knowledge, enthusiasm and hard work. I enjoy the work here more and more each year because of the independence of "rising or falling" on my personal relationship with clients, because of the satisfaction of getting new investors started on a solid investment program, and because of the earned respect of institutional fund managers for keeping them posted on money market conditions, industry trends, and attractive security purchase opportunities. Present clients now *rely* on my thinking.
>
> Sincerely,
>
> Doug Stevenson (*written*)

Obvious, isn't it, why the annual income of Doug Stevenson continues to move up. Not surprising that each new year is a record-breaker.

The case of Piero Gilardi

A slightly younger man than Doug in quite a different line has a similar record of an upped income when he took his particular talent to a new field.

Piero Gilardi, Swiss artist, had an inspiration as he walked barefoot in a dried-out river bed in France one day. "I am a man who is a product of a great period of technology," he told a reporter for the New York Times, "and yet I still love nature. I thought I needed a way to bring these two sensations together." According to the Times reporter, he went back to his studio and created a polyurethane floor covering that resembles foam plastic rocks.

His carved plastic "rugs" which can be vacuumed have brought him international recognition for a new art form and sell for top prices ($300 for a 40-inch square of pine cones to $5,000 for a large bed of plastic stones).

As an artist, he did not command these prices; but as an artist in a new field, he finds his work is a fortune-maker. Is there an area where you can do what you want to do that will bring you more money than you are now making? Think about this, and once you have your answer, *switch!*

From This Chapter . . .

Seventh Financial Recipe for Doubling Your Income

1. Think of what you do as "your thing" or as a commodity.
2. Determine where you can take this "thing" to sell it for double what you're getting. (Who needs what you have to sell?)
3. Make your move *now.*

Time for Review!

You have now read a third of the suggestions that have led others *and can lead you* to an improved income! Perhaps not every business suggestion in the seven chapters you have just read will have a deep meaning for you. But one of the described methods of conduct must, by its very nature, be one that you can put to work.

Read down this list of seven chapter heads and check the one that makes the most sense for you at this particular time.

Again, then . . .

1. ATTRACT A DOUBLED OFFER BECAUSE YOU'RE ABSOLUTELY TOPS
2. ACHIEVE YOUR GOAL THROUGH A STRATEGY USED IN ADVERTISING
3. EXPAND THE MARKET FOR YOUR SERVICES OR PRODUCT
4. DOUBLE YOUR MARGIN OF PROFITS—WHATEVER YOU'RE SELLING!
5. PUT YOUR TOTAL PERSONALITY TO WORK FOR WHAT YOU WANT
6. USE SOME MORE OF YOU
7. SHIFT TO A HIGHER-PAYING FIELD

For some who read this book, every chapter heading will serve as a business recipe that can lead to a bigger income. Do not put a check after each of the seven headings above, however, no matter how attractive each directive may be. Select only one which will for the present be the *key* for your upward swing. Before going on to Chapter 8 in this section, go back and read that *key chapter* again. Follow the code outlined in that chapter in everything you do for the next month. A change in your money life will begin to emerge.

Now Let Your Subconscious Go To Work

You have been doing some mental exercises which may be new to you, working on problems which you have never thought about before. Fine—but now let your brain absorb these new facts so that your subconscious mind can go to work. *Rest*—at least overnight—before reading the next seven income-doubling chapters. You will be surprised at what happens, especially in connection with the material in the one-out-of-seven chapters you selected as most meaningful.

With new thoughts now programmed into your mental computer, your buried creative mind will soon come up with a course of action. Follow that course and you will be successful. So don't push. Read on only when you feel completely rested. Then your mind will be receptive.

8

MAKE YOUR SPARE MOMENTS PAY OFF

Bibi Osterwald was an understudy for the role of "Dolly" in the big Broadway hit, "Hello, Dolly," for more than three years. In all that time, she never once went on stage for Carol Channing, the role's originator; went on only once for Ginger Rogers when Ginger lost her voice; went on just four times for Martha Raye.

So what do you do year after year when you work only five days and spend the rest of the time sitting around so that the money keeps coming in? What Bibi Osterwald said on Virginia Graham's "Girl Talk" was that she used her time, which she had plenty of, to try to make her money grow. She studied the stock market. And she did very well.

Later, Bibi wrote to us, as follows: "When I say I doubled my income, I wish to make clear that I mean what is left of my income after Federal, State, City and Agent's fees. I was able to put aside $100 a week."

Now let's see how she did this.

"When RCA split (I bought it at 32; it went to 62) I pulled out. I also bought Paddington, which is J & B Scotch. One year later, it split, and I had a gain of 25 points. I was also lucky enough to have purchased AMK at 15 and sold at 26."

We asked Bibi for tips; here they are:

"The trick is to buy well-recommended stocks when the slump is on (when most people panic and sell) and sell when it is on the rise. Many times the stock goes even higher, but you cannot be greedy, just smart enough to get the profit and reinvest when the market is low again. . . . Most of all, you must not panic and always keep some cash reserve on hand—and never buy on margin unless you can well afford to lose."[1]

[1] Other tips on stock purchasing appear on other pages.

Spoken like a protege of the late Bernard Baruch who said, "Nobody ever lost money in the market by selling at a profit."

Bibi Osterwald lost neither money nor time. Her years as a nonworking understudy paid off.

Seventy percent do work they don't like

According to Herbert Geiling, management consultant, 70 percent of the working population are doing work they do not like and hence are not successful. One of the basic steps to success, he says, is to organize one's time and use it effectively. We agree. And we also say that while you are waiting in a job that is not right for you for the right one to loom into view, use your spare minutes as Bibi Osterwald used hers—to learn something new.

When Bob Hope was getting nowhere as a vaudeville hoofer he used his spare time (and there was lots of it) to think up jokes; eventually he worked some thigh-slappers into his act and became a comedian. When Virginia Wren, Connecticut radio commentator, had time left over waiting to go on the air, she listened to old-time fiddle music and finally worked up a "fiddle" act with a friend of the family; now they're both in demand at fairs and exhibitions. Allan Sherman, $75,000 a year Goodson-Todman producer, worked up a comic routine in time left over after producing, gave it at parties for friends, and eventually recorded it as "My Son, the Folk Singer." He had to get a computer, his associates tell us, to count up his profits when that record hit the best-selling list.

Perhaps you have a job with a long vacation period. (You are a teacher, maybe, with three months off in the summer.) Sure, you can travel, go to school, get a part-time job—*or use this time to perfect a dream.* Or maybe you are a writer or artist or restaurant owner with a spare room where you can sell *stuff.*

Lots and lots of money for stuff

Artists with a good eye and a sixth sense for what sells are setting up shops from California to Maine (and, certainly, in our state of Connecticut) to sell just plain *stuff.* It's a good deal for them because they can live and paint or sculpt or operate their kilns in a studio in the back end of the house and put their wives or kids to work in the front end. There, they sell brass spittoons, metal banks, wooden decoys, Indian baskets, porcelain heads used by 1890 phrenologists, rocking chairs,

Indian apple heads, glass slipper pin holders, hatpin holders and dozens of other "camp" conversation pieces. As we say, it takes a good eye. Plus a native shrewdness and the time to go to auctions, second-hand and Salvation Army stores, and as many old attics as somebody's old aunt will let you prowl around in.

Vacation exchange club

Betty Ostroff, director of the Vacation Exchange Club, as principal of a school in the New York City public school system asked herself this question one day: "Why don't they have a service for teachers where they can exchange homes during their away-from-classes vacation time?" As a result, she and her associates created Vacation Exchange Club, with offices at 663 Fifth Avenue, New York City, which lists homes for would-be vacationers (now including any vacationers, not just teachers) where you can live free during your vacation in exchange for letting the owners of another home live in your home free during the same vacation. Cost of a listed membership in the club: $7.00. Not a get-rich-quick story, Betty tells us, but a pleasant and far-reaching activity that adds extra money outside of school hours, provides a welcome service to others, and makes better vacations possible.

Not long ago, we bought an outdoor wrought-iron table and chairs from a pleasant mature man in a discount furniture store near us. "First day on the job," he told us when he had to go to double-check the price. "You see, this isn't really my line; I'm an insurance salesman in New York City."

"What in the world?"

"I have eight children," he told us, "and Thursday nights and Saturdays free. I know the manager here, who asked me to come in twice a week and help out. I'm glad to get the extra money."

Off hours can be money-producing hours. Respect their usefulness.

And remember this: you get a tax reduction for transportation between two jobs; the Internal Revenue Service is specific on this point. "If you work at two places in a day, whether or not for the same employer, you may deduct the expense of getting from one place to the other. However, if for some personal reason, you did not go directly from one location to the other, you may deduct only the cost of going directly from the first location to the second."

Think of ways to use spare time to bring in more income. You will be surprised. There are many ways that spare minutes can bring in extra dollars not only away from your regular work but at your same old desk or in your same old job.

Mr. Toynbee's time-saving principle

Here is a time-saving suggestion from Arnold Toynbee, referred to earlier, which appeared in *Saturday Review.*[2] "Don't say to yourself: 'There, I have finished that piece of work, and it is really not worth beginning the next piece till tomorrow morning or till after the weekend. So for the rest of today or for the rest of this week I might as well let myself relax and take things easy.' The truth is that you might not as well do that; for the right moment for starting on your next job is not tomorrow or next week; it is . . . *right now.*"

Use odd moments to produce more. Not only will your output be impressive, but in addition your work will improve and more money will come.

From This Chapter . . .

Eighth Financial Recipe for Doubling Your Income

1. Collect all the spare minutes you can find.
2. Concentrate in your left-over minutes on new ways to make money.
3. Invest your new knowledge in a money-making venture either in or away from your regular work.

---

[2] See footnote 1, Chapter 8.

9

GO AFTER THE NITTY-GRITTY

"Forget the falderal," is the motto of Tom Kilbride, who became the young president of Knox Reeves Advertising Agency just five years after he moved from the food business to the ad business, "and go after the nitty-gritty."

So what does he mean?

"I mean if you want to double your income in one year, go after the job that can make this possible—and don't get hung up on having to have a better office or a big title or a long vacation as you make your play. These things can get in the way—when you're pushing for something special."

Tom's personal history reveals what he has in mind.

> I was working for a food company after I got out of the Army in World War II as a "sales supervisor." This was a step removed from the old food order-taker; it was really a kind of business advisory service rather than actual product-selling, which was done by this time by direct mail from the company to the grocer.
>
> My boss, who headed up the sales supervisors and reported directly to the president, suddenly was taken seriously ill and died. The shock of this left the president unprepared to fill the spot. I understand he offered the job to two different sales supervisors who were mature and experienced. But they both turned it down because it was a "hot spot" and they were quite comfortable in their present jobs.
>
> I'd like to tell you the job was offered to me, the youngest salesman in the place, but the truth is no one, least of all the president, thought of me at all in this connection. No one but me, that

> is. One day I walked into the president's office and asked him to give me a crack at it.
>
> Maybe he was desperate, but he said he would give it to me, even though I was only 28, if I did not insist on the title of my predecessor. That, I came to see later, gave him leeway to keep on looking for someone on the outside. Anyway, I did not insist, but after a few months, I asked for the title of sales manager, not sales supervisor, and the president agreed. This gave me a chance to function as I knew I was capable of functioning.
>
> Well, to condense some years in the next seven, the company grew five times its size—and, yes, I doubled my income in one year not just once in an eight-year period, but three times, at least.
>
> What amazed me afterward was that so many good men had turned down the opportunity I had gone after so eagerly. Perhaps, they saw it as a problem, I don't know; or they wanted a title the president wasn't ready to give or an office or some other concession. I asked for nothing—just the job. And I wasn't timid either. What I didn't know, I could learn, I told myself, and I did. The minute I became sales manager I joined the Sales Executives Club and learned everything I could learn from other older sales managers in the group. I have always done this—gone after the *nitty-gritty*—and let the details work themselves out afterward.

We have a young woman friend who went after a big job and got it in a large cosmetic firm. But unlike Tom Kilbride, she settled for a dazzled-up office and a high-sounding title, found out after two years she was doing the job of her predecessor *and her predecessor's assistant* for less than that assistant, alone, had made. All because the glittery doo-dads connected with work meant more to her than the price tag on her work, itself. Maybe she looked successful to others in her office, but as far as management was concerned, she had sold out cheap.

Remember this, for this is truth. *The man or woman who doubles his income in a year goes after the nitty-gritty.* The glamour office may be there, and the fancy title and the long vacation, but that isn't the successful person's first concern. The first concern is the price tag on the job itself—or the chance to tag it, himself, as he makes the job grow. That's why he's working in the first place, and he doesn't forget it for a minute.

Best time to make a deal

The day that you are making your agreement to go with a new company is the best time to make a deal that brings you in real money. And, of course, the more the company wants you, the better deal you can make. Here is the time, whether the company's stock has gone public or is privately owned, to ask for stock.

Get an option to buy stock at below-market cost

Recently, a marketing expert we know was approached to do a job for a new computer company with stock which had been floated at $3 a share, which was now selling Over the Counter at $9 and was expected by analysts to go up to $25. The marketing expert's request: to be given along with a fee for his services a warrant to buy within 3 years 500 shares of stock at $7 a share, which was 2 points below the current $9 selling price. If the sought-after consultant's deal goes through and the stock goes up to $25 at the end of three years, his stock will cost him $3,500 instead of $12,500—a good money-making deal. This does not necessarily indicate special shrewdness on his part; this kind of come-on is given constantly to men and women in business who are brought in to help make the company grow, thus helping to make the stock go up.

An even better deal is to get stock in a privately-owned company; best of all, one that is due to go public which will give those on the ground floor a real break. Let's say that you and two or three others organize an ad agency to promote the product of *one* client, selling stock for as low as 53 cents a share to get an office, typewriters, office help, drawing boards, etc. You, personally, keep 100,000 shares. Within three years, through good and well-publicized work for your one client, your agency attracts many more clients and now has billings of over $100 million, and you go public. Your stock sells for $15 a share, bringing you a million and a half dollars.

To tell you that the possibility of this second opportunity ever coming your way is rare is an understatement. Still, many agencies have gone from one-client shops to giant organizations and, in such cases, the original partners have made millions.

Don't be afraid to reach for the moon

"Only a lack of ambition can hold you back," successful men and women have been saying for years. "The money comes when you get to be tops in your field." And they have added, "So don't be afraid to *reach for the moon.*" But never before this generation has the advice been true *in fact.*

Take a look today at the money coming in to 55 astronauts (and eight widows of astronauts) who set out to reach the moon. For the accounts of their adventures, the designated astronauts (and widows) were slated to share a total of $1 million in the year following July 20, '69. Up to then, since the day of the signing of an announced contract with a major magazine, the astronauts and widows had been receiving about $3,000 annually; afterward, the take was due to jump to $16,000. Add to this what the astronauts working for National Aeronautics and Space Administration have collected annually in salaries (from $13,000 to $27,000), and the total take per astronaut is pretty impressive. Yet, from the first, the astronauts didn't look to their jobs for money, alone. Their aim was to reach the moon. *That was their nitty-gritty!* The money was a happy by-product on the way to a bigger goal.

Time out for self-appraisal

What job in your organization do you know you can do today that will pay you twice what you are now making? Keep your eye on that job—and learn how to do it well. It can be yours. (This does not mean that the man in the job you want is going to die or be fired; he may move up. The point is wherever and whenever he goes you can do the job, and you will be ready.) If there is no job in your organization that can lift your salary to where you want it to be, look outside for a slot into which you can move with the same confidence. Make up your mind now that you will fill that slot soon. Then work every way you know how to get to where you want to go.

Mickey Lolich's nitty-gritty

One of the greatest baseball players in the world concentrates on one thing when he gets out on the field—to pitch that ball over home plate as it's never been pitched before. His name is Mickey Lolich, and his spectacular pitching (along with that of another great pitcher, Denny McLain) won cheers from the nation in 1968 when Detroit came out on top in the World Series.

Lolich's success story is an Horatio Alger tale if there ever was one. When he was two, a motorcycle fell on him, damaging his left arm. To strengthen it, a doctor recommended throwing a baseball. The recommendation worked. A natural right-hander, Lolich developed a left arm so strong he uses it now for pitching. As a result, in '68, he became the second of only two southpaws in history (Harry Brecheen in '48 was first) to win three games in a World Series, and *brought the Detroit Tigers their first world championship in 23 years.*

Not everyone has as great a handicap to overcome as Mickey Lolich nor does everyone who concentrates on overcoming a handicap become as famous as this winning pitcher in a great World Series, *but you can bank on this. Concentration on getting good at whatever you do pays off.* So find your nitty-gritty and *push!*

Think now about the one factor in your work, or the work you want to get into, that can get you to where you want to go next. Are you concentrating on that factor or are you caught up in the razzle-dazzle? Dig for your nitty-gritty. Make it pay off this year.

From This Chapter . . .

Ninth Financial Recipe for Doubling Your Income

1. Look for the key factor in your eventual success.
2. Forget peripheral razzle-dazzle.
3. Concentrate on your nitty-gritty, passkey to success.

10

THOU MUST HAVE FAITH

This is not a book written to appeal to members of one special religious group. You can be a Jew, a Catholic, a Protestant . . . a Moslem, a Buddhist, even an agnostic . . . and most of this book's principles will work for you. But you will get to where you want to go with mysterious ease if you can accept with inner certainty that *the ideas that come to you come from beyond yourself.*

One of the greatest scientists the world has ever known was Albert Einstein. Blessed with a dismaying instinct for going to the heart of the most complex mathematical problem, he had a truly logical mind. Yet this brilliant scientist was deeply religious in the true sense of the word. "Ideas," he told a friend, "come from God." Then, he explained his *credo* which is carved today in German on the marble fireplace in the mathematics building at Princeton University. "God is subtle, but he is not malicious." According to Einstein, a scientist embarked on a given job can expect to find his project hard to do, but *never* hopeless.

You may not have Einstein's scientific bent, but you can work with his *credo* and find success.

Not long ago, we met a remarkable woman at a large party in Scarsdale, New York. From her life story which we gleaned in snatches from those around us, we knew that she must be in her 80s, yet her walk was the buoyant walk of a young and healthy woman, her smile was a joy. She was Mrs. Irene Ihde, formerly of Grand Prairie, Texas, and her life story is a lesson in faith. She wrote it down for us at our request when she became interested in this book we were writing.

> I was the victim of the depression like thousands of others. Besides lost securities I was left a widow with three small children

and a mother to support. My husband died very suddenly without insurance. I was $5,000 in debt. My meager income had to be doubled within a year in order for us to survive. I never knew beyond three weeks whether we could even live, let alone live together. One never knew when a small job would turn up. There were no jobs to be had. Bankruptcy everywhere was heading in like a flash flood ruining lives, homes, investments. Genius and education walked the streets. What chance had I? My father and father-in-law had died. I had no brothers.

My slogan had always been, "If there isn't a way, make a way." But how? I was almost out of my mind. I read the famous 6th chapter of Matthew from the New Testament: "Behold the fowls of the air: for they sow not, neither do they reap, nor gather into barns; consider the lilies of the field; they toil not, neither do they spin—yet Solomon in all his glory was not arrayed like one of these—take therefore no thought for the morrow, for God will take care of the morrow but rather, seek ye first the kingdom of God and His righteousness." What did this mean? I had read it so many times with little meaning, I guess. Today it seemed that the lily did nothing; the fowl of the air did nothing, and God did the rest. Yet life does not work that way. I re-thought the verses: the lily does all that is given a lily to do; the fowl does all that a fowl can do, and God does the rest. Had I done all that I could do? I began to write down all the things that I could really do. Before I was married I had been a Chautauqua entertainer; I was a speech and a music graduate from Northwestern University. But few could pay for entertainment these days, especially when an entertainer was unknown. We had lived in the Orient as teachers a number of years, but to teach required my going back to the university for a refresher course.

I had read somewhere that Henry Ford, Sr., once said that people had a need and if a person could find that need and do something about it, riches would come tumbling down on him.[1] He made a car that low-income people needed. His profit, I was told, was $1.00 on each car. This was true for him, but where did I fit in?

I began to write down people's needs. One thing they needed

---

[1] Don French, insurance broker with Connecticut General in Hartford, has doubled his income from one year to the next three times in his career by concentrating on filling a basic need. He never starts out to sell a policy but volunteers instead to help a new client plan his entire estate. He conscientiously takes into consideration all the dollars and all the property his client has now and can expect to have in the future. Thus he has a valid basis for counseling and builds a long-term relationship. Often he recommends new ways to save which are not in any way involved with what he has to sell. Yet, even without pushing to sell, he does better every year. "Serve first," he says, "and you can't escape being paid."

was faith. I was a Bible student seeking a larger faith. Wouldn't this search help others? People needed entertainment but could not pay for it. The churches needed money to pay their expenses. I wrote all this down.

For days many thoughts possessed my thinking. I slept little. I had read some place that a man acted, for one day, as if God really walked beside him and it changed his whole outlook on life. Then he read in his Bible, Matthew the first chapter, and after he got beyond all those "begats" he found this verse, "His name shall be called Emmanuel which being interpreted is, 'God with us.' " He said he began to go to the top. He said if he could believe that an ether wave could help his radio do that which he couldn't do, why not believe that God could do for him that which he could not do. That night I turned everything over to God and prayed, "O God, I have gone as far as I can. I don't know how to seek first the Kingdom of God and His righteousness." Then a sudden thought. "Righteousness" had among its many interpretations the righting of wrongs. Couldn't the little bit I had to give help to right something wrong? A peace enveloped me and I slept like a baby bird under its mother's wing in a secluded nest. At five in the morning I awoke, refreshed. Suddenly a whole program to put on in a church seemed to stand out clearly before me. Just like the time when my math teacher gave us three days to solve a problem in solid geometry. I had looked up all the theorems I could find that pertained to the problem. Nothing seemed to work. But on the third day, early in the morning, when I awoke I saw the problem solved clearly. And now, here was my church program as clear as clean cut-glass. I arose, put on my robe and wrote as fast as I could. I did not stop to yawn, or stretch. Coffee would taste better later. I was to put on a week's program in any church that would engage me.

The program would be on the order of the Old Chautauqua Week I once knew. I would give Bible impersonations each night. And I would give a concert number on the organ each night. I had memorized such numbers as "Tocatto in d minor" of Bach; and "The Storm" from the William Tell Overture, and several other entertaining numbers. I was to have the audience sing short, peppy choruses. The objective was to rejuvenate the depressed faith of discouraged church members; to encourage them to tithe their small incomes to help their church and social organizations such as the Red Cross. Getting their minds on something they could share, and sacrifice for, did something for them. People were amazed to discover how they improved in health and how things came their way. The church was to receive the offering each night except the last night. The pastor would say, "This is the only offering Mrs. Ihde receives for a week of religious entertainment." (There was to be no soliciting or begging.) Then I was to have circulars, with my picture on them,

> printed and sent out. The addresses I was to get from the General Conference minutes of my own denomination at first, later from other churches. I spent my last dollar doing this but I had confidence that what I had would meet a need for these times.
>
> The first weeks nothing happened but I believed it would. I kept on working the best I could. After weeks I was engaged for my first service. Then another in a few weeks. I called on preachers, visited women's societies, called on bishops. Three months before my year was up the program took hold. I could not answer requests fast enough. By the end of the year I had made it. I had doubled my income.
>
> I have had to double my income since—for instance, when the children were in college. I did not change the nature of my work but a larger vision and a larger program came to me; the same faith and the same philosophy went into it. To sum up: Your talent may be great or small. Write it down. You were put here to dovetail your talent to fit a need. Among the many whom I have tried to help, I have found that a person with a small talent, but with confidence, goes farther than a person with a great talent, but without confidence. Keep cheerful; keep your family happy as far as you can. Nothing is worse than keeping the ones with whom you live always in a turmoil. It lessens your faith; it lessens their faith in you and you need their faith. Don't hold a grudge. If someone does not speak to you, go to that person if you can and try "going the other mile" with him. You might say, "We have hurt each other. Whatever you think I did to hurt you I am sorry. As you know, there are some things in this life that cannot be straightened out. But we can forgive each other. Otherwise it will impair our health, so doctors tell us. It holds us back even in our business." You may not see results at once but keep working and believing and God will do the rest.

With faith like that how could Irene Ihde help but find success?

Learning from nature

If you are not a church-going man or woman, if faith of the kind Mrs. Ihde talks about is hard for you to come by, get in tune with nature. Get from your library the "Essay on Nature" by Ralph Waldo Emerson, who urges "going into solitude" in the country to get new understanding of the *beauty and discipline* in nature.

"The lover of nature is he whose inward and outward senses are truly adjusted to each other; and who has retained the spirit of childhood even into the era of manhood." *Keep wonder and belief in your life,* is what he is saying; *stay simple.* "Every natural act is graceful," he writes, and further on, "We know more from nature than we can at will communicate."

If you are reaching for a faith you do not now possess, let the light "flow into your mind," as Emerson suggests, from getting close to nature. When faced with a problem, either go back to the faith of your childhood or renew your childhood wonder at nature. Get over thinking you have to do everything *all by yourself!*

From This Chapter . . .

Tenth Financial Recipe for Doubling Your Income

1. List the things you know you can do.
2. List the needs of people that call for what you can do.
3. Have faith that those who need what you have to offer will come to you to fill them.
4. Make your childhood faith your mainstay, or get close to nature for your faith.
5. Avoid thinking that you have to do everything *all by yourself.*

11

BECOME A SELLING WRITER, INVENTOR, PAINTER OR COMPOSER ALONG WITH YOUR REGULAR WORK

Ask the next ten working men and women you meet if they would rather be writing books, inventing things, painting or composing songs than doing what they are doing, and at least seven of them will say "Yes!" Ask these seven why they don't begin now, after hours in their regular jobs, to do what they want to do, and at least six, and probably seven, will drop away. Most people want the life they believe is led by creative people, but few want to work with the constant diligence that such a life demands.

Our advice to anyone who wants to do something creative is to begin working at what you want to do *every day before leaving for your regular job!* Yes, we believe it is imperative that you keep your job and we also believe you should do what you want to do early in the morning. We believe this for three reasons: (1) You will need your present income until you have a market for your writing, inventions, painting or music. (2) You are fresh in the morning, can do your best creative work then. (3) You can be sure, if you get up early to do writing, painting or composing and stick to this schedule, that you really have talent and are going to do something about it. You will be calling your own bet.

The case of Shepherd Mead

Shep Mead, author of *How to Succeed in Business Without Really Trying*, was radio and television copy chief at Benton & Bowles Advertising Agency before he struck out on his own and hit the big time. All of the time that he was writing and supervising all copy, music, art and production that went into the agency's television commercials, he knew that what he eventually wanted was to write books. So he began—on his own time—before starting to work each day for others. Every morning at 8 o'clock he got to his office, which was scheduled to open at 9:30. For one uninterrupted hour he worked on a book in the early morning quiet. He turned out two big-selling books this way before hitting with his great money-maker that eventually was turned into a Broadway musical by Frank Loesser and Abe Burrows. Obviously, Shep Mead wanted to be a bigtime writer on his own, believed he would make this want come true, and had the inner discipline to pull it off, which he did in a big way. His 13th book, a novel about England, was recently published.

How do you know you can write?

If you are an adult with an income, as you must be or you probably wouldn't have picked up this book in the first place, what makes you think you can write?

Were you a good composition writer in school? Did you breeze through the vocabulary section in IQ tests? Did your writing find its way into print along the way, even if you got no payment for it? Do people come to you for ideas? Do you like to write letters? Do you like to read? Have you ever taken a writing course? Did you do well in it?

A born writer answers yes to all of these questions.

Let's say that you are a married woman with three children who does manuscript typing at home to augment your husband's income. You take in, maybe, $1,500 a year. Now, let's say that as you type an article on gardening for a local writer or a confession story for a fiction writer, you say to yourself: "Why am I typing this for someone? I can write better than this myself!"

Strangely enough, one thought does not necessarily follow the other. You are typing because you want to earn $1,500 a year doing what you know how to do. You may be able to write better than the writer whose work you are typing, but can you sell what you write? Until you know the answer to this second question, keep right on earning your regular income, but begin writing, too.

Five steps to take as you begin to write

1. **Take a course in writing.** Register for a writing course through the extension division of a neighboring college. Or take a correspondence course from Famous Writers School in Westport, Connecticut, or from the Palmer

Writers School, 500 South 4th St., Minneapolis, Minnesota 55415. (Write for full details before signing up.) Or organize a creative writing class through your local women's club or church group. The advantages of a class are (1) discipline, (2) encouragement and (3) criticism.

2. **Every single day write words that you eventually want to sell.** Every morning make yourself write at least a paragraph or two in a story, article, contest, something that you eventually intend to sell. Do this writing (personal letters, no fair) no matter what else the day brings forth. (Or if a morning hour is absolutely impossible, write at night.) A columnist has to write every day; a staff writer; an agency copywriter. To them, there is no such thing as "the mood to write." If you want to write for money, "mood" is a luxury you will have to give up.

3. **Write for local outlets.** Tell your club you will be publicity director and watch how your words go into the local paper; or write the copy for the annual director for your club; or volunteer for the writing staff of Community Chest. Seeing your words in print even when you don't get paid will be a spur for you.

4. **Keep up on national market information for writers.** Buy the annual edition of Writer's Market which lists 4,000 markets for free-lance writers. Send $7.95 to Writer's Digest, Cincinnati, Ohio, 45210.

When you decide what magazine may very possibly be interested in what you want to write, *study* that magazine. Get to know its needs.

5. **Test one idea a month on an editor.** If you eventually want to write a column for young mothers, write three columns and send them to a syndicate for consideration. Or send a story to a magazine, being sure its length matches the average length of their stories. If you have an article in mind, query the editor before submitting a finished manuscript. Boiling down your idea in a query for an editor will teach you much about writing.[1] So will rejection slips which can help you see what you are doing wrong. An acceptance, of course, means you are on your way.

If you are beyond the beginning stage but not yet making big money as a writer, you will have to ask yourself: "Is it better to take something other than a writing job and write outside of work, or to take a writing job and write on top of that?"

Many of the world's top writers worked at jobs far removed from writing to earn bread, and wrote what they wanted after hours. But for most writers, a writing job is the easiest job to get—so they become copywriters, reporters, publicity writers. For such writers this daily work often becomes enough; they do not need a larger creative outlet. But if their talent is great, they usually go on to a more personal type of writing.

---

[1] Long ago, I had an instructor at the State University of Iowa who told me the best thinking I would do for my story would come in my head before I ever typed a word. Writing a query to an editor makes it imperative for you to do this thinking.

The answer is, then, start to write now and continue day after day. Eventually, you will be led to the kind of writing that is right for you—*unless* you have been kidding yourself. In that case you will give the whole thing up.

What about that doubled income?

Unless the married manuscript typist we referred to has unusual writing talent, she probably will not make $1,500 as a freelance writer on top of her regular typing the first year. But if she has a flair for words, she will be led to a higher paying job in or out of her home that will demand some writing and can pay twice as much as plain typing. Examples: A secretarial job that demands letter writing for her boss on her own; a research assistant or an author working on a book in a specialized field (medicine, geology, history of art); an ad-writing secretary for a local real estate firm.

The doubled income will come although writing as a full-time career may not be the final destiny. Or then again, it may be. The only way to find out if you have a great best-selling book in you is to begin, which is a truth that applies to any creative work. Luckily, the more inventive your mind, the easier it will be for you to get to work. In fact, if the idea that comes to you for a book—or an invention of any kind—is really hot, you won't be able to leave it alone.

Skinned knuckles lead dentist to heat-pain theory

What do skinned knuckles have to do with a drilled tooth? What do coolants used by machinists in working with high-speed drills have to do with the development of the high-speed water-cooled drill in your dentist's office today? A lot, if you happen to have a mind like Dr. Chester Henschel's of Mahopac, New York, who happens to see the relationship between such things.

One day, Dr. Henschel, who is the director of the Department of Dentistry, Sydenham Hospital of New York, skinned his knuckles. Later, he washed his hand in very warm water and noted that the skinned area felt very hot in comparison to the unskinned areas of his hands. Knowing that skin is an insulator that protects against pain, he realized it was the heat that was causing the pain. This led him to realize that a tooth with its insulation removed by the ordinary drill, then used in a dental office, was painful because of the generated heat. A logical progression of thought that would have led him nowhere if he had not already made another mental note apparently not thought much about by other dentists. Several years before, he had noticed that coolants were used by machinists in working with high-speed drills to keep the heat generated from the drill from causing damage to the materials with which they were working.

His two observations led him to the research that helped perfect the high-speed water-cooled drill that makes a visit to the dentist today almost painless.

From parachutes to seat belts and more

Back in 1919 Leslie Irvin, of upper New York State, persuaded a Buffalo millinery shop to let him use a sewing machine to stitch up a 32-foot silk canopy parachute with 16 rigging lines, at the end of which was a harness. On April 28th of that year, Mr. Irvin strapped himself into the harness at McCook Field, Dayton, Ohio, and demonstrated from a moving airplane the first free-fall parachute jump. It won him a government contract and eventually made him a fortune making parachutes. Although Mr. Irvin is no longer living, the company he founded, now known as Irvin Industries, Inc., is still the world's largest makers of ordinary parachutes (made now of nylon, not silk, and retailing for about $300), but still parachutes are not the company's number one income producer. That harness Mr. Irvin strapped himself into led to his making a seat belt for the late racing car driver, Barney Oldfield, and other drivers. Later, a stockholder by the name of H. Kurt Blumberg saw a future in seat belts, and insisted on expansion in this direction. Today, seat belts and auto safety equipment account for 45 percent of sales; parachutes, 15 percent. The rest of the sales come from metal products, air cargo and airline equipment.

What about painting?

All of the rules that apply to would-be writers apply to would-be painters. Only a few beginning artists can afford to do painting, sketching, woodcuts, sculpture or anything else along this line, with no source of income except from art. Most artists work at a job and perfect their creative work after hours. Some again, become commercial artists or window decorators or art teachers or fabric designers and find these jobs are fulfillment enough. Others want more direct contact with an art-buying public. They become photographers, sculptors, potters or artists. Some have both.

The story of Les Rondell

Lester Rondell is a vice president and the executive art director of Grey Advertising in New York. All week he's busy administrating and supervising the activities of 50 art directors and the agency's art studio, searching for new approaches to art and photography for advertising. Come Friday night, and he pulls a switch.

For years, he has devoted his Saturdays and Sundays to his career of painter and sculptor. For this outside work, he has two fully equipped studios: one in New York in the winter, another at Fire Island in the summer.

His primary purpose is not to push up his income, which is good-sized, but "because my heart, mind and soul would shrivel if I were to stop." Even so, his work is represented in galleries in New York and San Francisco and hangs in national exhibitions. His paintings and sculpture bring from $250 to $1,500.

While the benefit that comes to Les from working over the weekend is not a doubled income, there are many things to be learned from this kind of discipline. Les counts up four.

(1) You can switch from one kind of hard work to another without fatigue. It can even be exhilarating. (2) You can use two facets of your talent without diminishing either. (3) You can earn extra money over the weekend and call your soul your own. (4) And who knows, posterity may even take notice.

The case of the busy toy salesman

A young and attractive owner of a sales organization for toy manufacturers has a weekend house near us. Successful in his work (he makes more than $30,000 a year), he nonetheless has a yen to do pen and ink sketches. Once a year he goes to Gloucester or Rockport, Massachusetts, and makes pencil sketches of boats and the sea; then comes home and does more sketches of around-the-county scenes. Finally, in his spare time, he converts his pencil sketches to pen and ink sketches.

As good a salesman for himself as he is for the toys he merchandises for clients, he takes his seascapes and pen and ink drawings of local scenes to libraries, restaurants, wallpaper outlets and encourages the owners of these places to place them on exhibit. He prices his work at quick-sale prices, sells everything he can turn out.

No doubled income for him as yet "but I'm working toward a retirement income when I decide to leave New York." In the meantime, he is developing a kit for other spare-time artists that he can merchandise through the outlets that carry his clients' wares, and he may well double his income through royalties.

If your urge is to be an artist, get started like this: (1) Take a course in art—through the extension division of a local college, from a local artist or by correspondence through a school like Famous Artists School in Westport, Connecticut, or Art Instruction Schools, 500 South 4th St., Minneapolis, Minnesota. Like "born writers," a few artists become successful without formal training, but they are rare. As advertising photographer Bert Stern, member of the guiding faculty of Famous Photographers School, puts it: "The average photographer will have a much better chance to make a good living if he has training. But there are some people who are just geniuses. They pick up a camera, get the wrong exposure, fall down and drop it, and everyone wants their pictures. You can't say you will make more money if you have training. But there is more *chance* of making money."

Many top photographers started in other fields

Like the study of the ocean, photography is new; so like many oceanographers, many photographers are self-taught and/or started out in other fields. Two top money-makers, Bert Stern and Irving Penn, started out in agency art departments; Alfred Eisenstaedt, Life's prize-winning photo-journalist, began as a non-picture-taking journalist for the magazine; Ezra Stoller studied architecture. All made their early experiences pay off in their photographic careers.

The story of Ace Williams

Ace Williams, in his early years, was an art director in an agency, and had a staff of 30 assistants working for him. Seeing early that photography was bound to eclipse drawings as illustrations for ads hell bent on realism, he switched from art to photography, making a deep study of color photography, then new. Once master of this medium, he moved on to movie-making, using his advertising know-how to make telling sales points in promotional films for Pepsi Cola, General Motors and other giant companies. Today, he and his wife maintain a handsomely furnished streamlined home at Heritage Village, Connecticut, and travel on assignment to all parts of the world. Ace estimates that his photographic assignments have kept him in glamorous places outside of the United States nine months out of every 12.

Switching over from librarian to author

Until a few years ago, Robert B. Jackson was a librarian in East Orange, New Jersey. One of the publisher's representatives who called on him was Beman Lord, who is an author as well as the owner of a business.[2] Well, one day Beman, who knew that Robert was a sports car afficionado, asked his librarian friend to read a chapter in a book he was writing to see if his facts were right. Robert obliged, and as a result the two men decided to collaborate on a book, *Sports Cars.* When they got into it, Beman was too busy with his own sports books (he's the author of *Look at Cars, Rough Ice, The Perfect Pitch, Mystery Guest at Left End*) to see this one through. He encouraged Robert to go on his own. Robert not only finished that first one but also sixteen others, including *Road Racing, U.S.A.*, and has now crossed over from library work to full-time writing.

So you want to compose a song

Writing a hit song seems easier to the average person, who may know a little music, than writing a book or painting a landscape. "A song is so *short,*" a bright boy told us the other day, "and the lyrics are so simple."

As with everything that brings in big money, song-writing is an art—and the chance of your writing a hit, if you are not working as a lyricist or composer for a Hollywood movie or a Broadway show, is a long shot. But it can be done. We called WINE Radio Station in Brookfield, Connecticut, today and asked what if a local guitar player composed a song—could he go to the station and play it?

"Indeed, yes," said the manager, "tell him to come up."

---

[2] Beman owns Lord Book Representatives, which employs 35 salesmen to represent eight publishers at libraries and schools. He writes his books in his head, he tells us, as he drives from appointment to appointment—says he seldom rewrites a word, writing all takes place in the head.

However, should the guitarist *record* his song, he could not have the record played on the station which plays only recordings registered with BMI and ASCAP.

Unlike writers and artists, musicians have to deal with unions as their work goes in front of the public.[3] This involves a set of rules too complicated to explain in its entirety here; anyway, it is not something to make you despair. If you want to write a song, write it. If you can sing, sing it on your local radio station, if you can get on, or at a local club. If it has something that makes others whistle it after they hear it, get it to a popular singing group near you and get them to sing it, whenever they want to, wherever they may be. Eventually, if your song has merit, it may be heard by someone who will help you get it recorded.

Take a tip from the uninhibited

Recently, we agreed to participate in a school enrichment program called *Rescue* (Regional Educational Services Concept through Unified Effort) which had its beginning in Danbury, Connecticut. In our first day, we addressed in five assemblies a total of 900 7th and 8th grade students on the subject of *how to write and do art for a children's book.* On the following day, much to the amazement of the school principal, 75 different students handed in an illustrated children's story. We were delighted, not only with the production but with the quality. Here was the work of minds unafraid to be creative, minds which had never heard anyone say, "*you* can't write or draw," minds that dared to soar.

Forget your inhibitions and write, paint or compose music that feels right to you. Discipline will come later.

Expose your work

Almost as important as the work you do as a musician, painter or writer is your ability to get it exposed. Once you get recognition (by selling or some other way), don't stop—keep going. Then, repeat and repeat and repeat, learning as you go. Does this sound like a push? That it is. But if you have talent, the push is worth the effort. Even if you are not a genius, you can eventually far more than double your income; with talent put to good use, you can become a millionaire.

[3] Inventors have to think about patents, too, which are handled by a patent attorney. As an inventor, go to your personal lawyer who will tell you what lawyer is right for you.

From This Chapter . . .

Eleventh Financial Recipe for Doubling Your Income

1. If you want to be a writer, inventor, painter or musician, begin *now*.
2. Work for at least one hour each morning when your mind is fresh.
3. Volunteer to do writing or art work or musical scoring for local affairs. Keep your hand in. Enter contests and exhibitions.
4. Offer your work for sale. Regard rejections as something to learn from, but do get a good patent attorney before talking about a new invention.
5. Don't get too worried at first about guilds and unions. Once your work begins to be recognized, go to the most successful writer or musician in your town and ask for an hours' time to determine what to do next.

12

DO FOR YOURSELF WHAT YOU HAVE DONE FOR OTHERS

One of the greatest merchandising minds we have ever been exposed to belonged to Mrs. Isabelle Ramey, founder of Ramey's, Inc., women's specialty shop in Davenport, Iowa. We were naturally interested when she told us about the job offer that pushed her into her own business.

"In the early 1920s, Killian's Store in Cedar Rapids offered me $9,000 to come there as a buyer. That was a fortune in those days. I decided that if hard-headed Al Killian thought I was worth that, I was worth more than that to myself. I opened my own shop." A smart move, because within a few years, Ramey's shop was grossing close to $400,000 a year—and its owner was on her way to becoming one of the all-time success stories of her state. All because she decided that it was about time she bet on herself!

Private enterprise pays off

Jerry LaSelva, popular owner of Jerry's Automotive at the south end of our little Squash Hollow Road, was born with no silver spoon in his mouth. The son of first generation Italian parents (divorced when he was eight), he didn't let any sadnesses in his childhood get to him, but knew from way back as long as he can remember that some day "he was going to make it." Now in his late 20s, happily married and the father of three, he is on his way. Personable, energetic and resourceful, he is a true believer in America's private enterprise system and is living evidence that it works.

Until March 1, 1969, Jerry worked at the Esso station and automobile repair shop, which he now runs, for a salary of $10,000 a year. Then, with the cooperation of the station owner, he decided to go into business for himself, even though at the time his only capital was a $3,000 equity in the small but attractive house where he lived with his family in a nearby development.

Here is what the owner asked in making the switch:

Rent for station: $250 a month for five years, at which time Jerry could have the option to buy.

Cost of stock (including tow truck, jack, oil, gas, etc.) $7,000, to be paid for with $3,000 down and the balance of $4,000 over a period of three years.

In thinking through the possibilities inherent in his business, Jerry figured as follows:

Present sale of gas: 6,000 gallons a month.

Repairs: $1,500 a month gross.

With any luck at all, he figured he could push up both.

Now, here were minimum monthly expenses he knew he'd have to pay:

Utilities:	$120
Insurance:	64
One helper:	320
Miscellaneous: (laundry, tools, etc.)	100

Jerry took a deep breath, borrowed the $3,000 he had to have from a local bank at 7½ percent, put up a sign reading *Jerry's Automotive* and went ahead. The night he took over, he told us that he would be content, if he could be his own boss, to realize at the end of his first year and every year thereafter $15,000 a year instead of his former $10,000, and *that would be enough!*

This is what he set out to accomplish. *First step:* he cleaned and painted the station inside (including toilets) and out until it was nice to look at. *Second step:* he stayed open two hours later each night and all day on Sunday. *Third step:* although he had another man working with him, he personally talked to every customer who came into the station for either fuel or repairs. *Fourth step was a break:* his wife won a TV prize which called attention to him and his station. *Fifth step, another break:* a population spurt in our county sent a third again as much traffic past his station as in the season past. *Sixth step, the best break of all:* his happiness in his work reflected itself in his ever-present smile.

Within the first three months that he was in business for himself, his gas sales increased to 15,000 gallons a month, and he was able to hire three part-time men. As his repair business increased right along with his gas sales, so did his courage, and he purchased an Allen Engine Analyzer for $2,500. Best of all, he began to see he didn't have to kill himself to make it in this business. When Jerry first took over, he worked from 7 A.M. to 9 P.M. After only one month, he realized that there was no point in making more money if he were going to cheat himself of the family life that is now so precious to him. So he began going home at 6 o'clock and took on a regular night man to close up at 9 P.M. He now enjoys Sundays at home with his family. Talk to Jerry LaSelva today about the "American Dream" and he knows what you're talking about. He's living it!

Going the way it's going now, Jerry's business will not only be bringing in what he anticipated making before going on his own but will far exceed that. Already, he smiles when he thinks how just a few months ago he promised himself that he would be happy for life if he could just be making $15,000 a year.

The story of Carole Stupell

By her own admission, America's foremost table-setting expert, whose Fifty-seventh Street shop in New York City carries dinnerware priced as high as $10,000 a set, has always wanted to learn everything about a job to be done, has always been "very aggressive." This very zealousness that has taken her to the top got her fired from her first department store job in 1929 when the buyer for her department thought she was trying to get her job. So, right then, Carole Stupell went into business for herself in the Barclay Hotel. She had no money (in fact, she was in debt), but she had no fear because she could do all the work herself (decorating, typing, everything) and had great confidence in her ability to buy and sell.

A year after she opened, Miss Stupell had a peculiar break. She doesn't drink, but this was Prohibition and everyone was drinking, so she wanted to have glasses to sell to guests who were stopping at the hotel. At a manufacturer's where she had gone to look for highball glasses, she saw an interestingly shaped glass and asked for "eight of those." The manufacturer became hysterical, said, "They're vases," and she said, "I don't care, I'll take them." She named the vases "Zombie glasses," put them on display, sold eight the first day, ordered and sold two dozen the next week, and eventually was ordering a hundred dozen at a clip. With that, she was on her way to fame as one of the great "originals" of our time.

A hard worker, from the beginning Carole Stupell worked from nine A.M. to eleven P.M., even did her own deliveries. She was determined to pay what she had to pay to get the effects in table settings she wanted, so she needed credit. And she wanted that credit to be A! Therefore, she went without eating to pay her bills on the 10th.

After the first year, she opened a shop in Southampton, Long Island, for the summer (New York summers in shops like hers are quiet) where she became a favorite of hostesses with great fortunes. One such hostess told her she used brandy snifters for water glasses. Carole Stupell began to get support for her idea that originality in table settings was desirable.

At the end of Prohibition when every little shop in New York stressed cocktail things, she called her shop simply "Carole Stupell" and went into selling decorative appointments of china, glassware, everything along those lines. Now her business got really big—so she took more space, and in a few years, even more. All during the depression she did well because she had extremely good taste, and, as she says, there are always some people around "with loads of money who will spend it if they like what you're selling."

From the beginning, Miss Stupell began going to Europe to find new and finer products. She also went to California twice a year. Her stock of beautiful things became immense. Even so, one day when she was setting a table for her window, she found that she didn't have flatwear, glassware, linens, everything for a perfect table. That's when she began buying correlated table things, but she called it "Carolated." Most of her customers through the years have bought, and still buy, "Carolated" table settings—and those customers are the Windsors, Princess Grace, Haile Selassie, the Fords, the duPonts, Perle Mesta, all the famous hostesses who love to entertain and like to be dramatic about it.

A woman can always earn money, if she wants to work, Miss Stupell believes, because most of them have some kind of talent—even though it may for a time be dormant. They've got to figure out, she says, what they are capable of doing, and then do it. Success will be inevitable! Not surprisingly, Miss Stupell also believes you ought to apply every ounce of flair and originality you've got to whatever you're doing—but she says, too, and she's right, that an original talent is God-given and that you can't learn good taste from books. Her taste is inherent. So is her knowledge of what advertising and publicity can do. One time publicity-minded members of a rodeo at the old Madison Square Garden asked if they could bring a bull of theirs into her china shop. She allowed this—and it cost her a whole table full of fabulous tableware but it gave her unparalleled publicity on a national newscast.

"The bull looked over my prettiest table and licked the table decoration—and down the damned thing went," she says. Far from weeping, she loved it. "That night on the news show, the film of that bull's tongue in slow motion as it licked the table was simply fantastic. The whole thing was great publicity."[1]

(NOTE: If you have a craving for the lovely things sold by Carole Stupell but not enough money to go all out, go to the Carole Stupell

[1] This quote taken from a tape made by Miss Stupell for the book, *"Money Talks,"* by Charles Sopkin, published by Random House, Inc.

Warehouse Outlet at 1749 First Avenue in New York where overstocks are sold. Linen, flatware, pewter, table mats, glassware, are sold at a fraction of what they're priced at in the store on Fifty Seventh Street. We bought a great glass cornucopia from Holland for about $80 which was originally priced close to $150 and used on a Carole Stupell Thanksgiving table. And we got blue glass goblets from Czechoslovakia there, and great big almost water-glass size wine glasses from Hungary. For so much less than at the main shop!) At the warehouse, you will meet Carole Stupell's husband. Once in the theater, he has been a helpmate to his famous wife, and handles all the business for the whole operation.

Doubling her income year after year after year, Miss Stupell buys carefully, sells enthusiastically, has beautiful taste and is supremely courageous. She is a legend in her time.

He quit to do better

Writing under your own byline on *The New York Times* would be enough for most reporters but not for Gay Talese, who quit to do livelier writing on his own. First big story: a breezy profile of *Times*' Managing Editor, Clifton Daniel, for *Esquire*. Result: a request by a publisher to do the history of the *Times* in the same dramatic way. Now when someone writes about Adolph Ochs, who bought the failing *Times* in 1896, and "Punch" Sulzberger, today's talented publisher, Talese, as an authoritative source, and his book get into the story, too. This close link with the *Times*' publishers could never have come had he stayed on at the *Times* as a reporter.

Don't stay in a comfortable job just because others might give their eyeteeth for it. The fact that you want more shows *you're not like the others:* get going on your own.

He dared to take new steps

As an actor, John Cassavetes had it good, co-starring with Mia Farrow in *Rosemary's Baby* and all that! But he wanted to do more with film than anyone had ever done before. So he wrote a script for a movie called "Faces" and directed it, too, using for actors and actresses small part movie players and his wife. Result: a deeply moving film about the boring lives lived by many affluent Americans that in a few months made Cassavetes almost as well known a performer turned director as Mike Nichols, another who has dared to take new steps along the way.

If you know you've got it, bet all you've got on yourself.

From This Chapter . . .

Twelfth Financial Recipe for Doubling Your Income

1. If you are working for another, and can do everything that person can do and more, go into business for yourself.
2. Cut down in every way on fat in your operation.
3. Be creative in every aspect.
4. Keep your goal of a doubled income in mind always.

13

BUY IN QUANTITY, SELL BY THE PIECE

Early in life, Charles H. Percy, United States Republican Senator from Illinois, acquired the "habit of industry." During the depression of the 30s, Percy's father, a neighborhood bank cashier, had to accept relief for his family when the bank failed. "Chuck," then 13, went to work. Today the Senator says, "I've been working all my life."

In the beginning, he stoked furnaces before going to school, delivered a newspaper route after classes. In high school, he worked in the school office for 30 cents an hour, and ushered in a movie theater at night. He did every kind of odd job, selling job, promoting job.

Just plain hard work was bound to put this boy from northside Chicago ahead of the pack, but the principle that took him way out front financially is one that is more familiar to chain store managers than to boys who work as ushers. At the University of Chicago, where young Charles went to college on a half tuition-scholarship, he became manager of a college co-operative, selling supplies to fraternity houses and university residences. Instead of approaching the job as a college boy providing a service for a fee, he applied the chain store buying method of buying in quantity and built up a $150,000-a-year business, collecting $10,000 as his share. In later years, Robert M. Hutchins, president of the University when Percy attended, observed, "Chuck Percy was the richest poor student we ever had."

Hard work, plus his natural talent for marketing, took Charles Percy to the top of Bell & Howell Company of Chicago, makers of photographic equipment, when he was 29 years old, causing financial writers to refer to the company's young president as the "boy wonder." Seventeen years later, after serving for most of that time as chairman of the board, as well as president, he left Bell & Howell with an accumulation of stock amounting to 3 million dollars. It is estimated that his net worth today is something more than 5 million dollars.

Besides hard work and an expert understanding of marketing, there was another factor at work in his advancement. We have touched on this factor before; we will do so again in the next chapter. He learned along the way from an expert in his field.

His mentor was Joseph H. McNabb, his Sunday School teacher in the Christian Science Church and president of Bell & Howell before him. During summer vacation when he was in school, young Charles worked for Bell & Howell. With characteristic directness he looked at his job one day and decided it should be abolished. He wrote this into a report which was brought to the attention of Mr. McNabb. Through his interest and by following his advice and example, Percy was elected to the board of directors of the company when he was 23 years old.

Obviously, many unusual qualities in his personal make-up contributed to Percy's financial success, but we will consider just one in this chapter. That is the chain store buying plan he studied and applied to his work as manager of the co-operative in college. You can apply this principle *beginning now,* to whatever you may be considering buying to divide up to sell later in small lots.

Strange story of a great South American diamond

Many years ago, a South American workman found one of the world's largest diamonds in a river. He sold it to a man who sold it again, and this man sold it once more; and it was sold even again. Eventually, a wealthy American bought the diamond for $235,000. He cut up the massive piece of hard crystallized carbon and sold off the pieces. He made exactly one million dollars from his sale of cut stones.

A 4 c. profit is all you have to have

With enough volume you can make millions from a 4 c. profit per sale. Morrison, Incorporated, a cafeteria chain, based in Mobile, Alabama, proves this daily as it takes in a profit of less than a nickel a meal on the 2,000,000 meals a month it serves in more than 60 cafeterias. A small profit per meal—but annual sales add up to close to $50 million.

Chairman of the Board J. Herbert Gibbons recently described his chain of cafeterias in *Time Magazine* as "the cafeteria that thinks like a restaurant." Certainly, his cafeterias look like restaurants. Waiters carry trays to the dining tables which are out of sight of the serving lines, and no two cafeterias, which are attractively decorated, are decorated alike. So much for surface appeal.

Behind the scenes, chain store buying methods are working for The Morrison Merchandising Corporations every minute. Menus, portions and prices are the same in every branch. By sticking to best-sellers like roast beef, chicken and fried shrimp (and by relying on an IBM computer to keep tab on customer preferences), losses from leftovers are kept down to 2 percent.

Emphasis on standardization, which is disguised behind good decor, keeps costs under rigid control. The Morrison Corporation handles the food buying, storage and processing for all Morrison cafeterias. Besides, the company has its own restaurant equipment, detergent-making and coffee processing companies.

This is the perfect example of a profit-making chain that makes profits by buying wisely in quantity at one end, and selling by the piece at the other end. A great profit per piece is not necessary when volume is high, as it is in this operation.

Pure sex by mail and otherwise

First a mail order business of sex aids; then a chain of supermarkets; now one of the fastest-growing retail businesses in Europe. That's the peculiar business run by Beate Uhse, attractive West German wife and mother of three grown sons, whose sales from 1964 to 1968 of contraceptives, mechanical sex stimulators and internal and external aphrodisiacs tripled in volume from $2 to $6 million. By early 1969, at least 13,000 mail orders a day were being filled for everything from "quick-lift" panties to sex-prolonging potions, and her second selection for her new book-of-the-month club, "Helga and Bernd Demonstrate 100 Love Positions," was being bought by thousands of buyers a week. Beate credits her phenomenal success to her unabashed determination to bring sex out in the open. "Lots of stores sell what we sell in a back room," she recently told reporters. "We put our products in the front window, *and it pays.*"

Simplify, simplify!

"Our life is frittered away by detail," wrote Henry David Thoreau more than 100 years ago. "Simplify, simplify." This advice is as sound in our complex society today as it was for this author at Walden. "But how can I make life simple when I have so many things to think about?" you may be asking yourself. Here are two rules that will help.

1. Keep your physical surroundings uncluttered.
2. Remember that dollars are simply multiples of pennies.

A cluttered desk makes for a cluttered mind and vise versa

At one time in our advertising career, we did work for an agency founded by an energetic salesman by the name of Milton Biow, who was as impeccable in dress and habitat as he was effective in the advertising business. Often, in the middle of a busy day, when desks were piled high with work in all departments, a memo would come around to everyone from the head office. "Stop working," it would say, "and clear off your desks. *A cluttered desk means a cluttered mind.*" Soon, the top man himself would walk past each office on an inspection tour.

"Autocratic," many muttered, but we learned much from this experience. After our clean-up pause when we had started back to work, we found ourselves doing faster, better organized work. Today, the habit instilled then has stuck. Now, whether we are researching or writing a book (even one as packed with detail as this one), we work from "chapter files" in separate uncluttered offices.

Take note, and you will see that most effective people—artists as well as business people—are non-messy. Keep your physical surroundings well-groomed!

Dollars are simply multiples of pennies

As your business grows, you may worry that your problems are growing bigger by the minute, too. Not necessarily. Clear away the details and you will see that your basic problems are exactly the same as they were when your business was small.

Let's say you once ran a small select shoe store for women. Because you knew fashion and also how far out the average woman in your town would go in price and fashion, you purchased shoes that your particular market liked and bought. Soon, your clientele grew—and so, in today's population surge, did your town. So now along with your first store, you own two others in outlying shopping centers. In your three stores, you sell maybe 100 times as many shoes as you did in your first little store—but are your problems 100 times as big? No, because when you peel away the details, you still are dependent on your awareness of fashion and the somewhat conservative attitudes of the women in your town. *Buy right and your customers will buy!* The same today as always! And your age-old problem of overhead vs. income is *fundamentally* the same, too.

The owner of a hamburger chain once told a meeting of his managers,

"Remember, the recipe for hamburger for a great crowd of people is simply a multiple of the ingredients for the hamburger you make for a few people." His plea was for perspective.

When details cram your mind with problems, *simplify*. Ask yourself: What is the basic recipe for selling shoes or making hamburger or doing anything else you may find yourself doing? Then, all you have to do is multiply. If your beginning facts are right, the multiplied facts will be right. If your basic formula makes sense, dollars will come where pennies used to be.

Story of an old rundown wharf

Friends of ours in the Caribbean bought an old wharf; then converted the ramshackle units (formerly used as stores and fishing shacks and boat houses) into simple but handsome and immaculate housing units. They sold these units separately as apartments in a condominium.[1] They doubled their money by the time a third of the units were sold, and have become some of the wealthiest persons on the island on which they live now that all units have been sold.

Other friends of ours did the same in New York City when they bought a West Side rooming house which was once a town house. They spiffed it up and made it into four cooperative apartments.[2] By the time two cooperatives were sold, the owners had their initial investment back. By the time the third was sold, they had back most of their remodeling investment. They live in the fourth unit, which actually cost them nothing. "And the market value of our cooperative apartment is going up every day," they told us the other night.

Mike Wallace's estate at Sneden's Landing

Ten or twelve years ago when CBS Newscaster Mike Wallace was doing his first big-time interview show, he and his wife made a shrewd real estate buy across the Hudson and up from New York City. At

---

[1] A condominium is an apartment house in which apartments or dwelling units are individually owned, each owner receiving a recordable deed enabling him to sell, mortgage, exchange, etc., his apartment independent of the owners of the other apartments in the building.

[2] Like units in a condominum, units in a cooperative apartment are individually owned, but unlike units in a condominium they cannot be sold as houses are sold by individuals. In a cooperative, the building is run by tenants for their mutual benefit and money-saving. Each owner must have approval of all other tenants before his unit can be sold.

Sneden's Landing near the Palisades in Rockland County, favorite living area of some of the better-paid creative people in Manhattan, they purchased the lovely old six-acre Dorothy Willard estate, which had a gate house, swimming pool and gardener's cottage around the bend from the main house. Immediately, the Wallaces spruced up the gate house and gardener's cottage, making needed repairs, and put both on the market, one with the swimming pool. Both sold almost immediately, and, as a result, Mike and his wife were left with a beautiful country home on three acres of valuable land for a total investment that Mike says now amounted to a comparative "pittance." Soon Mike's burgeoning career and edge-of-the-day hours made a home in New York City imperative. Next sale: the country house. Now the Wallaces had the money they needed for the handsome town house in New York City, where they live today.

Everybody came out on this deal. The three buyers of Mike's property, George Jenkins, scenic designer, David Thomas, ad man, and Leo Drechster, industrial designer, got three of the last good parcels of land available in a section where property is so scarce most comers have to rent. And Mike and his wife have a town house which through hard work and good figuring cost them little. Naturally, they have a soft spot in their hearts for Sneden's Landing—they rent to be near friends there every summer.

Buy by the unit, sell by the small piece. This economic principle, as old as money, is what Mike put to work at Sneden's Landing. It is a principle a child can understand but few people keep in mind day after day. It can make you more money than almost any other business plan you can think of. Keep it in mind always.

From This Chapter . . .

Thirteenth Financial Recipe for Doubling Your Income

1. Buy in quantity for as good a price as possible.
2. Keep your environment and your mind uncluttered as you work toward your goal.
3. Sell what you bought by the piece for a high enough price to bring in double your original investment. Apply this principle of buying and selling to everything from hamburger meat to real estate.

14

FIND A FOOLPROOF PATTERN FOR WHAT YOU WANT TO DO

Last year more than 600 million items of apparel were sewn at home. Some percentage when you consider that only a little more than twice that many dresses, coats, suits, slips and blouses were produced in factories! There are three reasons for this enormous output by individuals: (1) the desire to be creative; (2) the desire to get better workmanship than in apparel sold in stores; (3) the desire to save money on the end result. Whether the last two aims will be satisfied will depend on (1) the home sewer's workmanship and (2) the pattern or instructions she elects to follow.

Any man or woman can see the sense in the home sewer's selecting the right Butterick, McCall's, Simplicity or Vogue pattern[1] to get the result she wants, but often that same man or woman flounders along after a given goal, never bothering to follow a pattern which would guarantee the desired end result. Yet, no matter what you are doing, sewing, planning a career, building a business or anything else, there is a pattern available for you to follow if you will just look for it.

Where to look for your pattern

Suppose, now, after taking a look around you, that you have come to realize that men and women who are selling something on the road are making more money than others who are carrying out directions in a store or office for someone else. Let's say, for instance, that you are a clerk in a large paint store. You make a good enough salary as salaries go, by filling orders for customers who come into the store to buy. Now,

[1] Pattern sales in 1969 amounted to more than $225 million.

suppose you have recently come to see that salesmen for paint companies who come to see the owner of your store are making three, five or ten times more than you have ever made. You know that you know as much about paint as any salesman coming in the store. Would it be smart for you to switch?

Your number one step as you make your decision is *to talk to an expert.*

Look at that last word again, and put a line under it. *Expert.* This means just what it says. An expert in the field you are interested in!

You won't talk to your mother who may be a very good school teacher but who doesn't know anything about selling.[2] You won't talk to your father who is a good carpenter but has never sold anything in his life.[3] You won't talk to your buddy who is an engineer in your local radio station. Because none of these is a salesman. What you are going to do is to talk to the best salesman in your home town—and, after that, you are going to write to the best salesman you have ever known about anywhere.

Think for a minute. What salesman have you recently had experience with who sold you something you really hadn't intended to buy? Is it the automobile distributor who sold you a new car when you went in to have your old car fixed in answer to a notice that a part has been found to be defective? Was it the real estate man who gave you the courage to stretch for a higher-priced house than you ever thought you could own? Was it the dentist who sold you on the idea of having a bridge made when you went in for a cleaning? Or is it a local lumberman or contractor or insurance salesman or fruit broker or boat salesman who is going to town because he is a great salesman who sells everyone he meets? Make a list of five local salesmen whom you have had experience with or know about from the record. Go to see one or all of them and explain that you are deciding whether you should switch to selling. Ask how the man you're talking to started, how he knows when a sale is closed, how he gets a signature on a dotted line. *A good salesman will be flattered that you have sought him out.*

Never mind if you don't know the person you go to for help

When you have no hidden motive and all you are honestly asking for is 15 minutes of advice, you will find that anyone you call will be receptive whether you know him or not. (If not, don't push—go to the next on your list.)

---

[2] You will, however, talk to her and other teachers if you want to know more about teaching.

[3] You will talk to him and other carpenters if you want to know more about carpentry. The point is *you will make a point of talking to experts in the field in which you are interested.*

When you call someone cold, assure him that you have no hidden motive, have nothing to sell. You might say something like this: "Mr. Smith, I consider you the greatest salesman in town. Right now I am deciding whether to stay in the job I'm in or switch to a selling job. I have nothing to sell now, no hidden motive in calling you. But I certainly would like to talk to you for 15 minutes. Have you got the time?"

You will get your appointment. When you get your 15 minutes, tell the man you're talking to that you are determined to double your income next year. Any good salesman will be interested, and he will talk for longer than 15 minutes, too, and will send you on to others.

Write to a national expert

When you contact a local man, in the case we are describing, you aren't going to be choosy about what he's selling. But when you contact an out-of-town salesman, you are going to contact a salesman in the specific line in which you are interested.

Let's say now you are interested in selling paint. Find out first which of the salesmen who comes into your store sells the most paint, time after time, to your boss. Listen, if you can, to what he says; ask him to go to lunch the next time he's in town; notice how often he comes around. Find out how he got started; then find out which salesman in his company or competitive company he believes is the best he knows. Now write *cold* to that man and ask him if he is going to be in your town some day; if not, will he tell you if anything has been written about his success. Chances are you will get a reprint of an article about him and a letter in the next mail. Read and study his story. Don't become a pest—but later, if you have a specific question like "I have a choice of two territories, Illinois or New Mexico; which would you take?" ask him what he would do. It costs him nothing to answer, and he will want to help.

Once you contact men in the field you want, read about salesmen who have made it big.

Not just for salesmen

We do not mean to imply in this chapter that you must switch from the job you have to a selling job to double your income. We simply give the paint clerk's switch as one example. What we are really saying is that when you plan a switch to any new field, you are much more likely to do better if you consult an expert. In fact, you can save years of mistakes if you talk before you start to *an expert who is doing what you want to do!*

We cannot make this point too clear! Do not go to Betty Crocker for advice if you want to paint a barn; go to her if you want to ice a cake. Do not go to Dr. Spock if you want to know the correct way to extract a tooth; go to Dr. Spock if you want to know the correct way to handle a child.

Go to the expert in the field you are interested in when you are considering whether that field is right for you. And once you start in the field you know is right for you, read everything you can get your hands on written by men who are willing to pass along their secrets.

Read inspirational stories by and about men and women who have made it big

You can hardly pick up a magazine or newspaper[4] that does not tell the story of a man or woman who has risen to the top in a specific area of business. Read such stories in depth whether the business referred to is the one that you have in mind or not, because somewhere down in each story is a behavior hint that can serve as a spur in your push for success. And certainly, when you become particularly interested in someone who has made it big, read everything you can find that this person may have written for others, particularly any "how to" books or articles.

Anyone who passes along information about obstacles that he personally has overcome, or lessons he has learned, has had to cull his lifetime for stand-out experiences and has had to crystallize those experiences into a sound recipe before he can write an effective self-help book.[5] Keep a library of such books and re-read them when you are tempted to say, "It can't be done," or when you feel that you are in need of special encouragement or self-discipline.

Jeno Paulucci's five specific money-making commandments

Jeno Paulucci, founder and chairman of Jeno's, Inc., and author of "How It Was to Make $100,000,000 in a Hurry," (Grosset & Dunlap, 1969) followed five rules, he says, in building his Chun King Corporation

---

[4] *Time Magazine, Reader's Digest,* your newspaper's financial section, *Esquire, Forbes, Fortune,* all devote space to the step-by-step progress of Americans who have become successful in various fields. If you do not subscribe to these publications, read them in planes, in offices or in homes where you may visit.

[5] This is as true today as it was in the time of Benjamin Franklin.

into a multimillion-dollar operation which he sold a few years ago to R. J. Reynolds Tobacco Company. Here are his self-disciplinary commandments:

1. **Refuse to be flattered by those around you. Resist being buttered up.** Let your wife build up your ego, but at work insist on an honest professional opinion from those around you. That's what you're paying for.

2. **Don't be afraid to be unconventional.** Trust your personal hunches. Your product (or anything else you're selling) will never be noticed if you follow a formula used by everyone else. Your job is to find a way to stand out from today's great mass of hucksterism.

3. **Insist that those you hire stick to what you hired them for.** You can get all kinds of free advice about how to run your business, but that's *your* job. Insist that your advertising agency do your advertising and that others do the jobs you know they can do. *You run your business.*

4. **Get your selling methods talked about.** No one can talk about *how* you sell without talking about *what* you sell.[6] Your product gets free publicity when your TV commercials, ads, and any of your selling methods become conversation pieces.

5. **Turn a disadvantage into an advantage.** Don't be afraid to poke fun at a disadvantage.[7] If your story is appealing, prospective customers will be attracted to you, *because* of your disadvantage.

Exercise

Make up your mind now that you are going to double your income next year. Without question, you are going to do this. Ask yourself, "Is it possible to do this in my present business or will I have to make a change? Can I realistically double my income in the job I am now handling?" (The clerk in the paint store would have to answer No to this. His boss couldn't afford on his volume to double a clerk's income.)

If not, what switch can you make that will make your aim feasible? (If possible, make a switch that will utilize your present skills. If you are a cook for a country club, perhaps you will double your income by giving gourmet cooking classes at night to members of the club who have admired your special dishes.)

Write down the names of experts in your town who can help you; list

---

[6] A wacky TV campaign created by adman Stan Freberg made Chun King synonymous with Chinese foods all over America. Extra mileage came as irreverent, humorous commercials became talked about everywhere.

[7] Stan Freberg's message in Chun King commercials: Only a minority of people eat American-Oriental foods, but if everybody ate Chun King foods, they'd love them.

nationally known experts in the field to whom you can write; find books on the subject you can read.

Circle a date on the calendar when you will make your switch.

Put your plan into action that day and give it everything you've got!

From This Chapter . . .

Fourteenth Financial Recipe for Doubling Your Income

1. Write down the name of an expert in your town who understands the work you do or want to do.
2. Read a book on the subject of what you want to do.
3. Follow the advice they give you to double your income in one year.
4. Work like hell!

Time For Another Review

On page 105 you read a list of seven suggestions for doubling your income this year. And you checked one suggestion, which was the title of a chapter heading, which had a special meaning for you. (Remember, you went back at that time and re-read the chapter you selected as meaningful.)

We now are going to ask you to repeat that exercise, finding a *second* meaningful directive from the seven chapter headings you have read since last review time. Read down the new list.

Chapter 8. MAKE YOUR SPARE MOMENTS PAY OFF
9. GO AFTER THE NITTY-GRITTY
10. THOU MUST HAVE FAITH
11. BECOME A SELLING WRITER, INVENTOR, PAINTER OR COMPOSER ALONG WITH YOUR REGULAR WORK
12. DO FOR YOURSELF WHAT YOU HAVE DONE FOR OTHERS!
13. BUY IN QUANTITY, SELL BY THE PIECE
14. FIND A FOOLPROOF PATTERN FOR WHAT YOU WANT TO DO

There may be several truths that you can apply to your own business enterprises in the list above, but select only one for now. Then go back and *re-read the chapter with that heading* before going on to the chapter coming up.

When you took time out for your first review after Chapter 7 you checked a directive which you told yourself you could begin applying the next day. Now write that directive on a piece of paper and below it write one of the seven suggestions above.

(*Example:* Let's say you selected as your first meaningful directive "Achieve your goal with a strategy used in advertising"; and now, as a second, "Find a foolproof pattern for what you want to do." You are beginning to work out a set of personal rules that will lead you to where you want to go.)

Rest Again Before You Read More

Constructive ideas are now taking hold in your brain

A new, more positive approach to making money is overcoming any old, deeply embedded negativism. Attitudes that have been holding you back are changing. You are on your way!

Even though you see a light where there was foggy confusion before, do not go too fast. Give your subconscious mind a chance to digest what you have read. Rest now before reading the next seven chapters. There is much in them to absorb. Begin only when your mind is fresh. Right now, do something different or close your eyes and rest.

15

GET *SCORE* TO HELP YOU RUN A BUSINESS OF YOUR OWN

You have read time after time that small enterprises account for 91 percent of all business failures. So why in this book that guarantees a doubled income in a year *if you put its principles to work in a conscientious manner* are we suggesting that you take a precarious jump into dangerous waters.

The explanation lies in the reason for the failure of any small business in nine out of ten cases. Research proves that in the majority of cases *business collapse is due to bad management.* Change bad management to good management and you will correct the catastrophe that comes to the small business man, the most failure-prone individual in our economy.

Let's suppose now that the clerk in that paint store we talked about in our last chapter can see that his boss makes 10 or 20 times his weekly take, and he also can see he could do a far better job than the boss in running the business. So he decides that rather than travel as a road man, he will open a paint store. How should he start?

Free advice from retired executives

As his first step, he should talk to a member of SCORE, which is the bold, creative answer to a double-barreled problem which in 1964 faced Eugene P. Foley, then head of the Small Business Administration. Because it is the function of SBA to lend money to small companies for equipment, expansion and working capital, the government agency *and the taxpayer* lose money every time a small business fails. But what could

Foley do? His 3,300 field workers couldn't possibly cope with the problems of more than 4½ million struggling "little guys."

Gene Foley thought of the competent retired men he knew. Maybe they could give their talent to newcomers to business. He put out some "feelers" and had an immediate positive reaction to his idea from everyone he wrote to. *Result:* SCORE (which stands for Service Corps of Retired Executives) was launched full-scale from all 68 SBA offices. Hundreds of retired businessmen promptly offered their services—and all those "little guys" who would eventually be the recipients were even more responsive.

To qualify for aid

To qualify for help from SCORE you must be either (1) contemplating going into business or (2) an established concern with no more than 25 employees which obviously cannot afford $100-a-day management consultants. If you fit into either of these classifications, you can get free counsel from SCORE for as long as it is needed, occasionally, agreeing to pay the SCORE counselor $5 for travel expenses if he comes from as far away as 25 miles.

Back to the clerk who wants his own business

Suppose our clerk wants to talk to an expert in the retail paint business before going into business for himself. All he has to do is call or write to the director of the Small Business Administration in his state capital city. Or write to Richard M. Sweeney, of the SBA Management Assistance Division in Washington, D.C., to get the name of the director of the SCORE office nearest to him. (Your local chamber of commerce may know, too.) Once he has the address of the SCORE manager in his town or state, he can write and tell this man about his particular business problem and what he believes will be helpful in the way of counseling.

Let's say you are the boy behind the paint counter, going over the pros and cons of opening up your own business. Within a few days, you will get a call or a letter from SCORE, telling you that a former management consultant who has worked in your state is coming to call, or a one-time Sears Roebuck merchandising man, or the former manager of a giant discount paint outfit who used to be located in another part of the country. Now you can see how helpful SCORE can be. Where else can you get counselors *for free* who can and will help you figure out where, how and with what you can set up shop?

Play it straight

If you are going into business—or already in a business which is headed for failure—play it straight with your counselor from SCORE who comes to help you. Even though you may think you look foolish, let him have the facts. Then he can advise you as he has advised others. (SCORE has helped men and women in dress shops, books and records stores, filling stations, garages, trucking outfits, candy shops—you name it.) With experience and a true understanding of your wants or confusion or difficulties in front of him, he can get you headed toward success instead of failure.

What about going from a big business to a small business?

Rockland County, New York, Bucks County, Pennsylvania, Bergen County, New Jersey, and Fairfield and Litchfield counties in Connecticut, are filled with former New Yorkers who have worked in giant companies, agencies or publishing houses, and who have now set up businesses for themselves. One of the most successful is David G. Lyon who runs a money-making advertising agency out of his garage in Westport, Connecticut.

According to Dave, he was forcibly flung off Madison Avenue in his forties. In the first few months, he spent his days trying to get back on the gravy train; then, with a fairly decent lump sum of money in his pocket, he enjoyed an idyllic interlude of involuntary retirement. Finally, through a friend of a friend of a friend, he was thrust into the advertising business for a small local client. Today, he still writes his own copy, wraps his own packages, and closes his door sometimes at high tide for a two-hour scuba break.

Once again, you may never have worked in an ad agency, may never want to work in one, but David Lyon's advice to the man who has worked in a big business and is now thinking of starting in a small way in business for himself can prove invaluable to you no matter what kind of business you have in mind.

How to start in business for yourself

David Lyon has told the story of opening his own agency outside New York in a book entitled, "Off Madison Avenue," (G. P. Putnam's Sons). In talking of it, the author insists that this is not a how-to book but is really a how-I book. Dave says that in writing it, he hesitated to sway any business man to go into a "cottage industry," unless that man was absolutely sure that he could be happy away from the giants. He adds now, however, that for a man of the right disposition, a small business can give a sense of freedom, individuality and accomplishment.

For the man from the large agency who decides to run his own small agency, Dave has worked out 15 or 20 common sense rules, seven of which are printed here. These seven, we believe, are applicable to men in any large business who are either thinking of going into a small business or who have already crossed over.

1. **Know what to do if you are fired.** A man's first instinct when he is thrown out of a job is to try immediately to get another one. He is motivated as much by a need to regain status as by coolly considered economic judgments. He may go from a push for a big job to a smaller one, and then a smaller one. As his sights go down, so do his savings shrink. When he finally turns his attention to the possibility of going into business for himself, his bank account and his ego have been reduced to near zero.

If you are middle-aged when you are fired from a large organization, you will probably walk away with a decent sum of money. If so, you can use the temporary independence it gives you to set yourself up in business in the right way. Invest your time in finding a client (or a small business opportunity) that's right for your personality, your experience, your aptitudes. If you feel you want to go back to a big organization, invest three days a week in setting up a new business, two days in looking for a job. Eventually, you'll find that you can't spare the time for job interviews and you aren't interested anyway.

2. **Keep your overhead low.** A secondhand desk is fine as long as you don't sit at it and produce secondhand ideas.

3. **Be prepared to do it yourself.** As the proprietor of your own agency, you will find yourself doing many menial tasks which you formerly relegated to others. Accept this with good grace; realize that this is part of the price you pay for freedom from administrative responsibility.

4. **Talk to a bank about your credit problems.** The amount of capital you'll need to start in business depends on the nature of your business and your first client. Talk to your local bank and get its advice. If it will lend you the money to send cash with your first order, you're better off than if you tie up a substantial share of your personal net worth in a capital investment in your business. If the first bank you talk to doesn't seem to make sense, shop around.

5. **Get an accountant to set up your books and your billing procedures.** Find an accountant who is familiar with the operations of a small business and won't burden you with needless complications. If you can get your wife or some other trusted relative to handle the money-dispensing portion of your business, your entire bookkeeping can be simplified, because the accountant won't have to assume the possibility of dishonesty.

6. **Learn to trust your judgment again.** In a large organization you learn to subordinate your own judgment to the wisdom of the pack and never take a step without the crutch of research firmly supporting you. How satisfying it is to throw aside these fetters and to be a human being again! It is your ripened judgment that will establish your value now in this new business. Exercise this.

7. **Respect yourself.** The worst enemy you can have is a client (or customer) who tries to tear down your self-respect. Never let anyone feel that he is doing you a favor by giving you his business. Well-qualified men to handle small accounts are hard to find.

David Lyon, in the business of selling personal service, learned long ago that no man can sell himself to others unless he has respect for himself. The same holds true of any tangible product he may be selling. How can any man sell his product to others unless he really respects it?

Two stories about a man who loved his product

Do you respect your product? If so, would you go as far as William H. Danforth, late chairman of the Ralston Purina Company, to sell the product you or your company is selling? Here are two stories we heard about Mr. Danforth this week.

C. Victor Brown, well-known educational consultant who lives not far from us, was having breakfast in a Chicago restaurant one day with the unusual chairman of one of the largest breakfast food companies in the world. When approached by the waitress, Mr. Danforth asked for Ralston's for breakfast. "We do not carry that, sir," she told him politely. "But that is what I have every morning," he told her quietly, and again she replied that there simply was none in the kitchen. Now he asked if she could send out for the breakfast food he wanted, and after she conferred with the manager, she agreed that this could be done.

According to our friend, when the requested breakfast food eventually was set before Mr. Danforth, Vic whispered to his companion, "Why don't you tell her who you are?" Great salesman that he was, Mr. Danforth made this reply: "Oh, no, that would spoil it all."

On another occasion, when traveling on a train to the West Coast, Mr. Danforth asked for Ralston's Purina in the dining car; again, he was told that the train did not carry the product. This time, with the same quiet insistence, he persuaded the conductor to wire ahead to Santa Fe, New Mexico, for his product. When the dealer who delivered it arrived at the halted train, he nodded his head when he saw Mr. Danforth waiting beside the porter on the platform. "I figured," he said, "that you must be on this train. No other person in the world would have dared insist upon such an idea."

When you care about your product as Mr. Danforth cared, you and what you're selling are bound to be successful through good times and the problem times which are sure to come in every business.

Up again, old heart

Six or seven years ago, Murray Schefkind and his wife opened up a novel discount business on Route 7, between New Milford and Kent, Connecticut. Naming the business Ronal's (a tag that combined the names of the Schefkinds' two sons, Ronald and Alan), they began selling wallpaper at a discount.

"Because a manufacturer mixes up a new vat of paint every time he runs off a wallpaper pattern," Murray told us, "he never gets *exactly* the same color in two consecutive runs. So he sells the leftover rolls from a previous run to us at a discount. Also, when he brings out a new line of patterns, he sometimes sells us his entire stock from the season just past. We may get a discount of as much as 60 or 70 percent, which we pass along to the customer."

In this area where New Yorkers look for old Colonial houses to buy and restore for fun and profit, a wallpaper store selling at a discount was bound to prosper and did. Soon, cars were lined up at Ronal's as if it were a discount food store, so within a year, Alan, the one son still in Connecticut, decided to go into the business, too. As ambitious as his parents, he began in off hours to restore old houses, getting his paper, of course, from the family business.

Suddenly, tragedy struck! In a freak accident, Alan fell through an open stairwell in a house he was remodeling and was killed. Grief-stricken, the Schefkinds went on with the business as much out of habit as for profit when one of the major reasons for building the business was gone. Friends and neighbors were kind, and one boy, Larry Kisver, a friend of their son, offered to come into the store and help out. Soon, Larry found he loved the work and stayed on as an employee.

Then, tragedy struck again! Larry hadn't been a full-time employee for more than a month when Murray Schefkind died of a heart attack. Now, except for Larry, Mrs. Schefkind was alone. For months she considered giving up the business, which was now meaningless. But as she recently told us, "Even as I was saying I would quit, the business kept me going. I would go down in the morning and find hot muffins and coffee waiting from an old customer whose home we had helped to decorate and new customers waiting to buy for their homes. At night, when I would be leaving to go home, someone would bring in a cake or plant and stop to chat. People were wonderful and, of course, fate had sent me Larry. He *really pitched in!*

It has now been three years since Larry and Mrs. Schefkind have been running the business together. Still called Ronal's, the business is now Ronal's, Inc., and Larry is a stockholder. Still selling wallpaper at a discount in an area where the population is expanding and new houses are going up every day, Ronal's has doubled its income as the area's population has doubled, or even faster. "And it has been the best thing in the world for me," says its lady boss. "Talking to people here every day and helping them decide on what to do with their homes has saved my sanity. In fact," she told us yesterday, "Larry and I are talking now about buying up some old houses and doing them over ourselves."

Do you have the kind of stamina to take the violent ups and downs that come in life and still keep on with your business? If so, you probably can make more money working for yourself than for another. But, as you think about moving over from being an employee to being your own boss, take these steps:

1. Prepare yourself well in advance before you go into business for yourself.
2. Once in, be better than your competition.
3. Take a positive attitude; know around the clock that you're going to make it.

Do these three things, and you will be on your way.

From This Chapter . . .

Fifteenth Financial Recipe for Doubling Your Income

1. Get outside help when you're struggling with a business of your own.
2. If you can't afford a management consultant, call SCORE.
3. Be sure you can enjoy working away from the "giants," if you start a one-man business. Enjoy its compensations from the beginning.
4. Love your product.
5. When things get tough, keep right on working.

16

RUN A MAIL ORDER BUSINESS ON THE SIDE

Anyone who writes for a living—an ad man, a reporter, a publicity person, a ghostwriter, *anyone* at one time or another thinks of "running a little mail order business on the side." Some do this, too, and double their income from a side venture; others lose whatever it costs them for stock and advertising space and/or direct mail. Let's see what makes the successful ones *go!*

Fruit-of-the-month club

Harry and David, western fruit growers of Bear Creek Orchards, Medford, Oregon, first came to the attention of the average American consumer when they merchandised an idea called Fruit-of-the-Month. But even before that, one of their early ads, when they were advertising pears only, made advertising history and is now considered a mail order classic. It ran in *Fortune* and had as its headline, "Imagine Harry and Me advertising our PEARS in *Fortune!*" Purportedly written by David, it explained how he and his brother had decided to spend about what they would pay for a new tractor for space in a magazine to tell readers about the Royal Riviera Pears which they were raising in Rogue River Valley, Oregon, and shipping to fine hotels and restaurants in Paris and London. The ad's point: *Wouldn't you like to give a box of these rare pears to friends at Thanksgiving or Christmas?*

The medium for this message couldn't have been better—*Fortune,* a magazine read by rich and busy men, who could by following directions in the ad make up a list of business associates and friends and let Harry and David do the rest. The ad pioneered a new field for Harry and David and originated a form of merchandising which was the beginning of a new era in mail order selling. You will note that in the first ad, pears alone were advertised. The approach was so successful that the Oregon brothers originated their Fruit-of-the-Month Club a year later.

Mail order is done in two ways: (1) *By direct mail.* You go to your mail box, pull out a letter that tells you about a book that will help you to communicate more easily. A special price is offered. If the idea appeals to you, you send in a check and get the book by return mail, usually for a trial period. (2) *Through an ad.* You answer an ad that you see in a magazine through your post office, not in person. Let's say you see an ad for prime filet mignon (box of 16) shipped prepaid for $35. You send to the correct address and get your steaks by return mail.

"An easy way to make money," you say, thinking of the seller, and this is true *if you have two things going for you:* (1) A good basic idea; and (2) an exclusive idea (or an exceptionally good price on a popular item).

The reason so many persons are attracted to the idea of direct mail as a side business is that only a little capital need be involved. (For a test, you can run a small ad or send out 100 letters—which is quite different from setting yourself up in, say, a grocery store to get started in business.) Look closely, though, and you will see that the product offered by most direct mail sellers has real value (Maine lobsters by mail or shoes by an Italian craftsman or an engraved name plate for your Cadillac). So, once your trial run in a newspaper or through the mail tells you that you are going to get comers for your offer, you have to have capital to buy or manufacture wisely so that your offer can be priced to make you money when you ship.

Direct mail success formula

One of the direct mail success tales of our time is the story of the book company you ordered this book from. Let's see what makes this particular company so successful.

As we think about it, we believe there are three reasons for the phenomenal success of this particular operation.

1. **The "products" it offers.** Success in any business starts with the product. No business can stay alive very long if the product is not *right.* On this score, the books offered by this company are tops—not just in subject matter but in the appearance of their books—in their bindings, typography, printing and covers.

2. **The lists the company uses.** Some mail authorities say the lists are half the battle in mail order. We can't say whether the credit that goes to names you send to should be 50 percent—but certainly a key to success in mail order is the list of persons to get your announcement. Customer lists for the company that sells this book were built through the years from

lists of credit-checked customers who have been satisfied buyers of other books with the same basic appeal. This is a classic example of the wisdom of building a customer list for one property, then building new property to appeal to customers developed by the first property.

3. **The offers it makes.** You can have the right product and the right list—but you still won't make big money if your offer doesn't make sense. You've got to overcome the foot-dragging that is an automatic answer to most direct mail offers. The price and terms must be attractive in mail order or the prospective customer doesn't react. The books offered by this company are unique; the prices are right; the basic offer each time is fair (you have the privilege to return for full credit). There is much to be learned, too, from the presentation of the product in the mailer you receive. What made you send for this book? Undoubtedly, the announcement you received was in good taste, and complimented your status.

Check list as you consider selling by direct mail

You probably have no intention in your side business of selling books by mail. What you may have in mind is a blend-your-own powder or an astrology kit or the marketing of hand-crafted jewelry or a dormitory treat to be mailed once a month to children of clients away at school. No matter. The direct mail rules followed by book companies can make you equally successful, no matter what you're selling. So check your product as follows:

1. *Product or service*
   Is the product you have in mind a real value for the price you're asking?
   Can your customer get the same product by mail from another? At the same price?
   Are there many prospective customers in the market for your product?
   Does your product or service come under an umbrella which you can use later to sell related products?
2. *Your lists*
   How are you going to make up your list?
   Once you have a list, do you keep a second copy to avoid loss?
   Can you scan your list and find a certain "type" represented there (as on the list of Fruit-of-the-Month buyers)?
3. *Your offer*
   Can you come up with a newsmaking offer and still make a profit?
   Can your proposition contain an incentive? Free offer or gift, chance to win a prize, free trial, installment offer, price cut?

Are you sure that you have in mind the ideal introductory price?
If you have related items for sale, can you charge for your catalogue? (Some companies do this and make as much from the catalogue sale as they do from products.)

If you study these questions and work out your answers, you will begin to see that there is a pattern for success in a business founded in direct mail. And you will see whether the product that you may have to sell can measure up. If so, you may well be on your way to doubling your income in the next year from your present salary and a mail order business on the side.

Why mail order?

The basic point of this chapter is to encourage you to double your income by going into a *second* business on the side. So why do we concentrate on mail order? The answer is stated in the first few paragraphs. Mail order selling in many cases requires little capital until sales are actually made; marketing tests can be made for a very low cost. Also, success in mail order depends on common sense as much as it does on training—and mail order can lead you into new profit-making areas.

Story of a mail order writer

One of the few admen I know who actually went to school to learn the business of advertising is Al Goldman, executive vice president of Benton & Bowles, who went as a young man to the University of Missouri for this purpose. Upon graduation, he did not get a job in an agency, however, but as sportswriter for a New York newspaper.

The son of one of the great fight managers of the 20s and 30s, Sam Goldman, Al says he thinks today that he didn't do much consciously that led to success. He just went along *doing what came naturally*, and it took him further than he ever thought he'd go. Here is his philosophy.

Don't worry about all the moves— just make them

"My father always felt that the best fighter was the one who was doing what he did naturally. Something about the sound and fury of boxing attracts the young boxer in the first place. He tries it—as many kids do—with or without gloves—and finds he has an instinctive ability to use his feet and hands in the ring. This is the kind of kid a manager can look at and see that he is making all the right moves without knowing what or why. A manager knows that this kind of raw talent can be developed. The boy is a natural; he acts out of reflex."

"And," concludes Al, "that's how I always was with writing." (Also, Al liked to write for money—and he knew from the first that advertising would eventually pay more for his talent than editorial writing.) His friends who were in the ad business sensed that this man was a *natural* ad writer, soon beckoned him over to write "on the side" for them.

"A friend of mine was in the mail order business," Al said, "and he was first to ask me to do some mail order ads for him . . . and right there is where I first saw the power of one word as opposed in print to the power of another. We would offer a product under one headline, and it would fall on its face; put it out under another headline, and the money would roll in."

Soon, Al crossed from newspaper work to full-time mail order—made such a good record there that he eventually was beckoned into the agency business where he went quickly up. "Because I belonged in that ring," he says now, "it came naturally."

Learn from mail order about what makes people buy

"There is no better training than mail order for anyone who eventually wants to sell with little black words," Al Goldman says. "As with retail ads, a mail order ad either brings in money or it doesn't. You know in a hurry whether you have a winner or a dud."

If you have a yen to take a swing at a mail order offer, go ahead—but do it at first *on the side*. You will learn from your experience, whatever it may be, and if you keep learning, you will build up an income that will pay off; you just have to.

Mail order success story

Harold Fair, retired New York TV production company vice president, has had two hobbies for twenty-five years: sailing and building ship models. Two years ago, when a two months' illness took him off his feet, he combined his two hobbies into a profitable mail order business—and far more than doubled his income in his second year.

Harold's money-maker: a hand-carved wall decoration for boat enthusiasts. This novel gift consists of a bluejay mounted on a wooden plaque covered with a navigation chart of a lake or harbor where the sailor receiving the gift has sailed. First year, he offered the hand-made item for $21, including mailing, found by the time he paid for mahogany for hulls, poplar for sails, and jute for framing, he was losing money, so he doubled his price, found that he sold even more plaques for $42. Now he sells more than before, makes a nice little profit on something he likes to do anyway. Hardly has to advertise—publicity like this keeps the orders rolling in.

N. Flayderman & Co., Inc.

One of the most unusual businesses of its kind in the world is located right in our home town of New Milford, Connecticut. Begun a couple of decades ago in Kennebunk, Maine, by an ambitious young man, who had worked for a large corporation upon graduation but just couldn't get used to "pushing papers around," it started out as a mail order business which specialized in antique firearms and nautical items. The son of a respected antique dealer in Boston, who like many others in the luxury business had been hit by the depression, Norman Flayderman knew his wares but had no capital, so started on a shoestring. Fortunately, he was able to borrow money he needed to get started and to build up his working capital through sales.

By now, his company is actually in three distinct businesses: (1) It still sells antique firearms, militaria and nautical items via mail order in a semi-annual catalogue which sells for $2.00 a year. (2) It publishes books (11 to date) retailing from $6.50 to $19.50 which are concerned with military history and American weapons. (3) It operates in the retail and wholesale book sales business. Besides its own publications, the company lists and sells just about every known book on the subject of weapons (antique and modern) and issues a special 108-page catalogue, with reviews of each of these books, which comes out biannually.

Because there is currently no book available on the art of scrimshaw (carvings done on ivory and other materials by sailors on America's whaling ships and considered by many historians to be "America's first folk art"), the still young company president is now writing a book about scrimshaw, which he will offer through his catalogue.

Like many others written about in this book, the owner of this unusual company started with one simple step—selling firearms by mail. As his front foot was going down for this step, his back foot was coming up for the next, which resulted in the publication of a catalogue to tell collectors about his firearms, militaria and nautical items. As he took this step, the need for books on the subjects he was interested in became apparent to him. One simple step after another, and Norm was on his way.

Get your wife in the act

Let's say now that your wife is a potter, and a good one, and you and she have decided to start with a little investment and build up a mail order business. Your wife can turn out six, seven or eight elegant hollow tree trunk pencil holders (that will hold eight or ten pencils) on a Saturday morning. Maybe you have been giving her handsome clay pencil holders to executive friends as gifts and they are delighted. So you and your wife have been thinking of selling these items by direct mail. Let's say you want to give it a try. How do you begin?

You can sell your wife's pencil holders on a commission basis through a catalogue by going to a mail order gift item company that puts out gift items by mail. (Ask your State Development Commission if your state lists such a company, then go to see the owner. Or call the owner of a company whose catalogue comes to your house.)

If you want to take a swing at this operation on your own, start with something unusual that you make yourself, like the hollow tree-trunk pencil holder. Here are steps to take:

1. Take a black and white picture of your product in use. (Make a close-up of your pencil holder filled with pencils, sharp points up.)
2. Get a small local printer to print this picture on cards (on the side usually reserved for writing) that are the same size as Government Postal Cards. (Have just 100 cards printed but get your printer to hold the plate in case the 100-card mailing pays off.)
3. Make up a list of 100 male executives, who are members of a good men's club in your home town. (Many clubs have rulings that their mailing lists cannot be sold or used for mail order. If your husband belongs to a club with this ruling, you cannot use the mailing list—but you will know the names of local executives who are members and can take their home addresses from the telephone book.)
4. Mail out your cards three weeks in advance of a special day, like Father's Day. By mailing your offer early, you will get returns early and you can mail your gift by return mail in time for the special day.
5. On the right-hand half of stamp side of the Government card write the name and address of the *wife* of the executive whose name is on the list.
6. On the left half of the card, write this message: Father's Day, June ——Give "old dad" this handsome pottery pencil holder—(a Mary Smith "original") only $5 prepaid. Return this card with your check for return mail delivery.

The cards will cost you $5; the photograph you will take yourself; the printing will cost less than $25. We are assuming that your wife has a kiln—and the clay she will use for each holder will cost no more than 35 cents, if that much. Boxing and mailing each holder will run another 25 cents.

Costs you can see are easy to figure. Now, if you make seven sales, you will pay for your total investment (not counting your wife's time, of course), and every sale over that first seven will be a profit.

You will know, by trying a specific item like this for a given time, whether you have a winner. If you have a hot item, you are in business and can experiment with other items. If you do not do well, you will learn much about who reacts to what, who buys, how soon customers mail in replies, and whether your product has good appeal to the market you are going after.

You will lose little if you start in a small way, and in case you have a winner, you are on your way to a side business that can really pay off.

From This Chapter . . .

Sixteenth Financial Recipe for Doubling Your Income

1. Decide what mail order item you can make or buy for a low cost.
2. Carefully figure the cost of your production and mailing so that you can end up with a good profit.
3. Run a trial ad in a small newspaper, or send out a direct mail card to 100 homes. If this first try does not pay off, do not despair. Look at all facets of your operation and change your price or approach. Try once more. If this doesn't pull, try another item.

17

STAKE OUT A CLAIM ON A TIMELY IDEA

A few years ago, singer Aretha Franklin, who grew up on the frayed fringe of Detroit's Negro East Side, was cover girl on *Time*. Why? Because she is the greatest girl singer in the United States? (Many would say no.) Because she is the greatest Negro girl singer? (Surely, Marian Anderson has her out-classed there.) The reason is neither, but still it is easy to understand. At a time when America's key question about any performer is *has she* (*or he*) *got soul?* she was so loaded with whatever it is that she was known by her admirers as *Lady Soul.* Thus, what she had could be used to explain to others a concept which was puzzled about and delighted in by millions. No one could write about *soul* for months after the *Time* story without mentioning Aretha Franklin any more than reporters 40 years ago could talk about "It" without mentioning Clara Bow. Aretha had the franchise.

Lesson to be learned: In a year when *soul* is the thing, and you have it, get out there in the spotlight and sing, baby, *sing.* Get to be Lady Soul before someone else gets to be Lady Soul. The money will come.

Say you're a painter, and this is a year when everyone is hot for storytelling primitives, and you are good at this kind of painting. Start digging up legends from the past in your particular state. Were there slave auctions or Tory hide-outs in your county, if it is in the North? Indian wars and farm auctions that people have forgotten, if you live in the Middle West? Antebellum memory-bringers in the South?

Begin explaining legends in primitives. Historians as well as art connoisseurs will become interested in what you are doing. Now give yourself a memorable name that is somehow related to your own name. (Uncle Pete if your name is Peter; Foxy Brice if your name is Brice Fuchs; Grandpa Sage, if you are a 50-year-old John Sage, etc.) Then, begin entering your paintings *everywhere,* with a story of the subject matter printed on the back. Soon reporters will begin writing up your stories and illustrating with your paintings. You will become the painter in your state who tells stories with primitives. You will have a franchise on a timely idea. Anyone who follows, even though he is a slightly better painter, will be an also-ran as far as your regional story-telling paintings are concerned. (If you are a *great* painter, you don't have to be crafty in your "franchise" approach but this is the foolproof way.)

Now let's say you are a cosmetics manufacturer. Through careful research you find out that next year is going to be a year when the natural-looking, healthy girl will be in. Her clothes will be understated, no bouffant hairdo, no glittery eyelids; our neat heroine is going to be a brushed and shining biscuit-colored doll. So you won't bring out mahogany-colored nail polish with a lipstick to match, will you, or black paste-on beauty spots, or dead white powder? If you are a good merchandiser, you will ride the "natural" train with transparent freckle-revealing make-up base, honey colored powder, light lipstick. Once your wares are right, you want to be *first* with a descriptive name for your girl—"Honey," maybe, or "Biscuit Baby" or "Golden Girl." If your name ties in with a trend, and your products live up to your description, and your advertising budget is right, you are on your way to making money. Reason: your publicity is built in. You have a franchise on what the world wants and is talking about.

Different kinds of franchises

Your franchise may be a place, a job, a talent, an invention—one of a score of ownership opportunities. But in connection with the franchise idea we are discussing here, it will have three things in common with all other franchises of any form. It will be dependent on a trend; it will attract publicity because of that trend; it will be one of a kind or the best of its kind.

Let's look for a minute at a much-discussed trend and what opportunities there are in connection with it.

For our case in point, let's discuss again today's exploding population.

Much-discussed trend—our exploding population

Unless our current trend is interrupted or reversed in some way, the population of the United States, which is now 200,000,000, will double in the next 50 years. Let's look at opportunities made possible by this trend and/or our fear of it.

Birth control, food, housing

Birth control products will be in demand and in the news as our population expands and limited child production is encouraged. Already being talked about are pills for women to be taken after intercourse and others for men to be taken before; vaccines to prevent conception, and abortion aids, should such aids become legal. As interest grows, books about birth control measures will be in demand, printed material will have to be made available to women in and out of clinics, and special hospital equipment will be necessary. A whole new category of products will come into being as our expanding population threatens our freedom of movement, our open spaces, our food supply.

Even though birth control products will become more and more and more efficient, the population will increase because there will be more young marrieds who will want babies, less infant mortality and longer life spans. So we will need food for more and more human beings. Already being developed are synthetic foods like one which resembles and tastes like hamburger but is no more like real meat than nylon is like silk. Vitamins and minerals and protein can be added to such foods, so our health can conceivably be improved. Not just synthetic foods, but new and better ways to produce and process natural foods will call for a host of new products, processing equipment and marketing know-how. Crops grown on the ocean floor will be harvested for human consumption, which means that oceanography, as a field, will become increasingly important. Also, products and equipment for under-water exploring and fishing and farming will be money-makers.

All of this may seem way out to you, but certainly there is one familiar product which you can see has just got to increase in value. And that's *land!* Until new planets become inhabitable, the land on this earth is all we've got and, unlike the people who live on it, it's not going to increase in quantity. Buy land around major cities and you can make money by sub-dividing; buy less expensive land farther out and you can't lose that way, either. Because the more congested the cities become, the more men and women are going to be looking for places far away from the crowd where they can raise their children.

Suggestion: subscribe to the magazine, *Our Public Lands,* Superintendent of Documents, Government Printing Office, Washington, D.C., 20402. Send $1.00 annually for four issues which list tracts in remote areas for sale.

Sample buys in an issue we received today:

In Montana: 40-acre tract with ranch trail access—appraised at $800. In New Mexico: 40-acre tract of pinon-juniper grazing land—appraised at $900. In Oregon: 69 acres near Klamath Falls—appraised at $1,480. On seeing such an offer in your Public Lands book, what you do is write to the Bureau of Land Management in the state you want and ask for details and date of sale. Then, send in a sealed bid a certified check which must be equal to the appraised value or more. You will be notified if your bid is high; then you have to wait for 30 days to find out whether an adjoining landowner cares to meet your bid, which he can do. If no one takes advantage of this provision, the land is yours. (We have bought two 40-acre parcels, one in Minnesota and the other in Idaho, for our children and grandchildren, believing that in their lifetimes the land will become increasingly valuable. Buying for many this way is also a great "one fell swoop" Christmas present.) If you do not want to tie up a lot of money in a land investment of this kind, get 9 other people to form a land-buying company with you and watch for good buys in public lands. Right today, there is a 40-acre parcel of public land near Clark City, Nevada, appraised at $3,000, which has a road access, nearby electricity and a residential development potential. This means that 10 of you could possibly buy this tract for $300 apiece and a year from today subdivide into lots at a profit. Or you could hold until Harold Hughes buys up some more of the state.[1]

Something old in a standardized world

With all the giant apartment houses with standardized rooms and development type houses bound to go up as people multiply, there will be a desire on the part of many for "something old," a reminder of another time when life was less hurried, more gracious, less crowded. Nostalgia and the desire for something different will create a demand for old schoolhouses that can be converted to houses, old railroad stations, mills, chestnut barns, covered bridges, any old structure that can be made into a modern home, shop or restaurant.

---

[1] On a plane not long ago, we met Corbett Monica who told us he had just bought 160 acres of land near Las Vegas at $1,000 an acre, hoping for such a break.

Case in point: Nick Geraci, New York commercial artist, bought a barn in Norwalk, Connecticut, rubbed it, burnished it, brightened it through 15 years of living to within an inch of its life, eventually sold it for enough, he told us, to pay for all living he and his family have done in the barn for all the years that the children were growing up. "I figure I've been living rent free," he said, "for 15 years."

Second case: A young couple in New Boston, New Hampshire, saw a dilapidated mill on a stream pictured in a "fall color" section in an old *Life* magazine, went on a scouting trip, bought the mill for a few thousand dollars and restored it. Now they can get ten times over what they paid. "Because there *aren't* any more mills," a real estate man told us. "Who else has an old mill stream flowing under his back porch?"

Third case: In Peoria, Illinois, the most popular restaurant is a railroad station, complete with memorabilia, owned by one owner, leased to a restaurateur. People come for miles to see it and to dine.

Reminder: As the years go by, old things won't get any younger. And they will become more in demand as new things become more and more numerous. Something old that you can restore will become valuable because of its rarity and the publicity which it will automatically attract.

Attention-getting job in a crowded world

If you have ever been stymied in a cab on a New York cross-town street on the way to an 8:30 theatre curtain, you have wondered (aloud, probably) what the world is going to be like when there are twice as many people around. Someone else who did a lot of wondering was the late Commissioner of Traffic in New York City. Nobody needs to tell you that his name was Henry Barnes, because he was interviewed, quoted, written about every day of his life. Henry Barnes had a job that automatically put him in the limelight. In a snarled-up city, he was the man paid to do the unsnarling. Because he had the biggest traffic job in our biggest town, he became the best known authority on traffic problems in the United States. What's more, he had that job when the whole idea of a Commissioner of Traffic was new to most of us. While he lived, any TV director who wanted an expert on traffic immediately thought of Commissioner Barnes. He had the franchise. Now another man has inherited his job but not his headlines, because times have changed. By now, the whole nation has a traffic problem. So today's news-getter is Nixon's new cabinet member, John Volpe (a one-time hod carrier who borrowed $500 to start a construction company which grew into a multi-million dollar business). As he wrestles in our new Department of Transportation building with our railway, air and highway headaches, he will automatically attract headlines.

Suggestion: Get into position to solve a problem that arises automatically out of our increased population. Whether it's a garbage disposal problem, or air or water pollution trouble, or housing problems, or what to do about cemeteries (where *are* people going to be buried?) or highway engineering problems, *let your mind go!* Get a limelight job that will get more and more attention as our population increases. The money will come automatically with the publicizing of the need for what you know how to do.

Supply a growing market

Any business that is supplying any part of the mass market now is going to grow because the market is going to grow. All you have to do if you have a good business now is to tune up for more of the same. People are going to eat more, have more babies, build more houses, send more children to college, buy more cars, tickets on planes, *everything*. The trick is to get a larger share of the market, to get more business to come to you than to your competitor. Best way: make your name stand for an entire business as "Frigidaire" once stood for *all* refrigerators!

The tale of "Pledge and your dustcloth" is a classic marketing story. One year Johnson Wax Company decided to ride the aerosol trend and put furniture wax in an aerosol container. In discussing strategy, marketing experts there made a brilliant marketing decision. Instead of telling women that here was a furniture wax (which women were using *at the most* two or three times a month) in a new spray form, they told them that here was an aerosol product to be used "every time you dust." With this simple approach, the company changed a national wax-using habit. Women who had used paste or liquid wax three times a month suddenly began using Pledge three times a week. Pledge, the baby in a company selling wax in 42 forms, raced around waxes by all other names. In its first year, Pledge earned $7 million. Soon, other aerosol "dusting helps" jumped into the field, but today Pledge is still the household word for "waxed beauty instantly" and as meaningful to women as Chanel is in the perfume market.

Suggestion: To give consumers a reason to buy your product in greater quantity, tie usage to a second product used with frequency.

Stake out new claims as your market shifts

A good businessman stays as aware of shifts in his market as an elected official remains aware of the changing wants of his constituency. A business in our town illustrates how this pays off.

Back in 1912, when he was 10 years old, George Wells, with a business near where we live today, began hatching chicks and selling eggs in New Milford. By the time he entered the University of Connecticut's College of Agriculture (then Storr's Agricultural College) at the end of World War I, he had a flourishing little business. After college, while teaching Vocational Agriculture in the high school, he expanded the poultry business. Unable to get quality chicks, he began to hatch his own and then sold the surplus.

This was so successful that the business grew to the point where it produced over 3 million chicks in 1958, selling most of them in eastern Connecticut. A depression in poultry prices in 1959 resulted in a severe drop in chicks sold—and the hatchery business has never been quite the same since. (The George Wells Company reports today that far less than 50 percent of their '59 customers are still in business and most of the remaining are nearing retirement.) Because few new people have gone into the business, the company has shifted its emphasis to eggs.

While the firm still hatches 1,250,000 chicks a year, it produces 10 times as many eggs. The firm's new president, Stuart Wells, son of the founder and also a graduate of UConn's College of Agriculture, says the firm now produces more than 13 million eggs a year.

Like our town, the Wells Company has changed with the times. Until a few years ago, New Milford had 350 farms within its city limits; today it has 57. It is no longer a self-contained town; today its residents work in Danbury, Waterbury and other towns. So fewer residents raise their own chickens. And fewer families want baby chicks. At the same time, the population is going up, so more consumers are buying eggs. This points up another reason that there is less demand for chicks; more for eggs.

Even as it concentrates on producing eggs, Wells & Son is concentrating, too, on more productive use of its physical plant. Right now, it is in the process of switching to the raising of replacement pullets.

Whatever your business, make good use of your existing equipment and knowledge. But watch the market, too. And within this framework, shift your product emphasis as your market demands.

From flour to cake mixes

Pillsbury and General Mills supplied flour for home bakers of cakes and pies for a couple of generations, until cake and pie-baking from scratch became too time-consuming for busy young mothers and they reached for cake mixes, instead. So the two Minneapolis companies merchandised mixes of all sizes and descriptions which utilized the flour they used to sell "as is" in the processing plants.

From real potatoes to instant

For years, America's giant potato companies contracted for potatoes from growers in Idaho for resale to food chains. They still do, but now an ever-growing percentage of the annual crop goes to makers of instant mashed potatoes with processing plants in Idaho. Demands of time-conscious consumers made for the change.

From toilet paper to disposable diapers

A few years ago, a giant company bought a small midwest paper napkin company. With the help of its advertising agencies, it soon was merchandising facial tissues and paper towels along with its toilet paper. Then it brought out a disposable diaper—and that product took off until it now brings into the company and its agency, which collects 15 percent of its advertising expenditure, millions of dollars a year.

Like the hatchery that now makes as big a profit from eggs as it does from chicks, look for ways to merchandise related products. Such products can double your income—and maybe right before your eyes in your everyday operation.

Personal experience

During the past few years, since our children have flown from the nest, we have worked out a way of life outside of New York. In building this new life in Connecticut, we came upon truths of interest to others in our age bracket, eventually put our story in book form and sold it under the title, "Start with an Empty Nest." As the title became noticed and known, we sensed that we "had something" in this "Empty Nest" business; we copyrighted the title for sales promotion purposes.

See how one step leads to another: One of the first to take advantage of our promotion suggestion was a Minneapolis department store which co-sponsored with the Women's Advisory Council, Department of Human Rights, State of Minnesota, an "Empty Nest" symposium in the store's auditorium. As a result, *Parade* magazine asked us to write a story on the "Empty Nest" phenomenon for that magazine to be inserted in more than 13 million Sunday newspapers. This supplement piece led to our being asked to appear on "Girl Talk," the Mike Douglas show, the "Today" show, with Mike Wallace and on other network shows. About this time a part-time employment company asked us about the possibility of our helping management there to attract "Empty Nesters" into its labor force in various cities. Then *Better Homes and Gardens* asked for a story. Each step we took underscored our reputation as authorities on the "Empty Nest." As we wrote and made appearances, we studied our subject and collected more facts. Now, we have a franchise. When editors think about the "Empty Nest" they think of us *first.* By doing something every day to become better acquainted with this market, we have become the acknowledged experts. *Lesson to be learned: As you put one foot down for one step the back foot is already coming up for the next step. Be sure that front foot always goes down in the direction you want to go.*

Sense a trend—and go!

Rudi Gernreich, male headline-getting designer in today's women's fashion world, was first to see back in the 50s that fashion was growing freer and ever less inhibited in every way. His liberating design for swimsuits (a simple knit tank suit with no inner construction when women were used to stays and gussets) made sense. Ten years later, in talking liberation during an interview, he prophesied that women would soon remove their bras to sunbathe as French women on the Riviera have done for years. Deluged by calls asking if he meant it, he insisted that he did, and designed a topless suit on request for *Look.* To his surprise, he sold 3,000 topless suits which, some fashion writers insist, expressed the freedom wanted subconsciously by every woman. Today, no fashion forecast is complete without a reference to Gernreich who continues to insist that "Clothes are for fun" and creates them that way.

Result: Publicity and a reputation for the "free" feeling in clothes.

Down to his last city

On a recent television show, Bob Hope quipped about his pal, Del Webb, of Phoenix: "Poor fellow, he's down to his last city." Not Del Webb! This is the man of vision who has developed three complete cities, his most famous one being a resort-retirement community called Sun City, 12 miles from the capital of Arizona, in the Valley of the Sun.

We spent February, 1969, as his guests there right at the end of his biggest month of home sales in this or any community! *In one month, there were 282 sales of home units totaling $6.5 million.*

As founder and chief executive officer of the Del E. Webb Corporation, this still young man is successful because he saw along about 1960 the coming need for resort-type communities for energetic people past the child-rearing stage. *Result in Arizona:* a complete city with three shopping centers, more than 100 businesses, four golf courses, four heated swimming pools, bridge rooms, an outdoor sun bowl for Sunday afternoon concerts for such entertainers as Harry James and Guy Lombardo, studios, libraries, *everything!*

Because homes can be built in quantity from similar yet different master plans, prices are reasonable! And because of the few schools in the area, property taxes are 50 percent lower in Sun City than in other valley communities. The climate is ideal for outdoor living in the winter; homes are air-conditioned in the summer—and fast-growing Phoenix is nearby for excitement should the cruiseship atmosphere of Sun City become almost too idyllic. The whole mixture is a success recipe, as is now testified by close to 1,500 sales a year!

Bouncing boys

Thirty or more years ago in Cedar Rapids, Iowa, rclatives of ours went to Franklin High School with the Nissen boys, who won all ribbons for expertise in tumbling. As they performed, they sensed an oncoming trend. All boys might not want to be football or baseball players, they decided, but every one would like to be a part time tumbler, and would be especially attracted to the bouncing part which precedes the springboard take-off.

Result: They began manufacturing trampolines. They have made money and a reputation, making bouncing platforms which are accepted today with as much enthusiasm by girls as by boys.

Exercise: Stop reading. If you are at home, take ten minutes out and for relaxation lie on your back with your head down in a slant position (on a slant board, if you have one, otherwise on the floor with your feet up on a chair). If you are in a plane or on a train, put your head back against the seat and close your eyes. Think of your job or skill in relationship to the future. What do you do that can be applied to a long-term trend? Stay perfectly *still.* What big trend can you tie in with?

Billion dollar business

Twenty years ago, John Bardeen, Walter Brattain and William Shockley came up with an electronic brainchild which they called a transistor, saw it foster a multi-billion dollar industry, employing hundreds of thousands of workers, and found themselves recipients of the Nobel Prize. They had skills, an idea, and so not only sensed but also created a trend.

Don't wait for the giant thought

Your idea does not have to be a giant one, but it has to mesh with a demand trend. According to *The New York Times,* Mary Ann Strehlein, of Chicago, associated for most of her adult life with the women's clothing industry, saw the need for a garment fastener that avoids wear and tear of snap fasteners, and recently patented a fastener that closes with a click and stays fastened with no strain. To prove that it's never too late for a winning idea, consider Miss Strehlein's age. *She's over 80!*

What trends do you see ahead in the field where you do most of your work? What is the big need? Can you help to supply an answer to that need—even if it just means talking about it (as we do the Empty Nest) or analyzing it (as Helen Gurley Brown did when she took a long look at problems faced today by the single girl)? What do you have to say that's new on a timely subject? Find that, and you will be on your way to owning a franchise that nobody else is thinking about! Get hold of that franchise, and money will come. You will not only double your income in one year—but in the next year, too, and the next.

From This Chapter . . .

Seventeenth Financial Recipe for Doubling Your Income

1. List 20 trends you notice in your town. (Worry about air and water pollution; worry about riots; expanded population; interest in adult education; more horse shows, etc.)
2. Decide which of these trends you can tie in with. (Where are *your* interests?)
3. How can you capitalize on a new or coming trend with an idea no one is doing anything about?
4. Go to work to publicize your idea and/or product so the franchise becomes yours alone.

18

TAKE AN OVERRIDE ON THE WORK OF OTHERS

A carpenter in our town with a creative mind and the sure knowledge of how to put his ideas into a house for a price a particular home-owner can afford to pay was doing well 10 years ago, but he wasn't getting rich. Then he made a simple switch, and today his business account is sought by every bank for miles around. He thinks in the same old creative way and sells with the same old practical approach, but makes 20, 30, 40 times as much money as in the old days.

The switch: He stopped doing all the manual labor himself, began contracting work for workmen whom he pays to carry out his ideas.

We recently remodeled a schoolhouse and called on him to help. "All I want is 10 percent over what you would have to pay for labor and materials," he told us, "but I'll bring the job in twice as fast as you could bring it in and I'll have all the headaches."

In record time, the job was done, and we gladly paid our 10 percent over the bills our contractor let us see for hours spent by carpenters, plasterers, paperhangers. Fair enough!

A year later we had reason to have the paperhanger, charged out on our contractor's bill at $3.00 an hour, do a small job for us. Our bill from the paperhanger again was charged at the same rate, $3.00 an hour, but over coffee one morning he told us, "When I work for Bill (the contractor), I get paid only $2.75 an hour by him because he guarantees me a minimum of so many months a year." Rather than getting a 10 percent markup by charging us $3.30 over $3.00, our contractor had collected a 20 percent markup by charging $3.30 over the paperhanger's $2.75 base pay. Unethical? Perhaps, because the contractor was paying less for paperhanging than we thought he was paying; still, he was charging us only what we would have to pay on our own anyway, *plus 10 percent.* His native shrewdness in markups, his sales ability and creative eye, are the reasons behind his fatted income.

We are not advocating slippery business but we do suggest this basic principle: Get others to carry out your creative ideas—and take a markup. (A 10 percent override on the work of five men can make you far more than when you do all of the job yourself because you can do at least five [or anyway, four] times as much work in the same amount of time.)

Naturally, you can't just sit around as your men work. You have to work, too.

Success story in the life insurance business

George McNeal, Agency Manager for Equitable Life Assurance Society of America, in San Jose, California, is a living success story whose ever increasing prosperity we have been aware of for 20 years. The last time we saw him and his wife and four attractive children, the family was living in a handsome, sprawling stone house by the sea in Carmel—now the McNeals have an even more elegant place in San Jose, plus a boat, country club memberships and good schools and colleges for all the children.

We knew from first-hand accounts of good business men that George's success was built on two basic principles: (1) hard work; (2) the ability to attract hard-working salesmen for whose work he gets an override.

If you do not think a man can be successful today by starting from scratch, read this quote from a recent letter from George McNeal.

> After World War II where I was a B-29 pilot, I finished up at the University of Iowa. I met Colleen there and Dennis was born while we were still in school. Upon graduation in January, 1948, we loaded all of our belongings in a two wheel trailer and along with $200 headed for California.
>
> My brother was attending Occidental College in Los Angeles and living on the GI Bill. Colleen and I moved in with him and his wife for three weeks while I found a job. I went to Equitable there and was turned down because I did not know anyone in the Los Angeles area. I was hired by Texaco and was sent to San Jose, which I did not know even existed. After being in San Jose for a year, I again went to Equitable and was hired in June of 1949. I barely survived the first six months. It was the next year, my first full year in the life insurance business that I doubled my

income. It was merely a matter of working 14 hours a day, including Saturdays.

When I was made a District Manager in Monterey I again doubled my income. This was possible by hiring fellows like Grant Jennings, my first cousin, Jim, and my best friend in college, Don Thoms. In 1957 I came back to San Jose as a District Manager. In 1966 Grant Jennings and I were both made Agency Managers. In this job we have District Managers under us to train the men.

My brother, Don, moved out from Fargo where he was managing a Firestone store. This year he was promoted to District Manager and is hiring and training men. The manager receives a small basic salary and override on each of his salesmen's commissions.

The insurance business is crying for men who will accept responsibility and the desire for hard work. We find most men today are interested in an 8-hour job and time off, instead of the opportunity to work and make money.

There is a golden opportunity for a man who is not afraid of long hours and hard work in our business. Of the friends and relatives we have hired, James McNeal is a Million Dollar Producer in Phoenix, Arizona, Don Thoms is a manager in Santa Ana, California, Don McNeal is District Manager in San Jose and Grant Jennings is now Agency Manager in Portland, Oregon.[1]

Hard-working as ever, George began to make far more when he took on the responsibility of additional men than when he was doing everything all by himself.

Where to find workers

The best source for workers in the business you're in is to look for men (or women) who do what you do but who do not want the responsibility of contracting for themselves or others.

The carpenter referred to in this chapter became a contractor by putting other skilled carpenters to work and taking an override on their put-out. The good insurance salesman found other good salesmen, put them to work, took his override.

Suggestion: What business do you know? Can you find others to do what you are doing and take an override on *their* work in exchange for selling their wares? Good way to begin: Stick to your last! A shoemaker knows what to look for in other shoemakers; a farmer knows what to look for in farmhands; a baker knows what is needed in bakers.

---

[1] This promotion has recently given Grant Jennings a territory of over a million people.

Exceptions

There are two classes of people who can be put to work by businessmen who do not know at all how to do what these two groups of people know how to do: *First group,* creative people (artists, writers, television producers, etc.); *second group,* women who do part-time work.

Employment agencies and advertising agencies and other "talent pool" organizations have been formed by businessmen who are not at all creative themselves but who sense the need of businessmen looking for creative talent on one hand and the work and money needs of creative people on the other. The banker-type man who knows how to nurture talented men and women, what to pay for this creative help, and what to charge others for their work can make a fortune. Creative people usually would much rather do creative work than fool around with figures, social security, etc., so they appreciate being managed by such a person.

Usually, women looking for part-time help also dislike details that businessmen know how to handle. Such women make up a great portion of today's work force, and have made riches for many in the "temporary" employment field. Part-time work is great for women who do not want to commit themselves to full-time employment, and such help is a boon to employers with peak work loads a few times during the year and no need for a big group of workers at other times. A phenomenon of our time is the working grandmother.

Working grandmothers

Due to our increased population and longer life expectancy, there are more grandmothers living in the United States today than there are mothers who aren't grandmothers. And there are now (or will soon be) more working grandmothers than there are just plain working mothers!

According to the United States Department of Labor, 50 percent of all women aged 45 to 54 are now in the labor force, the highest percentage of any age group. This is a fact of life applauded by personnel directors. At a recent "Empty Nest" conference, in New Britain, Connecticut, Jolin Carpenter of Western Girl, Temporary Help Services, made the point that employers prefer the older woman to the "sweet young thing"—even in a receptionist's job.

"A woman's day-by-day experience in raising a family," he said, "leaves her with a built-in management viewpoint. Business men appreciate this."

John J. Husic, Jr., vice president of nationally known Employers Overload Co., and recent president of the Institute of Temporary Services, Inc., agrees. "Acceptance of the mature woman in offices is the main reason that the temporary help companies employ more than a million workers a year and gross over $500 million." He explained that part-time work is ideal for the mother who sees that her nest will soon be empty, begins to think about going back to work but doesn't want to commit herself to a full-time job.

Override of 35 percent

Every woman employed by a part-time employment company has all her bookwork done and social security details taken care of by the service sending her out on call. Thus, bookwork and appointment time is saved for her and also for the employer who needs her work. The temporary help service, serving as bookkeeper and as *broker* for her services, takes nothing from her fee but collects from her temporary employer 35 percent over and beyond what she is paid for her work.

Begin thinking now of how you can collect an override on what others do by working out an employment plan for them that they would find difficult, alone. The trick in being a good broker is to help everyone come out *better!*

From This Chapter . . .

Eighteenth Financial Recipe for Doubling Your Income

1. Change from doing everything yourself to hiring others to do what you do.
2. Take a mark-up on what those working for you take in.
3. Help those working for you to produce as much as you can produce.

19

SKIP A GRADE

A smart boy or girl in first grade whose teacher thinks he or she will waste time in second grade may be "skipped" to third. There are few places in later life (except for the Army, perhaps) where you can't follow this same principle as an adult and "skip" the business rung above you (or normal mark-up for an investment). This is, perhaps, the best way known today for doubling your income (or an investment) *instantly.*

For clarification, when we refer to "skipping" in this chapter, we mean passing over the accepted "next step" in the normal progression of things in business or investments to hit the Big Money rung faster.

Here are some recent examples.

In the cosmetics industry: Polly Bergen has joined the bigtime money-makers with a revival of a 1920 craze, turtle oil. In 1965, former model, TV spokeswoman and all-time stunner Polly invested $3,000 and a lot of enthusiasm in a new product, Oil of the Turtle Moisturizer Lotion, which in 36 months she built to a $2½ million business with seven products selling in a hundred leading stores. You know her ad campaign. Her face is next to a turtle along with the headline, "I have an ugly friend." Her only TV appearances today push "Oil of the Turtle" and by now she has a corps of assistants calling on stores.

Taking a page from Polly is real estate tycoon, Pat Palmer, who has cleared off a table in her New York real estate office at 22 East 67th Street, New York City, covered it with gold paper and placed on it little white jars of Sea Cream. The special formula, available only in her office, came to her six years ago when she found an apartment for an elderly European chemist, she says, who gave her a recipe for marine life a la cream in lieu of a commission. Already, her Sea Cream, which smells more like roses than shrimp, is a big seller.

In the art field: Anyone who owns a print of an engraving by an Old Master (whose original paintings and drawings are appearing less often today in the market place) can look forward to "skipping" a normal mark-up should he offer it for sale at an auction and rake in a really big profit. Analysts say there is a much greater rise in prices paid for prints in the last 15 years than in stock price levels. Since the middle 50s, Rembrandt prints have gone up in value 2,400 percent; Canaletto, 2,000 percent; Goya, 1,400 percent. The highest price recorded for a print ($89,700) was paid in 1965 for "The Women's Bath" by a 15th century German artist known as Master P.W., and in 1964, Goya's print, "Giant," brought $57,400 at auction. If you own a print of an engraving by a top artist, you can far more than double your investment. As these prints become more scarce, the value is bound to increase.

More money for what (and whom) you know

Salaries of $100,000 are fairly common in Wall Street investment banking houses, so at the end of the Johnson Administration when Manhattan's Lazard Freres & Co. announced the recruitment of three men, making $35,000, $29,500 and $28,750, you can bet that all three doubled their salaries. By understanding why a former Commerce Secretary, a former Under Secretary of the Treasury and a former Assistant Budget Bureau Director are important to an investment house, you can learn one of the easiest ways in the world to double your income. The first, D. R. Smith, who was once chairman of American Airlines, is familiar with the thinking and needs of airline management which will be needing capital to finance jumbo jets; the second, L. Deming, has international monetary experience that has made him familiar with the ins and outs of foreign loans; the third, Peter Lewis, was once a Housing Department aide, so understands urban real estate. With these men on its staff any international investment company stands to end the year with a better profit picture.

To push up your income, push up another's!

Man with a special quality: Few people outside of California knew Eric Hoffer until he was interviewed on network television by Eric Sevareid who says today that his Hoffer interview was his finest hour in 27 years of broadcasting. Writer, philosopher, lecturer at the University of California, Hoffer on TV experienced a turning point in his life. Speaking honestly of his admiration for Lyndon B. Johnson, he caught the President's attention, was invited to the White House, suddenly found himself on national commissions, saw sales of his books go up, became a celebrity, *could* become a big money-maker if money were important to him, which it is not. He loves to see his ideas in print, however, and now has a syndicated column.

Repair man with a better mousetrap: Back in the late 30s a high school boy named Bud McGlynn was earning 40 cents an hour working part-time for Burkhardt's Handbag Repair Service in Minneapolis. Shortly before he was drafted in World War II, Bud married the niece of his former boss, and when he came out, he and his wife bought the old business which they ran from home. *Big decision in 1966:* if he wanted more off-the-street business, Bud knew he'd have to move, so move he did to Nicollet Avenue where today he has close to 2,000 off-the-street bag repair jobs a year, plus all the big jobs he can handle for department store handbag departments. "I give the best service I know how," is his explanation of why his business grows and grows and grows, "and I took a plunge when I changed locations. Everything worked." *Including Bud!*

Handwriting column changed her life: At 16, Norma Buser, Brooklyn, was a bright sensitive kid who was writing articles on juvenile delinquency which were seen and commented on by J. Edgar Hoover. Believing even then that handwriting can be a psychological guide to personality, Miss Buser taught herself the science of graphology by studying handwriting analyses in newspapers and books, soon advertised her skills, began getting calls for her early $1.00 analyses. In the 50s, she became a consultant to the Dartmouth Tutoring Bureau, which used her analyses to help penetrate the reserve of introverted students. But she didn't begin making real money until late in the 1960s when *Harper's Bazaar* carried 13 lines of publicity about her ability to analyze handwriting, doubled her income in '66. (Note: We had *our* handwriting analyzed, found Miss Buser's analyses deeply penetrating and accurate. Cost for long helpful analysis, $5.00. Write 211 Park Street, Roselle, New Jersey, 07203.)

Toys for our times: Marvin Glass, America's top toy designer, got the idea for "Mr. Machine" in 1960 when talking by telephone to his former wife who told him, "You are nothing but a machine." This gave Mr. Glass, he says, his idea for a big, plastic, TV-promotable Mechanical Man which he believes is a psychological symbol for our times. In two years, sales of "Mr. Machine" amounted to $14 million, boosted Mr. Glass to the Big Time. He knows how to promote himself as well as his toys—sells no idea outright—instead leases his ideas to toy makers for a percentage of the gross. By now, 50 Marvin Glass creations chalk up annual sales of $100,000,000—representing more than $5 million in royalty to Glass' company. All this, and yet the designer *or his company* never manufacturers a single toy.

From 100 houses to 2,200 condominiums in the time it takes to dream

Three Connecticut brothers, Henry, Otto and Frank Paparazzo, enterprising offspring of an industrious German mother and an artistic, manually dexterous Italian father, went into the building business in the 1950s. From the first, their individual skills blended with their inherited sameness to make a perfect working team.[1] In their first 100-home projects at Essex[2] and Simsbury, Connecticut, they earned the reputation for putting together handsome as well as functional houses which fitted perfectly into the terrain wherever they were situated.

As a result of their first major successes which building experts call "stunning," the brothers were ready *to take a giant step.* Even though they may not have been quite aware of it, the knowledge of building and selling which they had been acquiring along the way had made them ready to "skip a grade." Their big chance came when Victor Borge of Southbury, Connecticut, offered for sale his 350-acre tree-studded country estate dotted with springs and laced with streams. Here along with 700 adjoining acres was the ideal place to build a creative condominium village unlike any cluster of homes America had ever seen. But there was a problem. The land was zoned for one-acre single family lots, and the town of Southbury had made no provision of any kind for multi-family housing.

As they were considering whether to purchase the land, the Paparazzos got a break. In that year, 1964, Connecticut passed a law permitting planned unit developments! Now Henry, Otto and Frank could move ahead with a plan for Heritage Village, which they envisioned as an adult community under condominium ownership. Still, they had another obstacle to overcome. *Local* zoning approval was needed! In order to secure Southbury's go-ahead, the builders knew that they must come up with an imaginative plan that would enhance, not detract from, the town's pastoral image. Immediately, they set out to find an architect who could appreciate and augment their desire to blend a cluster of more than 2,000 condominium units into their 1,100 acre natural New England paradise.

---

[1] Henry, who is president, is a graduate geologist from Indiana University and a born management man, a talent which has been honed to a fare-thee-well through 5 years of work with Howard Hughes. Otto, who is a graduate of the Rhode Island School of Design, is the principal design man. Frank, the grass expert, also has a solid background in construction.

[2] Essex has a few less than 100 homes; Simsbury has 121 homes.

Their selection: Charles Warren Callister of Callister and Payne, San Francisco, to whom they paid a $200,000 fee for his overall plan.

The choice of this West Coast architect proved to be a great one. Local approval for his sensitive plan soon came through from Southbury, but then *bang!* along came another problem. *Tight money!* Local banks couldn't come up with the large amounts needed to finance the project's first 119 units. But the brothers, *this* far along, weren't deterred. They went with their plan to Fidelity Mutual Life Insurance Company of Philadelphia and were offered, instead of the money they were asking for, a counter-proposal which was even better: 50/50 partnership between lender and builder to develop Heritage Village. The Paparazzos accepted—and now they were really on their way, as this record proves.

> *End of 1966:* $1 million sewer and water plant was in, the on-premises meeting house (once the home of artist Wallace Nutting) was ready for gatherings, an 18-hole golf course had been laid out, 25 model homes had been built—and 64 families[3] had signed up for occupancy.
>
> *End of 1967:* 225 condominiums ranging in price from $20,000 to $36,000 constructed and sold.
>
> *End of 1968:* 501 condominiums constructed and sold.
>
> *End of 1969:* 612 condominiums constructed and sold.
>
> *Projection:* 2,200 condominiums by 1971—and already more multiple dwelling projects for the Paparazzos are in the offing. (In 1969, the brothers constructed and sold 200 family homes in their new Avon-Farmington project near Hartford; and their eyes were turned to Maryland for another Heritage type village coming up. This one on the Chesapeake will have eight marinas.)

Recently listed in *Professional Builder* as one of the 50 "giants" in the construction business, the Paparazzo Construction Company now is visited daily by architects, builders, publicity people and investors. All are interested in Heritage Village *where the houses fit the land, and elegance blends with ease.*

Certainly, as building costs continue to go up and as Heritage Village reaches its 2,200 unit quota, the demand for homes in this unique setting will become greater and prices on individual units are bound to go up.[4] Therefore, the condominiums are attractive to buyers not only for everyday living but also for their long-term real estate value. Some investors are buying two or three condominiums at one time to rent to others in the over-50 bracket who prefer to try this kind of living on for size before doing any permanent investing on their own. And Empty Nesters who

---

[3] One partner of a married couple at Heritage Village must be over 50; no child can be under 18.

[4] Average cost per home in 1967, $26,000; in 1969, $32,000.

have invested in a home in Heritage Village (with its eventual quota set before building ever began) have come out very well. A condominium (with living room, bedroom, dining foyer, kitchen, master bedroom, den and two baths) which sold for $20,700 in 1967 was selling (as a new unit or as a resale) for $26,500 two years later.

There's an obvious lesson to be learned from the experience of the Paparazzo brothers who say they really don't think much about money, believing that *if the product is right, buyers will respond, and the money will come.* The lesson: *If a dream makes sense, even the most serious-seeming obstacles can be overcome.* And as one tough problem after another is solved, the person who is doing the solving rises to the top. Then, like the bright boy or girl who does the same in grade school, he is ready to *skip a grade.* He takes a giant step, and his income just naturally reflects this move. Without even realizing where he is headed, he upgrades himself when ready.

Versatility plus talent is bell-ringer for Sloane: Eric Sloane, our artist friend in Warren, Connecticut, is a writer, painter, historian, weatherman and expert on various pieces of Americana including the Liberty Bell. And he's an *all-round bell-ringer when it comes to making money,* which is something he isn't especially interested in, by the way.

To recap his story: Sloane left Yale Art School after a year and a half, became famous early for cloud paintings, worked in an early job as one of the nation's first TV weathermen. In his capacity as a cloud expert, he supplied information to the Army, Navy and Air Force and created the Hall of Atmosphere at the American Museum of Natural History. Later, he became as interested in barns and ancient American tools as he was in clouds, because, he says, "the story needed telling." His barn paintings now bring $6,000 a painting and his books (*How You Can Forecast the Weather, A Reverence for Wood, Diary of an Early American Boy*) are best-sellers, and his research done for his book *Sound of Bells* has led to a revival of bell-ringing instead of fireworks for home celebrations on the Fourth of July.

Mr. Sloane's belief is that if you concentrate on money "you can get it, but you work very hard! Better to do what needs to be done and let the money come." We agree, but it is our observation that men and women who say this usually acquire this philosophy after the money has started to come, not before. Or subconsciously see the potential income in an idea as they begin its execution. At any rate, Mr. Sloane became a top money-maker as he saw things along the way that needed to be done, and did them.

Heloise hunts for household hints: Best known newspaper writer to housewives is a San Antonio columnist who makes upwards of $100,000 a year. Heloise is her name, and she wafted to the big money bracket, her devotees would have you believe, in a cloud of nylon net, which she writes about often in her syndicated column. Actually, she writes about all kinds of little economies which she first began thinking about and collecting in China as wife of an Army man in World War II. Transferred with her husband to Hawaii, she began writing her "household hints" down for the Honolulu paper, and shot to the big time when she was syndicated.

Sub-sea fortune hunter: One of the most enterprising men in Bermuda climbed to riches by going down, not up. Encouraged by the Bermuda government, which has first option on his findings, he is paid handsomely for investigating shipwrecks on the reefs around Bermuda. As a kid, according to those who know him, he loved the waterfront and used to borrow diving equipment near Bermuda and make deep sea dives just for fun. During World War II, on a merchant ship, he dove in Far Eastern waters, repaired ships and cleared out wreckage. Back in Bermuda afterward, he and his brother began salvaging scrap metal in the harbors —eventually ran across the wreckage of an old ship, found after numerous explorations that it had been sunk in 1584 on its way home from the Caribbean to Spain. *That was the turning point*—the big break that boosted him from waterfront adventurer to the big time. Licensed by the government, this legendary gent has by now explored more than 150 wrecked ships. He uses balloons, airplanes, boats and magnetometers to locate wrecks, loves his life, which he admits is far from workaday and, almost in spite of himself, is a very rich man.

Things to be learned from skippers

1. They are good at what they are doing because they like what they are doing.
2. They see a need and fill it.
3. They get one big break which they in some way help to bring about.
4. They take an advantage of this break to hit the big time.

How to apply the skipping principle if you work in an organization, not for yourself, alone

1. At the turning point, let your boss know that *you* know you have scored and should be rewarded.
2. Jump to a rival organization for twice what you're getting; or
3. Take the offer you have received from the rival organization to your management, ask for an equal break at the home company; or
4. Make this the break-off point and go into business for yourself.

Is there such a thing as luck?

What about that turning point in a life that we talk about?

We asked this of America's top photographers a few years ago when we were doing some work for the Famous Photographers School in Westport, Conn. Here is what each said:

Irving Penn: "The skilled photographer knows how to pull the line when there's a nibble of luck."

Harry Garfield: "There must be more than luck. I think good pictures come out of a tremendous amount of experience."

Joe Costa: "The man who knows his business can anticipate what's going to happen and he is ready for it. So he looks lucky."

Philippe Halsman: "Napoleon said, 'Don't give me smart generals, give me lucky ones.' I think luck is in the character of the person. Something puts photographers in position so that they can foresee what will happen. Then they are ready with the camera. On the other hand, when the chronically unlucky photographers are changing the camera the bull is being killed."

Richard Avedon: "You have to make luck. You have to create an atmosphere that allows for a lucky accident."

Richard Beattie: "You call the weather man to see if it's going to rain. You have cameras that work. You cover yourself so you look lucky."

Bert Stern: "You create luck!"

Luck is inside *you.*

Get ready, get set, let luck come out!

From This Chapter . . .

Nineteenth Financial Recipe for Doubling Your Income

1. What skill do you possess that can be a real money-maker? Write this down.
2. The way things are going, what is your normal "next step" using this skill?
3. If you skip this step, can you collect a doubled income? If so, make the 2nd step up your goal.
4. Reach now for where you eventually want to be.

20

USE THE "DOUBLE A" METHOD TO GET ANYTHING YOU WANT

Apply the method described in this chapter to whatever you want to do next, and you cannot fail. The method is foolproof. Its name is "Double A," and it has been put to use by every businessman who has ever succeeded in anything, no matter what he tells you today. Follow the two simple "A" rules below, and it follows as the night the day that you will be successful. Here are the two "A" rules:

1. *Absorb*
2. *Apply*

There is one hitch. *You must be dedicated to what you want to do next.* In your case, otherwise you would not have picked up this book, what you want to do next is to *double your income from one year to the next.* Keep this purpose at the forefront of your mind.

With that aim in front of you, how will you put "A" #1 to work for you? Look at the word, *absorb.* Defined in the dictionary *absorb* means *to drink in,* as a sponge absorbs water. Dedicated as you now are to doubling your income, what you are going to absorb is *everything* that applies to what you want to do.

1st By-product: You will never be bored again. Like Will Rogers, *you will never again meet an uninteresting person.* Furthermore, you will never see an uninteresting movie, read an uninteresting book, go on an uninteresting trip. Every little thing that you see and do will have a special meaning for you. In some way from this life experience you will be *learning.*

2nd By-product: You will never bore anyone again, because you will be a rare person in a world of Big Mouths. You will truly listen to what anyone around you is saying; you will pay deep attention to *everything.*

3rd By-product: The world will become a great university to you. Day after day, you will learn, learn, learn. Teachers will present themselves to you at every turn—for you will have become aware of a great truth. People all around you are waiting to *give,* but usually no one wants what they have to offer. You do want, you are waiting, you will listen. Never fear, your teachers will speak.

Simple Test

Tomorrow, on a bus or a train or at a gathering where there is someone new—a child, an old man, a foreign-born person who knows little English, a passerby, the mailman, anyone you haven't talked to before—engage that person in conversation. Find out how this person has accomplished something he has wanted to accomplish. The child may have got an A this semester in a subject in which he got C last semester; the old man may have figured out a way to move from a crowded city to live full time at the vacation place where you are visiting; the foreign-born person may be here on an exchange program (what is it, where did he find out about it?); the passerby may have licked a dread disease (how?); the mailman may have plans for a new business once his retirement is set (what?) Talk 10 minutes and you will know what is on the other person's mind, for this, too, is a truth: *A man's accomplishment is something he doesn't forget.* Jog his mind and he will talk of what is of interest to him—the change he has brought about (or is bringing about) in his own life.

At the end of tomorrow, before you go to sleep, write down what you learned from the new person you talked to. Not a paragraph; the *gist.* Maybe the child will tell you that he got an A in American History, rather than a C, after he visited Williamsburg, Virginia, with his parents and came back and did some extracurricular reading on early America. Lesson to be learned: *Outside reading pays off!*

Never mind who gets the credit

As you become a listener in life, you will find your share of braggarts. Do not mind, because you are *learning!* Cull through the braggadocio for the meat of the speaker's accomplishment.

What has this man done in his life that you can learn from?

You may be associated in business right now with an obnoxious credit-taker. So—take a lesson from W. K. Kellogg, a self-effacing introvert, who for more than a generation was nothing more than the faint shadow of his dynamic extrovert brother, Dr. John Harvey Kellogg, founder of the Battle Creek, Michigan, Sanitarium, author, surgeon and entrepreneur. For years, W. K. played second fiddle, but today his is the name on the No. 1 ready-to-eat cereal in the world which he was first to package and sell *by the train load.*

W. K. Kellogg started to work in the early 1900s, running a health food business for his brother, Dr. Kellogg, which they advertised with "Live the Battle Creek Life for 30 days" with a five-dollar mail order package of "prescription" health foods. The mail order business was great, but W. K. saw possibilities bigger than his brother's five-dollar packages. He believed early in the game that corn flakes could be sold by the carload. In two years after suggesting this, he was selling them by the *train load.*

Here's what we can learn from W. K. Kellogg: (1) It doesn't matter who gets the credit as we are learning. (Kellogg learned that health foods have appeal, that a health "program" has appeal, found that corn in "toasted flake" form has appeal.) (2) The trick is to absorb what the credit-taker is saying and move on to the "A" #2 step. The trick after learning a principle is to *apply* that principle.

Apply what you have learned

Suppose you learn from the child you speak to tomorrow that he credits outside reading for boosting his grade in American History. Apply what *he* did to *your* life! Go to the library this week and get a book about a man in your particular business who doubled his income in a year! Just reading his life story will encourage you to read more. See his principles in use for him, and then each night write down how you can use in your business one of the principles which proved to be success-making for another. You will be on your way!

W. K. Kellogg's application

W. K. Kellogg played shadow to his brother for more than 30 years, but he was learning all the time. As his brother went on being the "big wheel" in Battle Creek, W. K. was applying what he was learning locally in the packaged cereal business to what he wanted to do *nationally*. He got what he wanted by proceeding along three avenues: (1) He publicized his own name on packaged corn flakes with this legend, "This package of the genuine bears the signature *W. K. Kellogg*." (2) He inaugurated a nation-wide sampling of the Battle Creek product. (3) He advertised the wholesomeness of his product with a "Sweetheart of the Corn" campaign. His name today is far better known than Dr. John's. And, introvert though he always remained, he, of course, made *millions*.

Don't be afraid to learn from your mate

Some men are too insecure in their maleness to learn from a woman. Too bad! Because a boy's mother—and later, his wife—can be a source of information that is ever-present and available. "Pillow talk," Mrs. Hubert Humphrey says, "can be of as much help to a husband as it is to a wife."

Take a look at any history book and you will see on every page that much can be learned by men from women.

You are familiar, of course, with the way in which Sarah Bush Johnston, stepmother of Abe Lincoln, encouraged her husband's boy to read and persuaded his father through the years to "let Abe be." Thus she helped to start the "learning through listening" process in the future president. Listening and learning became Abe's twin habits. According to poet historian Carl Sandburg, "Silence found Lincoln for her own. In the making of him, the element of silence was immense."

Several other poor boys made it to the presidency, and all were helped by women close to them. Millard Fillmore, born in a log cabin, had little formal education and didn't see a dictionary until he was 17. He was encouraged as a young lawyer by the daughter of a minister to "keep on learning." Seven years later, she became his wife.

The mother of our 20th president, James Garfield, stalwart widow who brought her children up alone on a poor Ohio farm, exerted an extraordinary influence on her son. "At almost every turning point in my life," President Garfield wrote later in life, "she was the molding agent."

Andrew Johnson, born in a North Carolina shack, fatherless from the age of three, had almost no schooling. He was fortunate to find books at 14 when he was apprenticed to a book-loving tailor. At 18, he moved to Greenville where a year later he married Eliza McCardle who encouraged her husband to continue educating himself and actually hired a man to read to her husband and teach him to write. Soon young Johnson joined a debating society and began getting public speaking engagements. His tailor's shop became a gathering place for townspeople, and Andrew was on his way.

Lesson to be learned from poor men who ended up in the White House: *Learn from your mother or wife, if she is willing to teach.*

Women have it lucky!

Women are lucky in an old affectionate daughter-father relationship which seems to make them have less resistance to taking help from men than men have in accepting help from women. Mia Farrow is first to admit today that she learned much from Frank Sinatra. Zsa Zsa Gabor learned from Conrad Hilton; Joan Crawford says she learned from all of her husbands.

Bonne Bell, executive vice president of Cleveland, Ohio's Bonne Bell, Inc., which specializes in therapeutic cosmetics for the youth market, couldn't even be in business if it weren't for men, she says. Her father started the business 38 years ago, and another male, her brother Jess Bell, is today's president of the company that bears her name and that makes lipsticks, creams and lotions to guard against the elements young women are exposed to when they sail, ski and golf.

The point is to *learn, learn, learn* no matter whether your teacher is male or female.

Franchiellie Cadwell of the Cadwell Davis Company, New York advertising agency, has always been a learner. Born in Bermuda in 1934, she graduated from Cornell College in 1955 and arrived in New York soon afterward to seek her fortune and more education. First step: a master's from N. Y. U. Then enrollment in the annual Career Course, conducted by experts in the fashion field, sponsored by The Fashion Group, Inc., 9 Rockefeller Plaza, New York City. Armed with knowledge absorbed from experts, she got a job with a furniture company in the ad department, moved upward quickly until the company merged one day and her whole department was discontinued. Undaunted, she opened her own agency which didn't take off. Undaunted, again, she opened another with present partner, Hal Davis, which did take off. Her present agency, of which she's president, bills $6 million and is doubling every year.

Her rule: *"Don't be afraid to give up a 'comfortable' situation or to refuse an account that isn't right for your business."* The Cadwell-Davis Agency turned away its first *six* potential clients (while hovering on the brink of financial ruin); finally, took an account they knew they could do well with. They did, and Frankie Cadwell's income not only doubled but came close to tripling between June 1965 and June 1966.

Use the "Double A" principle to lead you where you want to go!

Said in a single sentence: *Apply what you learn every day to your plan for getting ahead!*

From This Chapter . . .

Twentieth Financial Recipe for Doubling Your Income

1. Look for information that will help you in your climb every day, everywhere. Absorb this information until it becomes part of you.
2. Apply what you learn from reading about and contact with people who are getting ahead.
3. Refuse to give up if your first trial is a dud. Try again.

21

THINK OF MONEY-MAKING AS A GAME

If you enjoy playing draw poker, you will get special enjoyment out of this chapter. You will also begin to look at money-making in an entirely new way.

If you do not know anything about draw poker, here are a few card-playing rules you will have to know before you can translate the game of poker into everyday business.

In the usual game of draw poker, there are six, seven or eight players. A standard pack of fifty-two cards is used.

There are four suits in the deck and spades, hearts, diamonds, clubs, which are the suits in this game, have no relative rank.

The rank of cards is like this: A (high), K, Q, J, 10, 9, 8, 7, 6, 5, 4, 3, 2.

For draw poker, each player makes a bet before the deal. This is called an ante and it is simply a cash contribution to the pot which belongs to all the players before the betting begins. Then each player is dealt five cards, face down. There is then a betting period when each player who bets is asserting the fact that he has the winning hand. Afterward, each player can discard cards (one or more) that do not fit in his hand. He can then draw the same number of cards from the top of the pack, to restore his hand to five cards. After the draw, there is another betting interval (with new assertions) and, at last, the *showdown*. The person with the highest ranking hand wins the money in the pot.

The dealer can name the wild card or cards in a particular hand. For our purposes here, we are proclaiming all four deuces wild. In that case the rank of hands, from highest to lowest, is as follows:

1. Five of a kind. (*Examples:* four sixes and one deuce; three sevens and two deuces, etc. The highest ranking cards win—in this case, the sevens.)
2. Straight flush. Five cards in the same suit in sequence, 10-9-8-7-6 (with a deuce wild card, in this case, as a substitute for any card named). In a contest between two straight flushes, the one with the highest card wins. (When two players have high hands which are the same except for suits, they divide the pot.)
3. Four of a kind. (Between two hands containing four of a kind, the one with higher-ranking cards wins. With wild cards, there may be two hands with four cards of the same rank. Then the one with the highest *fifth* card takes the pot.)
4. Full house. Three cards of one rank and two of another. (The highest-ranking three-of-a-kind holding is the winner.)
5. Flush. Five cards of the same suit, not in sequence.
6. Straight. Five cards in two or more suits, ranking consecutively, as 10, 9, 8, of spades and 7 and 6 of hearts. Deuces can be substituted for any cards here. Player with highest top card wins.
7. Three of a kind.
8. Two pairs.
9. One pair.

During the second betting period (after the draw), each player can either check until another player makes a bet or make a bet which again asserts that his hand is best at the table. Or he can drop out of the game when it is his turn to bet and let a high hand of a remaining player take the pot.

A simple enough set of rules, but playing the game takes a many-sided skill. The consistent winner has to have a knowledge of cards, odds and people, *plus the courage to take a risk* when a risk is called for.

Translating rules for poker into rules for making money

For your real-life game which you are going to be playing with dollars, think of yourself as playing with a deck of 52 cards containing four suits. But instead of four suits in a card deck, your real-life suits will be as follows:

SPADES will stand for BUSINESS SENSE.
HEARTS will stand for KNOWLEDGE OF PEOPLE.
DIAMONDS will stand for CAPITAL.
CLUBS will stand for COURAGE.

It will be up to you to assess what you possess in each case.

To judge your Business Sense, take the following test:

Your Business Sense

I have better business sense than any banker I have ever dealt with.	If yes, give yourself the ACE OF SPADES.
I have more real business sense than any accountant.	If yes, give yourself the KING OF SPADES.
I have never lost money on any major investment I have ever made.	If yes, give yourself the QUEEN OF SPADES.
I usually make at least 20% profit on any major investment I make in real estate, a new business, stock or anything else.	If yes, give yourself the JACK OF SPADES.
I do pretty well at remaining solvent, keeping my checkbook balanced, earning enough to pay my current bills, etc.	If yes, give yourself a spade card ranking from 10 down to three, depending on how you see yourself.

Knowledge of people

A poker player has to be a good psychologist; so does the man who comes out ahead in the business world. (*Example:* When you are buying property, you have to sense through the real estate agent why the seller is selling and what is the lowest price he will take. At the same time, you have to be aware of what other buyers will pay for this property if you decide to "check" for the time being.)

Can you read why people act as they do and anticipate their future actions? Rate yourself with a heart card as follows:

Knowledge of People

I seldom start out to sell anything without accomplishing my purpose, whether I know the buyer ahead of time or not.	If yes, give yourself the ACE OF HEARTS.
I am never really surprised at what people do or say after a first meeting, so I am rarely if ever disappointed.	If yes, give yourself the KING OF HEARTS.
I have a "sixth sense" intuitive flash about people when I first meet them, but I usually go along expecting them to live up to the code I follow.	If yes, give yourself the QUEEN OF HEARTS.
I can spot a four-flusher a mile away and I am never taken in.	If yes, give yourself the JACK OF HEARTS.
I like games and I win my share or more.	If yes, give yourself any heart from 10 down to three depending on how you judge your gamesmanship.

How much capital can you raise?

The more money you have, the easier, as a general rule, it is for you to make money. Certainly, it is more convenient to have money than not to have it. Therefore, for the purpose of this book, now is the time to assess your worth in dollars.

Capital

I can raise $500,000 for a sure-fire investment in any given month.	If yes, give yourself the ACE OF DIAMONDS.

I can devote a year to a project without collecting a cent and without causing hardship to myself or my family.	If yes, give yourself the KING OF DIAMONDS.
Today, I am worth all told more than $100,000.	If yes, give yourself the QUEEN OF DIAMONDS.
I have enough surplus over and above what it takes to live to commit myself up to a $50,000 investment with no sweat.	If yes, give yourself the JACK OF DIAMONDS.
I can borrow up to $10,000 from my local bank with no problem . . .	If yes, give yourself the 10 OF DIAMONDS.
For $9,000 . . .	give yourself the NINE OF DIAMONDS.
For $8,000 . . . etc.—down the line to $3,000 and the	give yourself the EIGHT OF DIAMONDS. THREE OF DIAMONDS.

Do you have courage?

In a poker game, men sometimes lose their courage when they get into a game that has stakes too high for their bankbook, or when they are playing and they know their wives would disapprove, or when they are in the middle of a long losing streak. With courage gone, many good players lose all sense of values, forget how to figure odds, change from skillful players to poor ones.

Courage in the business world is every bit as important as it is in poker. The man who has a good hand and lets someone take it away from him is just as much a loser in life as is the man with no hand at all.

In a squeeze, can you out-gut the other guy? Here's your way to find out . . .

Courage

If I knew that my present source of income was to end six months from today and I was offered a chance to invest ¾ of my present capital in a real estate venture pretty sure to pay off *big* in three years, I would be able to assess the real estate venture for itself, alone, with no mixing in of thoughts about the chopped-off income.

If yes, give yourself the ACE OF CLUBS.

If I should suddenly be transported to a non-English speaking country, I have no fear that I could not make my work "speak for itself" alone—and I believe I would get along fine.

If yes, give yourself the KING OF CLUBS.

I cannot imagine any circumstances that could keep me in any job or business arrangement for more than six months after I once saw that I was being taken advantage of and not getting my just due.

If yes, give yourself the QUEEN OF CLUBS.

I would certainly discuss cheating done by a business manager, boss or banker who might be involved in my affairs with this person even if I were dependent on his good will.

If yes, give yourself the JACK OF CLUBS.

Given six months to live, I would get my affairs in shape for others to carry on without me before getting everyone emotionally involved with my goodbye . . .

Rate yourself 10, 9, 8, 7 or lower in clubs, depending on your anticipated emotionality in such a case.

How to assess your money-making ability so far

Decide which card in each suit *best* describes your ability there. Then, from a regular deck of cards, take out the spade that describes your Business Sense, the heart that describes your Knowledge of People, the diamond that tells about your Capital, the club that tells most about your Courage.

You now have four cards in your hand. You need one more before you can bet.

To complete the playing card description of your business hand, select the one of four deuces which stands for a particular trait you possess in a big way.

> Deuce of spades stands for *Resourcefulness.*
> Deuce of hearts stands for *Ability to Attract People.*
> Deuce of diamonds stands for *Excellence of Taste.*
> Deuce of clubs stands for *Dedication to the Job at Hand.*

In any situation, these cards will come in handy.

Now put the deuce of spades, hearts, diamonds or clubs, whichever describes best an ability *of yours,* in your hand with the four other cards you have picked out.

This is your five-card hand dealt to you by life that you can work with in business.

How much would you bet on what you have? How can you make this hand pay off? How can you strengthen it? These are questions that you must ask yourself.

How to strengthen your hand

Suppose in your hand you now have a king of spades, a king of diamonds, a deuce of clubs, an ace of clubs and the 10 spot of hearts. Obviously, you have a vigorous money instinct, but you are not so good with people. For the time being, forget *that!* Given a draw in poker you will probably discard the 10 of hearts and draw a new card. Do that then. What is the next best trait in your three remaining deuces? Resourcefulness, the man with 3 kings says. So instead of the 10 of hearts, he takes the deuce of spades, and suddenly he has four kings—with a back-up ace. A sure-fire money-making hand—made up of Resourcefulness, Dedication, Capital, Courage and Business Sense. His weakness is that he has no knowledge of people, which is something he can recognize and compensate for. Hopefully, his wife is good with people, his secretary is tactful, he has a good sales manager and a smart personnel director, agent or public relations person.

How to play the game

Now to play the game.

Keep your five cards that express your particular personality with you in your wallet or in the drawer of the night table beside your bed. Ponder your hand at the end of the day or when a new problem comes. Try to figure how you can put your known strengths to work for you more effectively. Also, learn how to determine what is in the hand of your competitor. (If he has A, K, Q, J, 10 of diamonds, his *Capital* is going to outclass your good Business Sense—so don't be too reckless in your betting. If any mistakes are made, let him make them.)

Every two months for the next year, come back to this chapter and reassess your hand. You may have a dealing with the top banker in your town and decide that your Business Sense tops his after all. Suddenly, then, your king of spades will become an ace. Now you will have four aces in your hand . . . with a back-up king of diamonds. Your aim now will be to change *that* king to an ace. With your Business Sense, you can do it. With five aces a few years from now, you will be winning all the rest of the way.

12 Rules to remember in poker or business

1. Don't try to beat the other fellow; work to strengthen your own hand and let him try to beat *you.*

2. Play as others play in the game you are in. (With conservative players, be conservative. They won't play without strong hands; neither must you. On the other side, with liberal players, play a liberal game. Others will resent you if you don't, and will force you out of the game.)

3. Treat the pot in any game as if it were a player. Any money you invest in a project *becomes* part of the project and no longer belongs to you; forget that you ever owned it.

4. In every game, calculate your chance of winning mathematically. (If there is $50 in the pot and it will cost you $10 to stay in, the pot is offering you 5 to 1 odds. Same theory goes in a business deal.)

5. Never play against a single opponent in any game unless you know through careful deduction that you have a better hand.

6. Try not to voice your bet first. The player who is late to speak always has the advantage.

7. To conceal your cards, adopt an "acting" style that is comfortable for you, but do not stick to it too intensely. Switch your technique.

8. The fun of the game is to use any strategy you want to use without actually cheating. Good players respect this.

9. Call when you suspect a bluff *only if your hand is good enough to win.*

10. In any game, don't try to bluff a poor player, a heavy winner, or a heavy loser.

11. Raise early in the game to avoid calling a big bet later.

12. The wilder the game the greater the smart player's advantage.

Think of money-making as a game instead of a chore, and you will have a good time instead of a headache in business from now on in.

From This Chapter . . .

Twenty-first Financial Recipe for Doubling Your Income

1. Don't be too dead serious about achievement; think of business as a game.
2. Play to win, but don't shoot yourself if the cards you hold don't pay off. Draw a new hand.
3. Concentrate on making money as good poker players work to win a pot. Your aim: to better your hand every chance you get.

Final Review

Just as at the end of Chapter 14, you selected one of seven previous chapter headings to adopt immediately as a personal directive for getting ahead, do the same here from the last seven chapters. Look down the list of headings:

Chapter 15. GET *SCORE* TO HELP YOU RUN A BUSINESS OF YOUR OWN
16. RUN A MAIL ORDER BUSINESS ON THE SIDE
17. STAKE OUT A CLAIM ON A TIMELY IDEA
18. TAKE AN OVERRIDE ON THE WORK OF OTHERS

19. SKIP A GRADE
20. USE THE "DOUBLE A" METHOD TO GET ANYTHING YOU WANT
21. THINK OF MONEY-MAKING AS A GAME

Which one of these ideas appeals to you right now? Put a check mark after it. Then go back and re-read the chapter under that heading. Do not read further in this book now! Once again, put a dollar bill here as a book mark. Re-read the chapter you have selected from the above headings. Then go on from this page and work out your personal Double-Your-Income Formula which follows next.

Personal Double-Your-Income Formula

If you have followed directions carefully, you have checked a directive at the end of Chapter 7; another, at the end of Chapter 14; still another, at the end of Chapter 21. And you have re-read each chapter under those headings.

In the following blanks write down the three directives you have checked, after numbers 1, 2 and 3.

1. ______________________________
2. ______________________________
3. ______________________________

These three pieces of advice, when followed correctly, make up your personal Double-Your-Income Formula.

Once again, read the three directives carefully. Think about each one. There are basic reasons for your finding these three directives particularly compatible with what you want to do next.

How to Get the Most Out of Your Personal Double-Your-Income Formula

If you are not in the field of your choice, take one step now to get there. (The suggestion for that step is in one of three chapters you have read in working out your personal double-your-income formula.) If you are in the field you want to stay in, take one step now guaranteed to boost your income. (Your suggestion, too, is in one of the three chapters you have selected as especially meaningful.)

When you take that first step, and only you know when you're really taking it, your back foot will automatically come up for the next step. There, you are on your way. Write down the date when you feel that you are moving positively ahead as you never have moved before.

Date of my first positive step: ____________________

One year from that date, if you have followed all directions as suggested in your three selected chapters, your income will be higher than you ever dreamed possible. It will be doubled before you realize it, if you conscientiously do what others have done whose pattern you are following.

Part Three

10 Ways to Beat Your "I Can't Do It" Hang-up

1

THREE GIANT OBSTACLES—AND HOW TO GET AROUND THEM

None of the 21 ways to double your income set down in the last section could be printed in this book without our being able to prove *legally* that others have followed the rules we advocate for the result we say can be yours. Yet, even now, unless you are someone with an unusual mind, *uncluttered with doubts,* you are saying to yourself, "Maybe for those other people—but for me . . . ?" We repeat: *Every rule set down in this book, if put to work as they have been by others, can lead in 12 months to twice what you are now making.* Only the negative thoughts in your own mind can hold you back.

Three negatives that make for a hang-up

If you are still saying, "I wish I could do it, *but* . . ." stop now to spell out why you believe you can't do what others have done. Chances are that your analysis will uncover these three apologies:

1. "I didn't have the bringing up that teaches you how to make money. My grandfather never had a dime; my dad was never a money-maker; I'll probably never have anything, either."
2. "Don't ever kid yourself, it takes capital to make money. I'm no Rockefeller."
3. "I've got too much responsibility to take a chance. It wouldn't be fair to my family."

Even with a Fortune Formula from the last section that you know in your heart is foolproof, you cannot succeed unless you eradicate the negative thoughts that are crowding positive action messages out of your brain. To get rid of your feet-dragging, take a long look at the three most common "I can't do it" excuses.

1. **"I didn't have the bringing up it takes."** So your father wasn't sophisticated in the ways of making money? Neither was the father of Jesse Livermore, Boy Wonder of Wall Street a few decades ago. The son of a dirt farmer who never made more than $600 a year, Jesse started as an office boy, made millions before he was 25—and then did it again—and again—and again. "I made 40 million dollars," he told a friend, "because I believed I could do it. I trusted *myself*."

Maybe you belong to a minority group. Let's say you're an Indian. So was Will Rogers, part Cherokee on both sides, born near Claremore in Indian territory (now Oklahoma), who grew up to delight the world with his rope-spinning tricks and his comments about politicians and foreign affairs. Eventually he earned $3,000 a week (when taxes were lower), not because he was trained since boyhood to make money, but because he trained himself to understand human beings.

"I believe man is capable of doing damn near anything he wants," another Cherokee Indian, who is making it big these days, said the other day. Principal chief of the Cherokees and chairman and chief executive officer of the Phillips Petroleum Company, William Wayne Keeler was born during a cattle drive outside of Dalhart, Texas. "My father was taking a herd of steers down from a winter feeding in Oklahoma, and my mother went along," he says. His mother was ill during his childhood and he was brought up by a grandmother who spoke only Cherokee to him. "But when my mother talked to me she spoke in English because she wanted me to understand the white man's society." The young Indian understood white society enough to rank tops in his high school class and to win a scholarship to the University of Kansas. During the depression, he had to drop out of school, and that's when he went to work for Phillips and began to move up first through laboratories, refining, and engineering, then through planning, and on up until finally he was *the big chief*. No hang-up from *his* membership in a minority group!

Another minority group member became the toast of Broadway in "The Great White Hope," a play about heavyweight champion, Jack Johnson. He is James Earl Jones, a Negro, whose earliest memories are of picking cotton in Tate, Mississippi, and who says he never saw white people until the day they took the cotton into town. He does not decry his hard childhood in the isolated farm system of the South; it gave him toughness. And he doesn't regret the handicap of stuttering he had as a child, either; it gave him his interest in speech and eventually in drama. The

1969 Tony Awards winner for that season's best dramatic actor and star of "The Great White Hope" motion picture, made from the play that brought him fame, James Earl Jones sums up his philosophy in five words. "It's what's ahead that counts!"

When you read about a man who is making it, don't kid yourself that he has it good because he was fed financial know-how with a silver spoon in childhood. Real estate tycoon, Harry B. Helmsley, recently paid $90 million for Metropolitan Life Insurance Company's Parkchester apartment complex in the Bronx, where he grew up. Beginning a little more than 40 years ago as an office boy, Harry listened and learned as he moved up in his firm, and saw his name become part of the title by the time he was 30. Now 60, he's so busy investing millions for Helmsley-Spear, Inc., he doesn't have time to be sad over having been the kid who had to leave school at 16.

If you are carrying within you memories of a childhood surrounded by people who "thought poor," be grateful that you can break the mold. Be glad that you see the light now. Remember what James Earl Jones says: "It's what's ahead that counts!"

Now let's look at that second belief that holds many back. Do you have this to fight against?

2. **"I'm no Rockefeller."** So who is? Take a look at 20 self-made millionaires and you will find almost without exception that in the beginning these people lived lean, taking shoestring salaries in order to pump profits back into their enterprises.

Vienna-born Charles Bluhdorn, today's Chairman of Gulf & Western Industries, Inc., came to New York when he was 16 and worked for a cotton brokerage firm for $15 a week. After becoming a U.S. citizen, he took a $60 a week job with an exporter and in his first year did $1 million in business exporting lard to Brazil and spaghetti to Italy for his absentee boss. At 23 he went into business for himself, and soon began importing coffee at the rate of *$1 million a day*—and at the same time also began speculating in commodities. A little more than 10 years later he quit the commodities market and went into the depression-proof business of distributing auto replacement parts, soon bought and merged Michigan Bumper with a Houston Auto Parts firm and renamed the combined company Gulf & Western, which now sells more than $100 million in auto parts every year. And that's just the beginning. Since 1958, Mr. Bluhdorn has bought more than 70 companies. His "conglomerate," which now includes Paramount Pictures and Lucille Ball's Desilu Productions, now has sales exceeding $1.5 billion a year. Surprisingly, this dynamo still in his early 40s who shops for top-ranking companies the way the Beautiful People shop for clothes, doesn't get his kicks out of just plain accumulating money. That's the by-product. His thrill comes from pumping cash, talent and ambition into a company and seeing its sales, profits and stock go up. "We attach a propeller," is the way he puts it, "and watch the business take off. That's where the fun comes in."

Of course, dollars are nice to have. With them you can make more dollars. But the lack of dollars does not mean you are doomed to a life of frustration. In the beginning, don't think about not having money. Think about getting it!

Recently, when our book, *How to Get 20 to 90% Off on Everything You Buy,* went to paperback, we got this letter:

> Your book, *How to Get 20 to 90% Off on Everything You Buy,* in hard cover, has been borrowed by so many of our friends we are now buying paperbacks to lend.
>
> The last time we were transferred, we followed the advice in your book and rented a house temporarily while we searched for the most house on the most land.
>
> We finally found it: 40 rooms, 20 baths and 60 sinks distributed over 27 acres. Fortunately, it was separated into three buildings an acre apart, with a pond, 7 acres of lawn with 20 acres of tillable land which we rented to the farmer next door. (The whole complex had been a nursing home.)
>
> Happily, it possessed good plumbing and heating, but many of the lovely details had been removed or covered up to facilitate clinical upkeep. We are currently authenticating the historic value of the house. (They say Lincoln slept upstairs, and we've discovered a map showing it was McClelland's headquarters during the Battle of South Mountain.) Walt is drawing it to scale for the architect who feels the back part of the house may be 200 years old.
>
> The first month we converted a hospital building to four garden-type apartments. Within 3 months, we added 2 more in the other unit. We were told the sinks were worthless, but they are selling for $12 each. We sold the jalousied, panelled heated front porch for $350 and are presently selling off the institutional equipment that can't be used (kitchen cabinets, lights, etc.). We bought nothing for the apartments that we could take from the house.
>
> The whole project has had a fantastic effect on the children. They are learning the advantages of American enterprise and ingenuity firsthand, while our do-it-yourself college fund is growing. (Five children, 13 months apart in college one after the other for 10 years will be costly!) Eleven-year-old Sue is in charge of the utility room with coin washer and dryer. Mike and Chris contracted for the weeding, 12-year-old Jack drives the tractor, and 14-year-old Jill designs gifts and flowers for a local boutique.
>
> Walt (who quadrupled his salary since 1954 as a computer

systems engineer) is plotting to acquire the 50 acres next door to engineer a housing development in his retirement.

For the past year, I have been working for a Baltimore paper doing news, interviews and reviews. An article on how to be a lovely landlord will soon be published in a national magazine. And an idea I had while taking a factory tour has become a writing-designing job for a large company. When I find a minute there are 3 portrait commissions waiting, illustrations for a book on flower arrangements and 2 magazine articles . . . all because of that energetic push I got from "20 to 90% Off."

(*signed*) Connie Stapleton

The credit doesn't go to our book. It goes to Connie and Walt, who may have been *inspired* by what we said to start a new venture but who had follow-through abilities within themselves. They are definitely making it—and they are definitely *not* Rockefellers.

Don't let a lack of money hold you back! Money comes when creative ideas flow.

Let's say that neither the first nor the second hang-up above gives you trouble. Your problem, you believe, is a concern for others. With the normal demands of a family, do you dare to take a chance? Analyze *now.*

3. **"I've got too many responsibilities to take a chance."** We have checked the families of dozens of men (and women heads of households) who have bet on themselves in a new venture and we have never found one whose members have said, "Don't go!" Many times, it is a wife or dependent parent or child who insists the one who wants to try his wings must take off. So why do we hear so many men and women give "responsibilities" as a reason for not doing what they say they've always wanted to do?

You know the answer to this one even as you read. The person who blames "responsibilities" for being in a job he doesn't like is secretly afraid this is the best he can do. Face this fact if you are using "responsibilities" as an excuse.

Do you dare to experiment?

Dale Hartford, father, husband and newspaper writer-photographer in our town, wanted to devote his full time to doing free-lance writing and picture-taking for magazines. With the encouragement of his wife, who was pregnant at the time, he took the plunge. To bank themselves against non-selling periods, the Hartfords opened an art and framing store in a converted second-hand store on a downtown side street; she sold; he did his "thing." Soon he was selling feature stories in quantity, making far more than in his old job. As his sales grew, she let the art supply business go overboard to work for Dale Hartford Associates, which now sells along with Dale's work a column by Eric Sloane, a radio show by Mrs. Harrison Salisbury and our Empty Nest show. Like most wives, she is *glad* to help.

"The average wife," a psychiatrist told us, "admires a man with the guts to do what he wants to do and will do anything to help him when he bets on himself. This is true especially when she looks around and sees that belief in self is what makes one man succeed over another."

Story of the lone inventor who made $50 million

Is the day gone when an inventor tinkering away in his basement can come up with a million-dollar idea? In competition with inventors working for large organizations with vast amounts of money and laboratory equipment, are such fellows doomed to failure?

"No," Chester Carlson told John Cunniff, Associated Press business analyst, shortly before he died in 1968 at the age of 62 and the possessor of a $50 million fortune from one invention. "The inventor working for somebody else feels pressed to make progress, so he usually works to make small improvements in an established field. The man working alone is using nobody's time but his own, so for him the sky's the limit. He dares to dream big."

During his lifetime, Carlson came up with an invention which became the Xerox copier, the leader in a photocopier field that now includes more than 40 companies grossing more than $1 billion. But though his faith in his basic idea was high, his way was not easy.

As a young boy in San Bernardino, California, Chester Carlson lived with his father, an invalid, and his mother, who became fatally ill when he was in high school. He had no brothers and sisters; therefore he became the main support of his parents who were desperately poor.

After working his way through college, he got a job with Bell Laboratories in New York but was soon laid off in the depression. By the time he landed his next job, he was fighting a severe case of crippling arthritis and he also had a dream, both of which were to stay with him for life. The dream was that there could be a machine to reproduce written and printed matter.

"I concluded," Carlson explained one time, "that the machine must be photographic in nature. I was sure that most companies in the field must have explored the possibility of photographic copying that was chemically based, so I decided to take a fundamental view of the process. This way, I would not compete. My aim: to find how light affects matter. In my search, I found photoelectricity. The process was purely physical, not chemical."

That was in 1938 and Carlson was filled with enthusiasm. But two decades of frustration went by before he saw his machine at work. Some companies looked but weren't interested; others were interested but had too many commitments to get involved. Finally, Battelle Development Corporation of Columbus, Ohio, helped make Carlson's invention into the Xerox copier.

Carlson's advice to the young man or woman inventor: "*Go beyond the obvious.* Discard the first idea that comes to you and consider the problem more deeply. You can't count your millions based on the first solution, because you are bound to find that hundreds of other good minds have thought of what you want to do. You've got to go deeper *alone.*"

Even though he made millions, he urged inventors not to let money rule their thoughts. "Concentrate on the idea; the money will come." However, he did warn inventors to go to a good patent lawyer. "There's no sense in coming up with a sensible solution to a problem and giving it away."

The priceless plus

Sheilah Graham, Hollywood writer, grew up in a European orphanage, was the product of an education that stopped when she was 14, came jobless to a new country as a young woman with no money. Yet Sheilah had a priceless plus over other pretty young women of a generation ago; she was sure she had something inside of her that could take her to the top. She was willing to work, and she believed in herself. Eventually she became one of the best known columnists in America, associated with the top-ranking writers, humorists and actresses and actors of all time.

Hollywood abounds with such stories. Harry Cohn, founder of Columbia Pictures, the son of Jewish immigrants, grew up in a four-room apartment in New York which housed along with his parents his three brothers and two grandmothers. And his story is not unusual. Take note of other successful men with lowly beginnings: Carl Laemmle was the German-born bookkeeper for an Oshkosh clothing store; Adolph Zukor, from Hungary, was a sweeper in a fur store; Samuel Goldfish, of Warsaw, was a glove salesman; William Fox was a cloth sponger from Hungary. The Schenck brothers from Russia ran drugstores in the Bronx; Marcus Loew, a fur salesman, was born of immigrant parents; Lewis Selznick, from Kiev, sold jewelry; Louis B. Mayer, born near Minsk, was a junk dealer.

In writing of them in his best-selling book, *King Cohn,* (G. P. Putnam's Sons) Hollywood's Bob Thomas has said, "Such men have two things in common; they know what the public wants; they are tough." We add a third: *all have the priceless plus.* They believe in themselves.

Point to remember: Don't let the lack of education, money or present responsibilities keep you from betting on yourself if you know inside yourself you've got what it takes to succeed. Put your bet on a winner —*you!*

2

SEVEN SURE-FOOTED STEPS TO TAKE YOU WHERE YOU WANT TO GO

Like the child in school who won't put up his hand because he is afraid of making a mistake, you may have been staying put because you are afraid of failure. Now it is time for the try.

We assume that you are not lazy or you wouldn't be reading this book.

We assume, too, that you are doing everything you can to keep from using alibis for holding back. Filled with ambition and stripped of your little pretenses, what do you want to do? If you are ever going to do it, now is the time.

Two honest fears

Let's say that for the first time in many years, you are being completely honest. Your games with yourself are gone. No more alibis! But you do have two fears. Here they are:

1. "I don't know enough about some aspects of what I want to do."
2. "I am afraid that I won't make my goal."

You must determine whether these fears are realistic.

Cases in point

Here are three men and women who have reason to have Fear #1:

a. A still photographer wants to produce TV commercials. He can handle a movie camera, has a small-budget client who will give him an assignment for three 30-second commercials in the next two months—but he doesn't belong to a union nor does he know the ins and outs of getting into one. He's afraid to chance it.

And so he should be!

To give up a going business to cross over before he finds out about his union requirements and gets his budgeting straightened out would be foolhardy.

b. A freshman girl in college decides she doesn't want school but wants to be a stewardess. In the middle of a semester, she is tempted to leave college and go to a nearby city to apply for an airline job. Her fear is that she may run out of funds before she gets a job.

And so she may.

Better to take a day off or apply by mail or telephone and stay in school for this semester which is paid for.

c. A young couple loves the country and dogs, wants to run a kennel, and finds the ideal spot. They are afraid to put all their money down on this place before learning more about breeds, show dogs, the veterinarian in this town, and competitive kennels.

Right they are.

They have more learning to do before taking the step.

Now let's look at three people with Fear #2:

a. A real estate salesman with a terrific two-year record in a town where he's always lived decides he's ready to take a broker's exam and go in business for himself. But he's afraid to take the step.

Why? He's proved that he's a natural salesman in a business he loves and in a town he knows. No reason to give somebody else part of his take.

b. A bookkeeper in a large real estate firm sees the big commissions earned by salesmen in his firm and decides he should be one. For three years, he dreams of switching, but every time he gets up nerve to talk to the boss he backs down. He's afraid the boss will say no.

And he probably will. The man isn't a salesman.

c. A good-looking saleswoman in a small dress shop knows all the women in town, makes record sales year after year by finding the right dress for the right woman. She decides one day she should be selling real estate in this boom time, makes up her mind to cross over. But she fears she may fail because she's never sold anything but dresses.

Who cares? If she can make a woman see herself in a new dress, she can make her see herself in a new house. The woman will succeed.

What about you?

If you know now that you are capable of doing what you want to do and it is only the fear of a change that is holding you back, make up your mind now to move ahead. To be sure of success take these seven steps:

1. Write down—in one sentence—exactly what you are going to do. (Our local newspaper man wrote, "I am going to be a free-lance writer and photographer doing stories on my own for magazines.")
2. Using your personal Fortune Formula, write down the most practical way for you to achieve this. (This same man wrote: "Start an art supply and picture-framing business. My wife can wait on trade; I will write in back room. When she's not there, I'll cover.")
3. Beginning today, stop in your church, whatever denomination, every single day. The quiet will clear your mind. If you do not have a church you feel comfortable in, go to a park in the city, or walk in the country. Picture yourself in this same place with your goal already achieved.
4. Until you have all phases of your plan worked out, talk to no man or woman. Once you have a plan, ask three people to listen to what you have in mind:

    (*a*) someone in another town or firm who is now doing what you want to do;
    (*b*) the brightest, most forward-looking person in your circle;
    (*c*) a money man or woman who can see the potential in what you want to do.

    Listen *carefully* to the comments they make.

5. Read one book by or about someone who is successful in the field you want (not necessarily a "how to" book). Does your mind work like this person's?
6. Now go to the man or woman who has the most reason to be fearful of what you want to do (i.e., your wife whose security depends on you; your dad who wants you to be safe; your best friend who knows your limitations as well as your strengths). State clearly to that per-

son what you plan to do as if you were already on your way. Is your listener sold? You are walking in the right direction.

7. Work for one month after completing step six to perfect every step of your plan. When all set, go to your calendar and circle a starting date when you will put your plan into operation. Write within that circle your present annual income. On a calendar for next year write in a circle on the same day and month a figure double this year's amount. This is your goal. Now go—you are on your way.

No more hang-up

Once you are committed to move toward the goal you want to achieve, your self-defeating hang-up will miraculously disappear. A year from today you will wonder how negative thoughts ever got into your mind. They will be gone! You will be functioning without fear. In this positive frame of mind, success will come.

3

FACE UP TO YOUR ALIBIS

"I can't make it because . . .

. . . I'm too old." Marlene Dietrich, who is close to 70, puts on a glittery gown, swoops her golden hair over one eye and slinks on stage in New York to wow younger men and women with her torchy ballad, "Look Me Over Closely." Packs them in year after year because she's *sexy*.

. . . I'm a Negro." Being black can be a plus. Billie Allen, TV actress, found this out recently when she was auditioned for a TV commercial and "popped off three." About the same time, Lorna Greene, an unseen voice until recently, got the nod for eight. Ad agencies are finding (as are magazines) that Negroes make TV and still pictures more real. The Negro with talent has a break today.

. . . I've been forgotten." "Eventually, you will attract quality if you are quality," says Jane Wyman, who dropped out of the limelight for a while; now in her fifties, she is *Big* again.

. . . I'm a woman." "All the better," says Tish Baldrige, popular author (*Of Diamonds and Diplomats*) and public relations woman whose father lives near us in Connecticut and whose brother, Mac Baldrige, is president of Scovill Manufacturing, with its home office in Waterbury. "To succeed all you need is a good hairdresser, a good nurse for the children and an understanding husband." She's kidding. All you need to do the things Tish has done (social secretary in Paris to Ambassador and Mrs. Bruce, in Rome to Mrs. Luce and in Washington to the Kennedys) are wit and wisdom, plus what she calls "the Art of Bluff." "Women are born knowing what to do when nothing can be done," she told us the other day.

. . . there's a shortage in what I have to sell." Then the demand is *greater*. David North, Executive Recruiter, thrives on this year's executive shortage, is called on to fill 150 to 200 positions a year at salaries between $15,000 and $125,000—because big companies need good top people and can't find them. Headhunter North charges from 20 to 30 percent of the filled position's gross annual salary, plus expenses, says that 70 to 80 percent of his searches are successful.

. . . the overhead in this business is too high." So cut it. Overhead in the restaurant business is figured at $1,000 a chair. (If you have 20 chairs, your building, equipment, etc., will cost $20,000.) Chuck and Donna Dreyfus, owners of jam-packed *Coach 'n Seven* Restaurant on Route 7, between New Milford and Kent, beat this one. For them, cost was less than $500 a chair, and their restaurant is far more attractive than any place else for miles around.

. . . everybody thinks of me in a particular way and I can't change my type." Tony Curtis beat the type-casting hang-up for "The Boston Strangler" by remembering that Lawrence Olivier told him to build a character from the *outside in*. "If you want people to see you as a lord, dress like a lord, walk like a lord, talk like a lord—pretty soon you will *feel* like a lord and people will think of you this way." Tony made himself a new nose out of putty, put rubber under his upper lip, changed his hair and eye brows to look like the man suspected of being the Boston Strangler. Then he got out his camera. Bosses at his studio saw his picture and said, "That's our man," before knowing this was Curtis. Sold now, they let him go ahead.

. . . there isn't any new way to make a fortune; everything's been done." Feel this way? So take a tip from toy companies, and do something that's been done before. For Christmas '68, the Yo Yo sold like crazy when it appeared as a Glow Go that lit up as it bobbed. The Mickey Mouse watch came back and sold 100,000 before Christmas buying started. Discs on a string, known thousands of years ago in Egypt, appeared and sold 1,000,000 at $1 each before Thanksgiving. Footsee (a plastic ankle ring with a weight at the other end) that landed under half the Christmas trees we saw, is as old as children. Whirlee Twirlee got its inspiration from old-time vaudeville jugglers twirling plates on a stick.

. . . I can't make money in land anymore; it's gone sky high." Buying cheap land takes some doing but it's possible. As suggested before bid on public lands offered for sale by the government. (Get names of regional Land Management offices from "Our Public Lands," $1 a year through U.S. Government Printing Office, Washington, D.C. 20402.) Recently, a New Mexico land office offered 39.64 acres near the Carlsbad Caverns for sale. Appraised value, $475—publication fee (which must accompany bid) $46.62. We bid $515 by mail, sending a certified check for $561.62 to New Mexico before the appointed day in a sealed envelope. We missed, but just barely. There were four sealed bids, the government reported; two for less than ours and one from Philip Shriver of Midwest City, Oklahoma, for $620. We were *green!*—$620 for 40 acres of New Mexico land. Yes, there are *still* good buys to be made!

. . . **I'm making hay now, but it can't last."** You're a model or a boxer or a pro football player. So take the advice of Izzy Lang, burly halfback for the Philadelphia Eagles. "Football is only a means to an end. When it's over, you better be ready." He's applying for a job with Snelling & Snelling, an employment agency teamed with the Officer of the Commissioner of Football, to place pro ball players in jobs. "Take the big name and big money in a short-term glamour job," he says, "but be working all the time on your lifetime career."

. . . **we can't produce as much as our competitors."** So make this add up to a good profit picture. The United States produces only 10 percent of the movies shown 'round the world. Yet they take up 60 percent of the world's screen time. Concentrate on marketing what you *do* produce.

. . . **people are getting so sophisticated. I don't know how to appeal to them anymore."** With the same basic stuff that appealed to them in the 30s, when life was simple and everybody listened to soap opera. They *still* do. The plot of "As the World Turns" is followed consistently by 8 million people.

. . . **I'm just a country boy."** Mike Douglas is a country boy from the Middle West who reaches more people per show than any other entertainer (40 million!). How does he do it? "I think of the woman in Nebraska," he says, "and tailor my show for her." *Nebraska!* In so doing, he has become the highest-rated show in New York City. People are about the same everywhere.

. . . **you've got to know more than I know about taxes to make it today."** So *learn.* Research Institute Recommendations, 589 Fifth Avenue, New York City, tells the story of two executives who get the same annual bonus of $3,000 year after year after year. At the end of 10 years, one has $20,166; the other has $36,018—$15,852 *more* and all of which can be a low-taxed capital gain. Sure you have to be sophisticated about tax laws. If you have no mind for such things, find a first-rate accountant.

. . . **I had to start at the bottom."** In 1936, Howard Harder, Chairman of the Board and Chief Executive Officer of CPC International Inc., began as an office boy at $75 a month. He hadn't finished college (another common alibi) so he took night courses at Columbia, later attended Harvard Business School, all of the time staying connected with CPC and moving steadily up.

. . . **money, alone, isn't enough. I would like to do something worthwhile for my community but still get paid."** As a starter, call your County Clerk and volunteer for jury duty. If called, you will be paid $10 a day, plus 10 cents a mile for trips to the county seat.

. . . I'm not a drone and I want some fun out of life." Let's go back to Howard Harder at CPC International again. He attributes his success to the fact that he has *always* had fun out of life. He has fun on the job. "I think a man should be able to go home and tell his wife after a hard day of creative work," he says, "that he had a great time that day." Work is fun. Check your alibis and enjoy it!

Are You Still an "Alibi Ike?"

Even after reading all of these alibis, and perhaps laughing about how some people kid themselves, are you still saying about your own case, "yes, but"? If so, try now to shake yourself loose from excuses for not getting ahead.

If your alibi is not one of those listed on the previous few pages, write down what you think is holding you back.

____

(*Example:* "I have had a lot of sickness in my family.")

Directly underneath this, write down the name of someone who has had far more reason than you to look for an alibi in this area.

____

(*Example:* "Patricia Neal")

Now write down what that person has done to make your alibi look silly.

____

(*Example:* "After a series of strokes at the height of her career, Patricia Neal taught herself to walk, talk, and even think straight again; returned to acting to get rave reviews in 'The Time of Roses.' ")

Change from being an "Alibi Ike" to an "Anything's Possible Anna!" Life will be better tomorrow!

Part Four

Why Money Is Nice to Have

1

"MONEY IS THE SEED OF MONEY"

Two hundred years ago, Jean Jacques Rousseau wrote down his views on political economy. "Money is the seed of money," was his conclusion, "and the first guinea is sometimes more difficult to acquire than the second million." His point applies today and will apply two hundred years from today. The first money that you make is much tougher to come by than your later dollars for two reasons: (1) The second time around, you have a pattern for making more money. (2) After you acquire money, you and your dollars can work together.

Top TV personality

One of the biggest money-makers on daytime and nighttime television started out at the age of 10 as a hawker of papers and peanuts and has been selling ever since. Today, the shows he originates and appears in and the commercials he performs in bring him in a six figure annual income. And he practically doubles this take with secondary enterprises including a talent agency, production company and specialty stores.

Even though he obviously loves his on-camera life, he undoubtedly would be the first to agree with the founding father of the famous Kennedy clan who said one time, "You work a lot of years for money. Then you finally get smart and put your money to work for you. And that's when you *really* make it."

Most money-makers keep right on working as long as they're able to, even when their money is at work in a dozen outside places. They love their work, and then with a bigger bank account the old money game becomes easier all the time. There is an obvious reason for this. *Money comes easier when there is no need.*

Why need gets in the way

"Necessity never made a bargain," said Benjamin Franklin, and our New England banker agrees with him. "You can't make money in a bank from rich people," he told us, "because they always have another way to go. So they want a special deal. The little guy who's got to have the money to get going is the one who makes us money. He'll pay anything to get in the game."

When opportunity knocks

By the time that Walter Hickel, Nixon's Secretary of the Interior, became Governor of Alaska in 1966, he had acquired more than $14 million. How? All because he recognized the fantastic money-making opportunities in the 586,400 square-mile state he lived in. His special interests: hotels and natural gas. He invested in both, and made money. So he was ready when opportunity knocked, which was often, with more money. Millions came.

The stuff of legends

A few years ago, a pretty girl ad-maker named Mary Wells jumped from making $40,000 a year in one New York agency to making $60,000 in another. *The absolute tops* everyone said, but she knew better! So she and two male co-workers decided to start their own business. At the end of its first fiscal year, their agency had billings of close to $40 million; and when it went public in another year, it provided our heroine with $1 million in cash and made her worth $5 million on paper.

Did Mary become the Golden Girl of Madison Avenue (with a salary of $225,000) because she is brainy as well as pretty? *More!* She believed enough in herself to give up a big job that any other girl would have given her eyeteeth for and *go it on her own.* Then, as the money came in as a result of her talent and effort, she managed that money wisely to bring in more money. Such is the stuff of legends.

Money allows for diversity

We had occasion recently to spend some time with Harold B. Kerr, one of the original founders of The Merchandising Group, Inc., one of the most novel and effective organizations in the United States today. TMG was conceived as an organization which would put to use 30- to 45-year old women in leading American cities, trained in the past in sales, publicity, promotion, advertising and other phases of merchandising, to back up a sales effort by a particular magazine, fabric company, clothing group, paper company, or like group selling through retail stores.[1] Today, women working for TMG do local publicity, make local TV and radio appearances, present, sell or document manufacturers' promotions, "police" retail advertising, conduct opinion surveys, provide all kinds of services not originally spelled out by The Merchandising Group. And more is to come. The day we talked at 477 Madison Avenue, New York City, Harry Kerr was making plans for TMG's first film-making venture.

Today, 300 women living in 80 major markets operate as free-lance independent contractors on an hourly basis for The Merchandising Group, Inc. As appliance manufacturers, liquor producers, lingerie manufacturers, textile manufacturers, food companies, magazines and many more clients use their services, more services are called for. The diversified company keeps planting seeds in new areas. These seeds flower and TMG just naturally becomes more prosperous as clients prosper.

Some efforts of a company go great guns; others may not be so successful. Money for diversification permits experimentation without great risk.

Conclusion: Money begets money; money saves money; money cuts down risk.

Make money your friend!

---

[1] Write to Nancy Nicholas, Vice-President, The Merchandising Group, Inc., 477 Madison Avenue, New York, N.Y. 10022, for further service information or possible employment.

2

BLESSED IS THE CONVENIENCE

On the night of the great blackout all along the East Coast a few years ago, we were separated. (One of us was home in New Milford, Connecticut; the other was stranded in a cave-black railroad station in Boston, Massachusetts.) In order to reassure the half of the partnership at home that the other was all right, the one in Boston had to fish out two nickels or a dime from somewhere to dial an operator to call collect from the blacked-out telephone booth. No dime was to be found, so all communication between us was impossible because one of us did not have the needed coin for the right slot. Nothing in our experience has pointed up more dramatically the inconvenience that comes when needed money for a specific purpose is not available.

"Being rich is better"

"I have been poor," Sophie Tucker said one time, "and I have been rich, and believe me, *being rich is better!*"

We agree. This is not because we yearn to give each other yachts and helicopters and baskets of jewels for birthday presents. What we resent when we are without money is the inconvenience that is caused by the lack thereof.

Possibilities unlimited

In the early 1960s, when our children finished school, married and started out on their own, our nest in New York emptied as we have explained and we accepted our freedom as a chance to start a new life away from Manhattan. Even though our advertising agency work had paid exceptionally well, our expenses in putting six children through school had been big, too, so our assets when we moved to "do our thing" in the country were modest as we looked ahead to the long haul. In our first six months in the country we had no regular pay checks. Therefore, as we were casting around for our first contracts for books and agency work from home and were making our first real estate sales through Possibilities Unlimited, our country real estate agency, we "pulled in our horns" and found the short-term experience extremely trying *for one reason.* For the first time in years *our daily life was inconvenient!*

So you get into Danbury on the train and have 20 minutes to get to another appointment at home in New Milford—and find the connecting bus 40 minutes late. What do you do? Wait for the malingering bus or take a cab for seven dollars to the next stop? Even stopping to consider was an inconvenience.

After years of being assisted every minute by able secretaries, we found ourselves limping through life with haphazard typists. What now—make do with occasional help until our future course was set?

The dilemma was a bore. There were letters to get out. We were never fearful, but we had daily discouragements because of our concern about spending too much before we were sure that our long-term plan was right.

A great land buy came up. 187 acres with a beautiful house, barns, 3-acre lake, acres of road frontage. All for $60,000! Common sense told us we could make the house a beauty, sell off the land in chunks, come out with a huge profit. As we talked to bankers, friends and family, putting forth a case, another buyer bought. We watched with regret as we saw him begin to do what we could do better.

"If we ever have plenty of cash on hand again," we said one night, "we will never cease to be grateful." Until now, we have not remembered this, so of course we are not everlastingly thankful that we have cash to move around with, but we do remember our crossover from New York with gladness that it is behind. Certainly, we don't want another period when every purchase is a choice between extravagance on one side and inconvenience on the other.

It is this inconvenience, to both of our minds, that is the real pain in the neck when you are without cash to function in the way that your psyche finds comfortable.

3

IN THE END YOU CAN FORGET IT

James Norman Hall sought to devise "some scheme of life to banish fear that lurks in most men's eyes."

Common fears today: the fear of not having as much as others in your circle; the fear of not "making it" the way you once thought you would; the fear of not being paid as much for your talent or skill as you know you are worth; the fear that you may not be able to maintain your present way of life in later years. These are the fears that haunt the *drivers* in life!

The common fears just named make men uncomfortable, but the drive for more and more money can also make men uncomfortable. No one wants to live with 100 percent concentration on money. So what is the answer?

Suggestion: Once you achieve your goal to make twice what you are making per year, promise yourself now that you will not push for more until you give yourself a hiatus. Look forward to this hiatus from money thoughts as devotedly as you look forward to your doubled income. Pursue and find this goal and you are in for a glorious surprise! During your hiatus your income will go up even more. As artist Eric Sloane says, "When I stopped driving for money, it really rolled in." Others say it in a different way.

When Joseph Kennedy, father of the late President John Kennedy and the late Senator Robert Kennedy, was asked when he started to make really *big* money, he said, "When I stopped pushing for it and went up and sat on the Cape and gave myself time to think."

As you look forward to the hiatus that you are going to give yourself once your goal is reached, think of the place where you want to spend your quiet time. Where are you most peaceful? Where can you do your best thinking? Where is your "Cape"?

Maybe you work in a great city and know that your talent is now and always will be expressed in a city more than in the country. But when you are not at work, where do you want to spend your weekends and vacations?

Assume now that you are going to have that doubled income soon. At the same time, make plans to get a place where you can be at peace and *forget about money.* (It may be a desert place, or an island in the Caribbean or a roof-top penthouse in New York City.) The point is that you must hold the place where you want to get away from it all in mind. Your aim eventually must be to do the work you want to do without worrying about the pay you are going to get for it. That is when you will *really* begin to make money.

Final goal

Again, as that famous Italian designer says: "Do something good and money rolls into your lap."

We agree that more money, for its own sake, should not be the final goal. But each man who makes a point of this—the Kennedys, Pucci, Eric Sloane, all the others—either have always had money so that "making it" has never been a problem, *or* a big lifetime money goal has been reached and thus other life goals can come forward.

Your goal is the development of your talent which we described earlier as "anything that you do easily that others find difficult." When you finally reach the place where you have all the money to live as you want to live, you can concentrate on talent alone. Once that talent is recognized by others the money will come—and you can forget the push.

The point is now that you have to have the money you know is right for your way of life to get the freedom to concentrate on what you really want to do. So pick up your foot for the next step, a doubled income. Move toward the hiatus. All the time keep developing your talent. Once that's working for you the way you want it to, you can forget about money, for it will always be there. This is a law! You will see. You will not have long to wait. You are on your way!

Where We Got Our Data

The data included in this book on income opportunities, taxes, personal accounts, overall economic trends and company earnings and expenditures come from various sources. These include business columns, annual reports, U.S. Government documents, professional magazines, *Who's Who*. Elements in some of the success stories have been told in first person on TV and radio and in magazines, newspapers and books. In a few such cases, we have reported figures as told there. Usually, however, we have interviewed direct, and in the majority of cases, we are well acquainted with the business men or women whose success we have described.

BIBLIOGRAPHY

American Heritage History of the Presidents, 2 Volumes. Distributed by Simon & Schuster. American Heritage.

Crawford, John R. *How to Be a Consistent Winner in the Most Popular Card Games,* Doubleday, New York, 1953.

Hicks, Tyler G. *Smart Money Shortcuts to Becoming Rich,* Parker Publishing, West Nyack, New York, 1967.

Kinney, Jean and Cle. *How to Get 20 to 90% Off on Everything You Buy,* Parker Publishing, West Nyack, New York, 1966.

Lasser, J. K. *Your Income Tax,* Simon & Schuster, New York, 1968.

Lyon, David G. *Off Madison Avenue,* G. P. Putnam's Sons, New York, 1967.

Mead, Shepherd. *How to Succeed in Business Without Really Trying,* Simon & Schuster, New York, 1952.

Reagan, Ronald, with Hubler, Richard G. *"Where's the Rest of Me?" The Ronald Reagan Story,* Duell, Sloan and Pearce, New York, 1965.

Rickenbacker, Edward V. *Rickenbacker,* Prentice-Hall, Inc., Englewood Cliffs, New Jersey, 1967.

Singer, Leslie P. *Economics Made Simple,* Doubleday, New York, 1958.

Sopkin, Charles. *Money Talks,* Random House, Inc., New York, 1964.

The Complete Essays and Other Writings of Ralph Waldo Emerson, The Modern Library, Random House, Inc., New York, 1950.

Thomas, Bob. *King Cohn,* G. P. Putnam's Sons, New York, 1967.

Toynbee, Arnold J. *Experiences,* Oxford University Press, New York.